Tolley' Share and Business Valuation Handbook

(Fifth Edition)

Techniques for the valuation of shares in
private companies and businesses including
intellectual property and transfer pricing

by

Leslie Livens, ATII, AITI, QDR, MAE, MOI, TEP, SBV
of Atlas Consulting

Tolley Publishing

A member of the Reed Elsevier plc group

Published by
Tolley
2 Addiscombe Road
Croydon, Surrey
CR9 5AF England
0181 686 9141

Typeset by Kerrypress
Luton, Bedfordshire

Printed in Great Britain by
Hobbs the Printers, Southampton

ISBN 1 86012 915-3

Foreword

Valuing shares or a business is an immensely responsible, challenging and satisfying professional activity. All at the same time it can have the excitement of a voyage of discovery, the beauty of logical structure, and the drama that arises from real human conflict or anticipation. On top of all this, it can be the ultimate determinant of someone's financial worth. Consequently, it needs from its practitioners the highest professional disciplines, understanding and knowledge. Over the last fifteen years it has advanced steadily from its previous life as an adjunct activity of the auditor to become a discrete profession in its own right.

The objective of this book, now in its fifth edition, is simply to present in a useful format the broad techniques of share and business valuation. In the process, some guidance is given on how to structure a valuation exercise and how to present a valuation report. Occasionally, I have made personal observations on matters of dispute or debate — notably in the realm of tax related valuations, and sometimes these are a little provocative. There are still open issues that need resolving and there is a healthy professional interest in seeking answers (although, in some tax related valuations the lack of the occasional defining line often offers the gladly seized opportunity of negotiated settlement).

One of the most important recent developments in the field was the creation of the Society of Share and Business Valuers. This Society will undoubtedly contribute significantly to cementing the foundation of this profession and to improving standards and consistency in approach as regards the presentation of valuations, conduct in negotiation and also in the debate of valuation issues and the identification and clarification of those awkward areas.

If this book contributes in some small way to the process of education and professional improvement it will have been a worthwhile endeavour.

Leslie Livens
May 1999

Of valuers . . .

"It seems to me that their opinions are indeed properly described as guess-work, though of course it is intelligent guesswork . . ."

Mr Justice Danckwerts, *Re Holt, Holt v IRC*

Contents

Contents

Contents

Contents

Abbreviations and References

PRCR	=	Planning & Compensation Reports
QB/QBD	=	Law Reports Queen's Bench Division
RR	=	Revised Reports
SLT	=	Scots Law Times
Sol Jo	=	Solicitors' Journal
TC	=	Tax Cases
TR	=	Taxation Reports
WLR	=	Weekly Law Reports

Table of Cases

Table of Statutes

Chapter 1

Introduction
Share Valuation Techniques

Background

1.1   Many occasions give rise to a valuation of shares in a private company and most, if not all, have some immediate or future tax consequence.

1.2   Whenever there is a direct tax consequence (e.g. a non-arm's-length transaction) it will usually be necessary to prepare a formal valuation report (see Chapter 10) for submission to the Inland Revenue in support of the value of the transaction. That valuation may differ from the value that one or other of the parties to the transaction has in mind. A formal independent valuation report is a statutory requirement under the *Companies Act 1985, s 108* or *s 109* in the case of:

   (i)   shares being allotted for non-cash consideration on re-registration of a private company as public,
   (ii) shares being allotted for non-cash consideration by a public company, and
   (iii) shareholder transfers of non-cash assets to a recently new public company.

1.3   Arriving at a share valuation on paper is not always the end of the matter, certainly not in the case of valuation for tax purposes. A tax valuation has to be agreed by the appropriate Inspector of Taxes or other Inland Revenue officer (Chapter 11), and he may well (and is obliged to in certain circumstances) refer the valuation to the Shares Valuation Division of the Inland Revenue. This department is staffed by highly experienced examiners who have available to them a vast amount of information on share valuation and other asset valuation matters, including files accumulated over many years dealing with settled valuations of private companies of all shapes and sizes, ages and complexity. They also have access to information concerning the company whose shares are being valued, including details of any previously notified dealings in the shares.

1.4   Without careful and thorough preparation, it is most unwise to commence negotiation with the Shares Valuation Division. Unfortunately, if a difference of opinion does arise between valuer and the Shares Valuation Division the correspondence can run on for months or even years. It is therefore important to collect complete and unambiguous evidence supporting any tax valuation; and the background to the valuation — i.e. the precise purpose of the valuation, the principles adopted and the calculation — should be presented clearly in the valuation report.

Valuer's opinions and negligence

1.5   A detailed formal valuation report is not always required — such as where, under a company's Articles of Association, the company's auditor (acting as expert, not arbitrator) is required to state his 'opinion' as to the 'fair value' of the company's shares. This matter is dealt with at 2.57 *et seq*. Also, some valuers find it less inhibiting simply to give an opinion statement (a 'non-speaking' valuation) rather than a full valuation report (a 'speaking' valuation). The reason is that the cases that require an 'opinion' are often ones where the value is important to two opposing parties.

Whatever value is arrived at, one party is likely to be dissatisfied and it is not inconceivable that litigation might ensue. The more detail presented, the more can be brought into dispute, and the share valuer's credibility tested. A 'non-speaking' valuation hitherto has been less likely to be set aside by the court except where it can be shown that the valuer had acted negligently or fraudulently (see *Johnston v Chestergate Hat Manufacturing Co Ltd*, *Jones (M) v Jones (RR)* and *Jones v Sherwood Computer Services plc*).

In *Macro v Thompson* it was held that if a valuer merely makes a mistake in doing what he was authorised to do, the valuation is still binding and the parties have no remedies against that. However, if he does something he is not authorised to do (in this case he valued the assets of a different company from that which he should have been valuing) the parties are not bound by his conclusion. This was echoed in *Morgan Sindall PLC v Sawston Farms (Cambs) Ltd*, which found that a valuation might be overturned if the valuer failed to carry out the task prescribed in an agreement, but not merely for a mistake having been made by the valuer in carrying out the valuation.

Consider the proposition that a valuer's responsibility when required to determine a value as an expert is to provide a *conclusive* value. That sounds sensible, but this objective may be lost where the value is accompanied by a detailed report that nevertheless does not carry persuasive explanations of how the valuer has chosen one figure rather than another or one piece of information to the exclusion of another and so on. An opinion of value either will suffer this shortcoming or otherwise be supported by undisclosed information and any subsequent legal argument could well throw doubt on aspects of an expert opinion and consequently may destroy that opinion. That argument would be unlikely to determine a better value but notwithstanding there has to be some question over how long the courts will suffer the inviolability of valuation opinion over explicit valuations or arbitration between such valuations or formal mediation processes.

1.6   Lord Denning's judgment in the case of *Campbell v Edwards* usefully summarises the position, simply stated, that a valuer when acting as expert can be liable for negligence, whereas if acting as arbitrator he cannot be so liable.

1.7 In summary, the valuer himself is not personally liable unless he is dishonest or negligent. See also 1.27.

1.8 The case of *Banque Bruxelles Lambert SA v Eagle Star Insurance Co Ltd and Others* considers a negligent real estate valuation and finds that a lender can recover from a negligent valuer on the borrower's default. The case made the perhaps obvious point that the valuer's duty to the lender in the absence of special conditions was to take reasonable care to give a reliable and informed opinion on the open market value of the relevant land at the valuation date. However, in the absence of special instructions it was no part of the valuer's duty to advise on future movements in property prices, and the valuer was in no sense a guarantor of the lender's investment decisions.

The House of Lords held that the proper measure of the damages was the difference between the negligent value and the correct value. However, the point was made that whilst it could not be said that this negligent valuation caused the loss which arose from a subsequent fall in the market value, the knowledge of a probable fall in the value of the property was not too remote from the valuation to be removed from an assessment of loss. This is a principle that makes the case important for all valuers to consider not just real estate valuers. If I tell you on Monday that today's value is £100 but that it is my expectation that within the week that value is likely to be £1, and I know that you will take my non-speaking valuation to a poor uneducated banker, what is my liability if anything — to the banker? In *Omega Trust Company Limited and another v Wright Son & Pepper and another*, a disclaimer of liability to third parties was upheld.

1.9 In the case of *Whiteoak v Walker* it was held that if the valuation has been carried out by a company's auditor under the terms of its Articles of Association, the standard of skill the auditor must bring to bear is that to be expected of an accountant in general practice, not that of a specialist valuer. However, the judgment, given in 1987, was made in respect of a 1932 valuation and included the following prophetic words: 'Of course, as the art of share valuation develops, which may very well be due to the existence of a specialist body of valuers, so the standard of skill in valuing to be expected of the accountant in general practice and of auditors will rise'.

1.10 Where a share valuation is prepared for tax purposes, the valuer's opinion is clearly not binding on the Inland Revenue until agreement is reached, by which time that opinion may have shifted or have been sacrificed to the greater cause of expedience. If two *unconnected* parties ask for an independent assessment of market value for the purpose of a disposal by one party to the other the valuation would be accepted by the Inland Revenue (but see *TCGA 1992, ss 29–34* (value shifting)). If the parties are related or connected in tax terms, the Inland Revenue would pursue its own assessment of the market value and the normal appeal procedures would be available in case of a dispute.

Sale/purchase/merger

1.11   On a straightforward sale or purchase of company shares there is clearly a need to value what is being bought and sold. The number of shares being sold as a percentage of the entire issued share capital is relevant as will be seen at 3.76 *et seq*, but the other circumstances surrounding the transaction must be made clear to the valuer because, either for taxation or company law purposes, there could be wider consequences. Chapter 9 covers the various tax situations and in any share transaction the parties should satisfy themselves of the tax position before committing themselves. Problems can arise where the transaction takes place for a consideration other than cash, or at an undervalue or overvalue. The transaction may be a compulsory purchase under the *Companies Act 1985, s 461(2)(d)*, which will also require a valuation.

1.12   In a merger the share valuation principles will be applicable to each of the companies independently in the first instance. As far as the individual shareholders are concerned they will probably be converting their shareholdings from those in the original pre-merged company into new shareholdings in a new entity. The permutations of approaches are large. The question arises whether the whole post-merger entity is more valuable than the sum of its parts and if so whether the respective shareholders have each been credited with an appropriate share of this premium. The post-merger entity may, initially, have less apparent value to the shareholder rather than more, because of costs of the merger or of dilution of the shareholding by virtue of the introduction of venture capitalists or new management shareholders. It is at this point, particularly, that a discounted cash flow basis of valuation may be appropriate whether to the resultant entity or the pre-merged entities or both. See also 1.17, 1.21 and 8.4.

Variation of rights

1.13   If there is a variation in the rights attaching to any shares it is probable that value has been removed or added with a consequential increase or reduction elsewhere.

1.14   There may well be commercial reasons supporting a variation of rights and there may be actual consideration passing, but whatever the case it is wise to check the capital gains tax rules relating to value-shifting and depreciatory transactions. Inheritance tax may also be in point if the value of someone's estate has been reduced. If the variation is in respect of shares held by employees, *ICTA 1988, s 135* and the *Finance Act 1988, ss 77–89* may apply (see Chapter 9).

1.15   In all these events a valuation will be necessary — probably by reference to the reduction or increase in value. However, if the prospective variation had already been taken into account in an earlier transaction, it may be that there is no further tax consequence and no further valuation requirement.

1.16   It is important to understand the purpose of any variation in rights, which may have been contingent upon the happening of another event (such as targeted profits being achieved), or simply the desire to make a gift of value.

Financing

1.17   A valuation may be necessary if shares are to be held by a bank or other financial institution as security for a loan. The creation of a mortgage or charge over the assets of a company may affect the value of the shares in issue notwithstanding that the creation of the charge will bring new finance into the company. This will depend upon all the circumstances, not least of which will be the reasons for raising the borrowings.

1.18   Some financing arrangements call for a subscription of new equity and the issue of new shares and/or debentures. The valuation basis for a new issue may be quite different from that for existing shares. Thus a minority shareholding subject to pre-emption rights should not be valued for tax purposes in quite the same way as, for example, risk capital put up in tandem with a convertible secured loan by a financial institution that may be investing in a number of companies on the basis that a small proportion will be outstandingly successful. For the valuation approach recommended to capital venturists by the British Venture Capital Association, see Appendix 3. See also 1.21 and Chapter 8.

Flotation

1.19   Prior to a public flotation of shares the 'value' can vary daily for a host of reasons — mostly to do with the market mood of institutional investors. If any prior estate planning is undertaken by the original shareholders (such as transferring shares into trust) there will be a separate valuation exercise under the traditional principles of tax valuation rules which, depending upon how close the events are to each other, may be influenced by the price at which the stock eventually floats. This matter is discussed in 2.96, and see 1.21 and Chapter 8.

Buy-back of shares

1.20   Provided it is authorised to do so by its Articles of Association, a company can purchase its own shares, thereby effectively cancelling them (*Companies Act 1985, s 162*). Such a purchase by a company will be treated as a distribution of the purchase money, and taxed accordingly, unless the complex provisions of *ICTA 1988, ss 219* to *229* are complied with. Neither the *Companies Act* nor the *Taxes Act* contains any directions as to how a company should fix the price to be paid on a purchase of its own shares, but to avoid the suggestion of value shifting a valuation on normal principles will be necessary.

Demergers and management buy-outs and buy-ins

1.21   On any fundamental alteration to the capital structure of a company, be it simply a reorganisation of share capital or a more traumatic piece of financial surgery, there will be a requirement from both the commercial and taxation points of view to value what is going, what is coming in, and what is staying. Not only can these matters be complicated, they can also have tax consequences ranging across the entire spectrum. Note especially the requirement to value non-cash consideration received by a public company (not necessarily a quoted company) for a share issue (*Companies Act 1985, s 103*). Typically, in a demerger situation, new money is being attracted from a bank or other institutional investor. The value is therefore often determined more by reference to the practice of that particular investor than by any market value concept. That value may not reflect the true open market value on the date of the demerger, but more a basic value, after infusion of new money, by reference to which the future performance can be judged. See also Chapter 8.

Share schemes

1.22   Whenever approved or unapproved share option and incentive schemes are introduced (including a transfer of shares from an existing shareholder to an employee as such), the shares must be valued for income tax and capital gains purposes (see Chapter 9). In the case of an approved scheme the Shares Valuation Division will agree a value for the purposes of the scheme, which may not necessarily have a bearing on other valuations for tax purposes since the Inland Revenue are simply concerned that options are granted at 'not manifestly less' than open market value. The agreed option price should be used only for the purposes of the share scheme for employees in determining any future income tax or capital gains tax liability arising out of the scheme.

Matrimonial proceedings

1.23   The value of shares held by either party to matrimonial proceedings may be relevant. A valuation may have implications for the future even if no immediate transfer of shares takes place, because a value for the shares at a point in time has been struck. In determining the value of assets for the purposes of divorce, the open market value would be taken, untainted by specific tax value assumptions (as explained in Chapter 9). The courts can, however, look unfavourably on detailed and costly valuations of capital assets such as businesses or shares which are not to be sold but provide a spouse's main source of income (*Potter v Potter*; *B v B*).

Death

1.24   Valuation of shares on the shareholder's death may be required to establish the value for inheritance tax as well as for capital gains tax. Although no capital gains tax is chargeable on death, valuation is necessary to establish the new base cost in the hands of the beneficiary. See Chapter 9 for details.

Other occasions

1.25   Valuations may be necessary on a distribution by a trust and also for the purpose of various 'deemed disposal' transactions for tax purposes (dealt with in Chapter 9).

Starting a share valuation

1.26   Assuming the principles (Chapter 2) are clear, the starting point is the shares themselves (see Chapter 3). Having identified the rights and restrictions attaching to the shares, the next step is to decide which of the valuation bases is most appropriate (see 3.78). A minority interest will usually suggest the dividend basis (Chapter 4), a majority interest the earnings basis (Chapter 5); although it may be appropriate to adopt a hybrid basis (Chapter 7) where the valuer is not satisfied that one of the other bases is wholly appropriate. An asset basis (Chapter 6) will be appropriate in a case of impending liquidation or if there is extraordinary asset value involved. Other methods of valuation are given in Chapter 8. The case of *Hawkings-Byass v Sassen* contains an interesting, detailed analysis of the choice of valuation base on the facts of that case.

1.27   The valuer needs a wide range of skills, including a knowledge of the legal principles of valuation. He must be able to interpret financial statements including consolidated accounts. In any particular case, he must understand the basis adopted for depreciation, bad debts and reserves, and the other accounting policies adopted by companies. He must be able to distinguish extraordinary expenditure and exceptional expenditure, and he must be able to take a view, often by reference to past performance, of the future earning or dividend capacity of the company. It clearly helps to understand business and business people, management and managers. He must also have the skill and experience necessary to convert the information, by reference to the appropriate market for shares and comparable values, into a specific value that reflects all the multifarious elements surrounding the company, its earning 'machinery' and the wider world.

1.28   Although it is generally understood that an auditor undertaking a valuation under the terms of the company's Articles of Association is required to bring to bear that standard of skill that is to be expected of an accountant in general practice, and not that expected of a specialist valuer (*Whiteoak v Walker*), note the comments made at 1.9 which signify an important development in this rule towards a recognition that the standard of skill required may now be (or soon become) the skill expected of a valuation specialist.

1.29   Should the valuation specialist be one who specialises only in an industry or sector? How far should specialism go? A valuer who undertakes a valuation that requires the consideration of matters specific to an industry or sector and who is not fully aware of these matters may be treading on eggs. On the other hand, a valuer who slavishly follows sector rule-of-thumb valuation principles may be similarly accused when, eventually, a valuation proves to be inaccurate.

1.30   There are rules-of-thumb for many types of business which can be important indicators of value, but great caution is necessary (see 12.34 for a wider discussion of this issue). It is difficult to deny that someone with specialist valuation experience and expertise in a particular area will know what he is talking about. That experience must, however, be rounded by general current valuation experience to avoid the 'ivory tower' syndrome. This debate also moves into the question of valuation bases, particularly the application of the discounted cash flow basis — see 8.4.

1.31   There is a clear and proven need for specialist valuers in certain asset valuation fields, such as real estate, plant and machinery, certain intellectual property, commodities, shares and even market prices for goods of all kinds. — see 1.30. Perhaps the area to watch with caution and concern is the hiking in quoted share prices caused by internet trading by Sexy Sector Shares Syndrome — currently internet company shares, but watch developments. Students of economics may recall the South Sea Bubble Company debacle.

1.32   It is important to differentiate between business assets which are necessary to generate the earnings of the company, and assets that are surplus to these requirements. The company's earnings must be capitalised by reference to an acceptable price-to-earnings ratio (5.22) or some other required yield (4.46; 5.45) — this is a matter that will exercise the valuer's skill and experience, and is often the arena for dispute between experts. The company's dividend policy (or lack of it) must be investigated to see what the future can promise for shareholders in dividend terms (see 4.12).

1.33   If a Hybrid Basis (Chapter 7) is to be used, all or some of the factors — assets and surplus assets, earnings and dividends — may be given an individual weighting according to their perceived relative importance to the shareholding in question. The share valuation will be constructed from the duly weighted values by dividing the total value so determined by the number of shares in issue and multiplying by the shareholding being valued. This may then be discounted to reflect the problems of marketability (see 2.126) of the private company shares — including the problem of pre-emption rights and restrictions on transfer (see 2.101) often found in a company's Articles of Association.

1.34 The valuation of shares is one thing; the valuation of particular assets, such as real estate or intangible assets is another. A share valuation is often influenced by tangible or intangible assets that the company owns or has rights over. The valuation of these assets may have to be determined by a specialist valuer — see Chapter 6. As regards intangible property, see Chapter 13, and as to goodwill, see Chapter 12.

1.35 All the foregoing matters are considered in greater detail in the following chapters of this book. A guide to the preparation of a valuation report is given in Chapter 10, and a sample valuation is given in Appendix 1. The following valuation checklist broadly follows the arrangement of Chapter 10, the Share Valuation Report. This checklist may appear to some to be one designed for a 'due diligence' exercise rather than a valuation. Well, it might be argued that the valuer is conducting such an exercise for himself if for no-one else. Although (it might again be argued) the valuer should be able to take at face value the raw information he is presented with, and leave due diligence where it is necessary to someone else, he would have difficulty hiding himself from an omission to consider all clearly relevant matters. He is, after all, a specialist who might be expected to know and understand a few things! Such matters should be resolved in the valuer's engagement letter.

1.35   Valuation checklist

General
- ❏ Client's name
- ❏ Subject company name
- ❏ Terms of appointment of valuer and terms of reference
- ❏ Relationship of client to company
- ❏ Relationship of client to shareholders

Identifying the subject of valuation
- ❏ Share capital
- ❏ Shareholders
- ❏ Shareholding to be valued
- ❏ Date for valuation
- ❏ Purpose of valuation
- ❏ Previous sales and transfers
- ❏ Sources of information
- ❏ Subject company profile
- ❏ Basis of valuation
- ❏ Statutory rules applicable (especially regarding tax)
- ❏ Mem & Arts relevant clauses
- ❏ Resolutions and agreements
- ❏ Special rights, votes
- ❏ Financial and economic rates and data

Company financial profile
- ❏ Financial and management background
- ❏ Flotation, takeover, liquidation likelihood
- ❏ Balance sheets and account
- ❏ Consolidated accounts
- ❏ Accounting policies
- ❏ Dividend policy
- ❏ Management projections and profit forecasts
- ❏ Directors' and chairman's statements

Specific issues that may impact upon value
- ❏ Directors and personnel

- ❏ Environmental exposures
- ❏ Health and safety at work regulations
- ❏ Regulated industry compliance
- ❏ Assets and real estate
- ❏ Liquidity
- ❏ Intellectual property rights
- ❏ Liabilities
- ❏ Order book
- ❏ Suppliers, joint ventures and commitments
- ❏ Bad debts
- ❏ Exceptional, extraordinary expenditure
- ❏ Foreign trading and currency exposure
- ❏ Tax computations and liabilities
- ❏ Other industry or sector issues
- ❏ Off Balance Sheet items and pension scheme surpluses
- ❏ Insurance and risk management issues

Supporting documentation
- ❏ Future trading prospects
- ❏ General economic outlook
- ❏ Valuation approach (concepts reviewed)
- ❏ Comparisons (quoted or other cos)
- ❏ Calculation
- ❏ Taxation
- ❏ Review
- ❏ Terms of appointment of valuer and terms of reference
- ❏ Accounts
- ❏ Mem & Arts
- ❏ Resolutions and minutes
- ❏ Material contracts
- ❏ Asset valuations
- ❏ Financial data
- ❏ Directors etc. statements

Chapter 2

Concepts in Valuation

Background

2.1   As stated in Chapter 1, there are many occasions that give rise to the need for a valuation of private company shares. Given that there are also likely to be very different circumstances applying to each company or set of shareholders it can be seen that each case will require an approach, an emphasis and attention to special factors that taken together will be unique. Nevertheless, there is a solid foundation upon which valuation rules are based.

2.2   A number of fundamental concepts in share valuation have sprung from or have been clarified by a range of judicial decisions and *dicta*. Most of the cases are concerned with valuations for estate duty, stamp duty and land duty. Many cases have concerned company law, compulsory acquisition, administration and negligence.

2.3   The tax and company law statutes themselves are of minimal assistance in understanding valuation principles, and the courts have had to have regard to common sense and practical interpretations with the result that the major share valuation principles were expounded and developed by the courts and are of wide application.

Open market value

2.4   For valuations of private company shares for fiscal purposes it is necessary to base the valuation on an assumed sale of the shares in the *open market* at the appropriate time (see Chapter 9). The concept of open market embraces the place of the market; the purchasers; the willingness of both seller and purchaser to do a deal at a price; the information available and the time of the transaction.

2.5   In *IRC v Clay*, Swinfen Eady LJ said:

'The market is to be the open market, as distinguished from an offer to a limited class only, such as members of the family. The market is not necessarily an auction sale.'

2.6   For non-fiscal valuations, the special factors that are drawn into a valuation by tax statutes — such as no discount for flooding the market, and information (see 2.24 *et seq* below and Chapter 9) — will be absent. However, it is likely that an 'open market' valuation will be required, and it would certainly be wise to work on that basis unless some specific requirement dictates otherwise. For example, a transfer of shares between two parties under terms set out in, perhaps, the company's Articles of Association or other agreement, may require a 'fair value' to be ascertained. 'Fair value' is discussed below, and may be otherwise than 'open market' value.

2.7   Whatever value is taken for any transfer, if there is likely to be a tax consequence then it is probable that an adjustment will be made to the value to ascertain the required open market value for tax purposes. An example may be the issue of new shares to an employee, where the Inland Revenue view of the open market value differs from the company's and the employee's views of the value of the shares. A compensating adjustment for tax purposes may be required (see 1.22 and Chapter 9).

Hypothetical open market

2.8   For tax purposes, at least, a hypothetical sale is assumed to take place in a hypothetical open market which includes any 'special purchaser' (see 2.77). In the case of *Re Lynall*, Plowman J said:

> 'It is common ground that the shares must be valued on the basis of a hypothetical sale . . . in a hypothetical open market between a hypothetical willing vendor . . . and a hypothetical willing purchaser on the hypothesis that no-one is excluded from buying and that the purchaser would be registered as the holder of his shares but would then hold them subject to the Articles of Association of the company, including the restrictions on transfer.'

2.9   In *Re Holt*, Danckwerts J uttered the following memorable lines:

> 'The result is that I must enter into a dim world peopled by the indeterminate spirits of fictitious or unborn sales. It is necessary to assume the prophetic vision of a prospective purchaser at the moment of the death of the deceased, and firmly to reject the wisdom which might be provided by the knowledge of subsequent events.'

2.10   *Re Holt* concerned estate duty, but the principle espoused by Danckwerts J is fundamental to any valuation requiring an open market basis. In *Walton (Executor of Walton, deceased) v IRC*, Gibbons LJ said: ' . . . the statute requires one to assume a sale but it should be assumed to take place in the real world'.

2.11   In *Smyth v IRC*, Hanna J, rejecting the Revenue's restrictive contention that the most likely purchaser of shares (in this particular case) would be someone desiring a block of shares, emphasised the openness of the hypothetical market by saying:

'In visualising the hypothetical open market I consider that it may contain some persons looking merely for a return of their money in a going concern, or some members of the family anxious to buy, and perhaps willing to give more than the ordinary buyer, in order to keep the business in the family, as well as the block purchaser, who wants to wind up the company for some reason, or to have a profit on his speculation.'

Willing buyer and seller

2.12   In the hypothetical market it has been considered necessary to have a hypothetical willing seller and hypothetical willing buyer. Harman LJ in *Re Lynall* explained that the willing vendor is a person who must sell and cannot simply call off the sale if he does not like the price; but on the other hand there must be a willing purchaser so that the conditions of the sale must be such as to induce in him a willing frame of mind. The willing seller was defined in *IRC v Buchanan* and distinguished from a sale which is made by reason of compulsory powers. Swinfen Eady LJ said: 'It does not mean a sale by a person willing to sell his property without reserve for any price he can obtain'. He went on: 'she was willing to sell at a price, she was offered a price less than the maximum which the intending purchasers were willing to give, and she took it'. He held that she was a willing seller.

2.13   In *Buccleuch v IRC*, Lord Reid imputed a willingness on the seller when he said:

'What must be envisaged is a sale in the open market on a particular day. So *there is no room* for supposing that the owner would do as many prudent owners do — withdraw the property if he does not get a sufficient offer and wait until a time when he can get a better offer'.

2.14   In *IRC v Clay* (on the meaning of 'willing vendor' in relation to *Finance (1909–10) Act 1910, s 25*) Pickford LJ described the person as 'one who is prepared to sell, provided a fair price is obtained — not an anxious seller'. This seems to strike the right chord.

2.15   Whether or not the vendor is 'willing', the purchaser has to be a willing purchaser at the right price! Lord Fleming, in *Findlay's Trustees v IRC*, describes the willing purchaser as a person of reasonable prudence, who has informed himself with regard to all the relevant facts such as the history of the business, its present position, its future prospects and the general conditions of the industry; and who also has access to the accounts of the business for a number of years. How far can this be taken? See 2.20 *et seq.*

2.16   The concept of a willing seller was introduced in the *Finance (1909–1910) Act 1910, s 25(1)* but the term is now found in fiscal legislation only in respect of *the information* that is made available to prospective purchasers by a 'willing vendor' — see 2.24 *et seq*. Otherwise tax legislation simply assumes the sale to be in the open market at the relevant date. As shown above, the case law takes care of the assumption that the vendor is willing.

Every possible purchaser

2.17   A number of cases have come before the courts on the matter of open market value. In the land value duty cases of *IRC v Buchanan*, Swinfen Eady LJ said that 'a value ascertained by reference to the amount obtainable in an open market shows an intention to include every possible purchaser'.

2.18   In *A-G v Jameson*, Fitzgibbon LJ said that one must look at 'the price which would be obtainable upon a sale where it was open to everyone who had the will and the money, to offer the price which the property . . . was worth'. Again, in *IRC v Buchanan*, Swinfen Eady LJ said that 'the market is to be the open market, as distinguished from an offer to a limited class only . . . The market is not necessarily an auction sale'.

2.19   In the estate duty case of *Duke of Buccleuch v IRC* Lord Reid, discussing the proposition that the sale takes place *in the open market*, expressed his view that 'the phrase requires that the seller must take such steps as are reasonable to attract as much competition as possible for the particular piece of property which is to be sold. Sometimes this will be by sale by auction, sometimes otherwise'. See also 2.77 *et seq*.

Available information

General

2.20   'The sum which any bidder will offer must depend on what he knows (or thinks he knows) about the property for which he bids.' (Lord Reid in *Re Lynall*.)

2.21   It has to be assumed that information is available to our hypothetical purchasers. In *Re Lynall*, Lord Morris of Borth-y-Gest, in considering what information could be available to hypothetical purchasers and vendors in the open market, said:

'this must mean whether it would be openly available to all potential purchasers and vendors in the market or markets in which relevant purchases and sales take place. There may be different markets or types of markets for different varieties of property, but . . . the market which must be contemplated, whatever its form, must be an "open" market in which the property is offered for sale to the world at large so that all potential purchasers have an equal opportunity to make an offer as a result of it being openly known what it is that is being offered for sale. Mere private deals on a confidential basis are not the equivalent of open market transactions.'

2.22   In valuing unquoted shares and securities for capital gains or inheritance tax purposes the legislation states:

'it shall be assumed that, in the open market which is postulated . . . there is available to any prospective purchaser of the asset in question all the information which a prudent prospective purchaser of the asset might reasonably require if he were proposing to purchase it from a willing vendor by private treaty and at arm's length' *(TCGA 1992, s 273(3))*.

Herein lies one of the great tax valuation debates. The first point is that the information that is to be available is that which the prudent prospective purchaser might *reasonably* require. Does the purchaser have to determine what information it is reasonable to ask for in the knowledge that the reasonable directors of the company may have problems about what they can reasonably disclose and therefore accept what his lawyer advises is all he is reasonably entitled to request? Or, does the purchaser ignore all obstacles and simply take the information that the potential purchaser needs to make his own informed valuation? The legislation requires the latter, because that has the least uncertain outcome, however, we must then consider what in all seriousness the directors simply will not disclose to the potential shareholder. Does their fiduciary responsibility extend to giving information to prospective shareholders? That would be a most onerous position. The legal interpretation is considered further below.

The second point is that the section puts this information requirement into the context of a *private treaty at arm's length*. This recognises that the words *reasonably require* would, in isolation, have fallen into the first postulated scenario. In a sale by private treaty the rest of the world is excluded, more information may be expected to pass to the prospective purchaser because the danger of indiscreet disclosure of information is lessened; further the prospective purchaser is the only purchaser in town, but the absence of the '£1 more' purchaser removes excesses in the negotiated price.

So, at first blush it would seem that the second postulated scenario is more appropriate. Yet, there is an obstacle. The deal, the private treaty, is between shareholders; it is not between prospective shareholder and the directors (per se) of the company (see 2.28). Thus, up pops the question about what responsibility the directors of the company have towards the shareholder who is negotiating a private treaty sale. This question widens, because the vendor might be a control shareholder or a minority shareholder — fundamentally different animals.

2.23   In two consecutive appeals before the Special Commissioners *Clark v HMIT* and *Caton, deceased v HMIT* the question was whether unpublished information about profits (in the first case), and about profits, budgets, forecasts and a possible sale of the company (in the second), were to be assumed to be available to a purchaser. The first case considered a minority holding of 3.16% and the second considered a minority interest of 14.02%. Both holdings were in the same company.

The Special Commissioner interpreted the word 'require' (in *TCGA 1992*, s 273(3)) to mean 'demand as a condition of buying': 'information is "required" if the purchase would not proceed without it'. Expert opinion and other evidence presented held strongly that if the outlay was substantial then, whatever the size of the holding, the purchaser would enquire about possible sales approaches and about management accounts and budget forecasts.

The taxpayer argued in *Caton* that the subject company would have provided the information on these matters, whereas the Inland Revenue argued that information provided by the directors would not be complete and information about a possible sale of the company might not have been released. It was held that because the consideration was in the region of £1M the purchaser would require and receive this information notwithstanding that the shareholding constituted a minority holding.

The finding in *Clark* was that unpublished information about the profits of the company would be available but that information about a proposed sale of the company would not. The proposed investment was not large enough to suggest that the purchaser would have been reasonable to require the same level of information. See also 2.31.

The *Caton* and *Clarke* cases have added spice to the conundrum concerning the quantum of the purchase price as a catalyst for obtaining information by osmosis from the corporate entity through the shareholder to the prospective purchaser. These cases also suggest that the information which the intending purchaser would require can include any information, whether unpublished or confidential, and information which might prejudice the interests of the company. Yet, what the purchaser can *reasonably* require will depend upon the circumstances of the case, and particularly the amount being paid for the shareholding.

The cases have suggested that (for the appropriate tax purposes) there can be a significant difference in power and influence between minority shareholdings of 3% and 14%, but depending upon how much money is being paid. If the amount paid for the 3% is significant then the intending shareholder may be entitled to full disclosure of information which would put that shareholding on a par with larger shareholdings as far as the information stakes is concerned and possibly at a level of entitlement which public company shareholders do not enjoy.

2.24   There is a divide between minority shareholders and the directors of the company. True it is a divide that can be very different from one company to another, but it is there. The directors rarely have a duty to support the sale of shares by a shareholder. Indeed, that is what pre-emption rights and directors' powers of not registering share transfers is all about. This is why it can be said that for disclosure of privileged information to have an effect on a valuation that disclosure has actually to take place or be proven that it would have taken place in the real world. This is what happened in the *Caton* case.

The legislation, for all it says, does not say nor does it imply that the divide between shareholder and company is breached.

2.25   The Inland Revenue are pulling up their bootstraps on the information issue to suggest a direct relationship between size and performance in the information stakes —

Voting capital:

- < 5%   entitled only to published information unless large sums of money are involved;
- <25%   depends;
- >25%   fairly full disclosure (especially if the holding is on a par will or greater than others);
- >50%   all information available to directors would be disclosed to the purchaser of a control holding.

The Inland Revenue also says that if the cost of the investment is substantial it is reasonable to assume that a potential investor would reasonably require more than just published information, but they are unable to say what constitutes a substantial investment, including from whose perspective that is determined. There is also a marked disinterest in whether directors would simply ignore a private treaty taking place between minority interest shareholders.

2.26   It perhaps would be helpful to consider the directors' personal position in all this. The directors will be concerned that their actions should not jeopardise their own positions nor the business interests of the company, nor the interests of other shareholders — perhaps particularly of minority interest shareholders. For example, the divulging of details of business proposals or proposed special dividends could spur a share transaction that might redirect the intentions of the directors, even benefit the directors. So what? So, perhaps the continuing shareholders would consider the disclosure a breach of the directors' duty to safeguard the interests of the existing shareholders. The best scenario here is one of uncertainty for the directors.This matter is considered further in general at 2.28.

2.27   *TCGA 1992, s 273(3)* applies for income tax purposes to determine the market value of unquoted shares given by way of a stock dividend — see *ICTA 1988, s 251(6)*; and in respect of a charge to income tax on gains from shares or options accruing to employees and directors under *ICTA 1988, ss 135–140* (see *sections 140(3), 162(10)(d)*) and *s 185* etc. (see *section 187(2)*); and

> 'In determining the price which unquoted shares or securities might reasonably be expected to fetch if sold in the open market it shall be assumed that in that market there is available to any prospective purchaser of the shares or securities all the information which a prudent prospective purchaser might reasonably require *if he were proposing to purchase them from a willing vendor by private treaty and at arm's length'* (*Inheritance Tax Act 1984, s 168(1)*).

'Reasonable' directors

2.28   In relation to the question of how far information concerning the value of shares could be made public, Lord Reid in the *Re Lynall* case said:

> 'The furthest we could possibly go would be to hold that the directors must be deemed to have done what all *reasonable directors* would do. Then it might be reasonable to say that they would disclose information provided that its disclosure could not possibly prejudice the interests of the company'.

2.29   Interestingly, he went on:

> 'Not all financiers who might wish to bid in such a sale, and not even all accountants whom they might nominate, are equally trustworthy ... I could not hold it right to suppose that all reasonable directors would agree to disclose information such as these reports [being reports which made it very probable that a public issue would be made in the near future] so widely as would be necessary if it had to be made available to all who must be regarded as genuine potential bidders or their nominees.'

2.30   In a private treaty sale for a majority interest it is probable that such information would be divulged; not necessarily however, or perhaps particularly not, in the case of a minority sale.

2.31   In a major acquisition of shares it is usual for the purchaser to require that the company's books and records be made available to his accountants for confidential scrutiny. How much information would be allowed to be divulged by reasonable directors would largely depend upon the size or importance of the share acquisition. The amount of information that reasonable directors would divulge in a disposal of a minority interest would probably be less than in a subscription for new shares. Indeed the directors may see no good reason at all for disclosing any confidential information to minority shareholders; this, however, may not override the provision in *TCGA 1992, s 273(3)* and elsewhere which assumes information to be available — see 2.22. The question whether and to what extent a purchaser would require and directors would provide information may rest on:

(*a*)   the size of the shareholding,
(*b*)   the potential purchase price,
(*c*)   the potential purchase price as a percentage of the whole value of the company or the capital of the company,
(*d*)   whether the share sale is associated with a capital injection into the company.

2.32   The sale of shares to a director was considered in the case of *Percival v Wright* and it was held that the purchasing directors were under no obligation to disclose to their vendor shareholders matters which are 'merely incidents in the ordinary course of management'. Such matters included large casual profits, the discovery of a new vein (it was a colliery company), good prospective dividends, and negotiations for a sale of the company undertaking. Equally, a director selling shares is under no obligation to disclose losses.

2.33 In general, a director is under no legal obligation to make confidential information available; indeed no director should disclose confidential information without the consent, at least, of the board of directors.

Memorandum and Articles of Association and minute book

2.34 Information not available to a prospective purchaser may well be available to the share valuer, who would commence his valuation exercise by an examination of the company's Memorandum and Articles of Association; the company's minute book might also be inspected. Under the *Companies Act 1985, s 383*, the minute book must be kept available for inspection by members, but not by the general public. Therefore, although the valuer might inspect it for evidence of proper conduct of statutory duties and any other relevant matters, the information in the minute book would not normally be available to a prospective purchaser (other than possibly a majority shareholder) prior to an acquisition. Confidential information, which, if known to the purchaser, might affect the value of the company's shares should not necessarily be adopted as a factor affecting that value unless it is reasonable to assume that the information would be made available to that purchaser on the principles discussed above.

2.35 The company's Memorandum and Articles of Association, register of directors and secretary, register of mortgages and charges, annual return and accounts, or modified or abbreviated accounts, are all available for public inspection at Companies House. Any prospective purchaser of shares would probably carry out a company search as the first stage and so would know the full entitlements and rights attaching to the shares. This course of action should be followed whether the acquisition is from an existing shareholder, or is of an issue of new shares by the company.

Warranties and indemnities

2.36 The purchaser of a majority interest would probably require warranties from the present directors and shareholders (especially if they were involved in the management of the company or if the acquisition is from a holding company).

2.37 The warranties that might attach to a share sale agreement relate to liabilities in respect of matters such as taxation, property and fixed assets, company law, trading and profit and loss account, finance, employment, trading activities and contracts and environmental pollution. A full set of warranties can be most intimidating and much time can be spent simply negotiating which warranties will remain and which will be left out — the vendor wishing for none; the purchaser requiring all. The valuer might therefore consider:

(*a*) whether the acquisition is one in which warranties and indemnities would be required, and given; and

(*b*) if so, whether the discovery of confidential information after the sale would give cause for an action by the purchaser under the terms of the sale contract, either for rescission or, more likely, for damages, and whether a liability would be likely to be incurred because of the indemnity given by the shareholders.

2.38   So, any adverse facts that it would be reasonable to expect would be covered by warranties should not be ignored in a valuation. Equally, the fact that no-one would give warranties to the purchaser of a minority interest might be considered to be a discounting factor. Even if a shareholder gave general warranties, unless it could clearly be established that he had access to adverse facts that were known to the directors of the company, it would be difficult to take action against him unless, unwisely from the vendor's point of view, the warranties were of a specific and categoric nature. No mere shareholder would give such warranties.

Transferee standing in shoes of transferor

2.39   In *Stanyforth v IRC* Lord Warrington of Clyffe said that the property for sale in an open market:

'would have to be put up with all its incidents, including provisions for defeasance either in whole or in part, powers vested in persons not controlled by the vendor to create charges taking precedence of the property sold, and so forth.'

2.40   Thus, where a power to affect the value of any property adversely or to destroy it vests in some person over whom the purchaser has no control, this 'incident' of the property cannot be disregarded. In the context of company shares, existing options, deferred shares, restrictions on transfers (see 2.101 *et seq*) and the like are relevant.

2.41   The transferee must stand in the shoes of the transferor. Chief Baron Palles in *A-G v Jameson* said that the hypothetical sale and purchase must be of the entire legal and equitable interest therein, of that interest by virtue of which the transferor was entitled to be a member of the company in respect of the shares; it must be a sale whereby the purchaser would be entitled to have that which he has bought vested in him in the same manner as it had been vested in the (hypothetical) seller, and consequently under which he would be entitled to be registered as a member of the company in respect of those shares; and this assumption must be made whilst excluding from consideration any provisions in the Articles of Association as actually do prevent a purchaser at the time of the sale from becoming a member of the company and registered as such in respect of the shares.

2.42   In the same case, Walker LJ said that the test of value (for estate duty purposes) is what the shares would fetch if sold in open market — a hypothetical open market — upon the terms that the purchaser would be entitled to be registered in respect of the shares but would himself thereafter hold them subject to the provisions of the Articles of Association, including those relating to alienation and transfer. This price he said, was not limited to the 'fair value' (see 2.57 *et seq*). This matter is more exhaustively dealt with in 2.101 *et seq.*

2.43   The *Jameson* case was thoroughly reviewed in *IRC v Crossman* (qv) and upheld in the House of Lords. The more recent case of *Alexander v IRC* applied the *Crossman* (*inter alia*) decision to the transfer of a leasehold interest in a flat, so that the value of the leasehold interest was the price that the hypothetical purchaser would pay to stand in the shoes of the leaseholder and that would take account of incumbrances to which the leaseholder was (and would be) subject.

Date for valuation

2.44   The date upon which the valuation is required should be regarded as a frozen point in time which cannot be influenced by events which have not yet taken place and which would not have been known or foreseen on the valuation date, even though at the time of the valuation exercise there is knowledge of sales, transactions or influential events subsequent to the valuation date; this applies certainly for fiscal purposes and usually for other purposes (but see 2.49 and 2.69 *et seq*).

2.45   In *Duke of Buccleuch v IRC* the taxpayer contended that a landed estate which was inherited could not possibly be sold at the time of death but would take several years to dispose of. However, Lord Morris of Borth-y-Gest said:

> 'the value of any property must be estimated to be the price which, in the opinion of the Commissioners, the property would fetch if sold in the open market at the time of the death of the deceased. "At the time of death" must not be paraphrased or altered so as to read "within a reasonably short time of the death". It follows from this that the section is envisaging a hypothetical sale at the time of death. This is quite inconsistent with a notion that the value of a piece of property is to be estimated by postulating that preparations for an actual sale would be commenced at but after the time of death and that a sale would later follow after such preparation.'

2.46   Lord Reid in the *Duke of Buccleuch* case said that as the valuation was required for a particular time (i.e. the date of death of the taxpayer):

> 'There was no room for supposing that the owner would do as many prudent owners do — withdraw the property if he does not get a sufficient offer and wait until a time when he can get a better offer. The Commissioners must estimate what the property would probably have

fetched on that particular day if it had then been exposed for sale, no doubt after such advance publicity as would have been reasonable.'

2.47   The value of some assets can be particularly susceptible to cyclical or seasonal fluctuations. Residential property, for example, may be more easily sold or may command a higher price in the spring and summer months than in autumn and winter.

2.48   In the case of *IRC v Marr's Trustees*, a herd of cattle was considered, and for valuation purposes the definite ascertainable condition of the herd at the valuation date and at no later time was taken. 'At that date a cow may be two or three weeks from calving. In the course of three or four months, the risks of calving and the risks to the life of the young calf are largely over: the two conditions are completely different things.'

2.49   In a case where an offer to purchase shares was made one day after the date at which an independent valuer was to assess their value, the judge took the pragmatic view that the valuer could take account of the offer (in *Re Company No. 002708* and in *Re Company No. 004247*).

See also 2.123.

The price the property would fetch

2.50   No allowance for notional expenses on the notional disposal can be taken for fiscal valuation purposes. In the *Buccleuch* case, Lord Guest said that the 'price the property would fetch' (in *Finance Act 1894, s 7(5)*) means not the price which the vendor would have received but what the purchaser would have paid to be put into the shoes of the deceased. He went on to say that this means that the cost of realisation does not form a legitimate deduction in arriving at the valuation. Indeed, he said, in *section 7(3)* a specific deduction of 5% was allowed in arriving at the value of foreign property for estate duty and this only emphasised the fact that no costs of realisation are permissible deductions in arriving at the valuation of properties within the UK for fiscal purposes. The 5% deduction for estate duty purposes is statutorily available for foreign property under the inheritance tax regime (*Inheritance Tax Act 1984, s 173*).

2.51   Before 13 December 1979, in relation to assets subject to exchange control restrictions in the UK, the 'market value' for capital gains tax purposes was, under *Capital Gains Tax Act 1979, s 150(5)* 'subject to such adjustment as is appropriate having regard to the difference between the amount payable by a purchaser and the amount receivable by a seller'. As to valuation costs for capital gains tax deduction purposes, see 9.30.

2.52   Nothing was said by Lord Guest about the costs of the purchaser — professional fees and stamp duty for example — and the extent to which these costs would influence the price that the purchaser would be prepared to pay;

however, these considerations are more likely to be relevant to assets other than shares.

2.53   In the case of *Earl of Ellesmere v IRC*, Sankey J pointed out that a sale in the open market does not necessarily mean the price which would be fetched upon a sale to a single purchaser. He cited the case of an owner having property including a colliery and a draper's shop, suggesting that if the colliery and the draper's shop were sold separately the best possible price might be obtained for each. On the other hand, a purchaser who was anxious to buy the draper's shop might not wish to be encumbered with the colliery and *vice versa*. What is meant by the words 'the price which it would fetch if sold in the open market' was the best possible price that is obtainable and that is largely, if not entirely, a question of fact.

2.54   Lord Reid in the *Duke of Buccleuch* case tempered this by explaining how, if applied as a universal rule, it would create enormous difficulties. He cited the case of the owner of a wholesale business who dies possessed of a large quantity of merchandise. It would have been possible by extensive advertising to obtain offers for small lots of something near retail prices and thereby realise the stock at much more than wholesale prices. It may not have been reasonable and it may not have been economic but it would have been possible. He said that 'there is no universal rule that the best possible prices at the date of death must be taken'. The principle of dividing up the assets is not so much directed at a disposal of shares as at separate assets but, theoretically, there may be instances where a break-up of a single shareholding or a combination of different classes of share would bring this principle into play.

2.55   The case of *A-G of Ceylon v Mackie* considered the situation where a better price was obtained by aggregating shareholdings than by subdividing them. In that case, it was clearly established that a higher price would be got on a sale of the combined holding of ordinary and preference shares because of restrictions in the Articles of Association which made a sale of any of the shares in isolation untenable from an investment point of view. This case is regarded by the Inland Revenue as having no application to capital gains tax because different classes of shares are treated as different assets. However it remains relevant for inheritance tax.

2.56   When valuing shares for fiscal purposes it is important to remember the inheritance tax related property rules and estate concept, which could lead to a minority holding being valued as a *pro rata* proportion of a majority holding, whereas for capital gains tax, it would be valued in isolation (see Chapter 9).

Fair value (and other expressions of value)

2.57   Often, a company's Articles of Association include provision for transfers of the company's shares to be made at a 'fair value'. The situation usually envisaged is a transfer under the pre-emption article from an existing registered shareholder to another such shareholder or possibly a transfer by virtue of an employee shareholder leaving employment. Sometimes, sale agreements, options and other private commercial arrangements may also call for a 'fair value' instead of an 'open market' value; but invariably the expression refers to transactions between known parties.

2.58   In these cases the quantification of the value is usually left to the company's auditors or some other independent party and usually that party is required to act as an expert, not an arbitrator.

2.59   In fact, the expressions that may be used include 'full value', 'market value', 'open market value', 'fair market value', 'fair open market value', 'fair value', 'arm's length value' or even 'par value' or 'nominal value'. Dealing with the last two first, ascertaining the par or nominal value of shares should not be difficult. There may be other problems arising, however, because in such a case a transfer may be taking place at a considerable under-value for tax purposes. Wherever transfers are to be made at such value care should be taken to ascertain the full facts relating to the agreement and the reasoning behind the transfer. Par value or nominal value cannot be taken for share valuation purposes if the 'worth' or market value of the shares is different (*McIlquham v Taylor* and see also 2.101 *et seq*).

2.60   Those responsible for drafting a company's Articles of Association sometimes attempt to clarify the 'fair value' of a share by adding an explanation of what is intended. If that addition is unambiguous it makes the valuer's job that much easier, as in, for instance:

'the fair value shall be determined by the auditors for the time being of the company on the following basis, namely:

(*a*)   by determining the sum which a willing purchaser and a willing vendor would agree for the whole of the issued share capital of the company; and

(*b*)   by dividing that sum by the number of shares in issue'.

2.61   Where such additions are ambiguous however, or do not accord with the actual share capital or attendant rights and restrictions (such as convertibility), they can simply create further problems of interpretation, e.g. what does the following mean (which is an actual case)?

'a fair price for the shares of the company as a going concern with no account being taken as to whether or not the transfer affects control of the company'.

2.62   The valuer could not be criticised if he makes his own reasonable interpretation of such a clause, but his view may not be what those who drafted the clause had in mind.

2.63   The fact that shares can only be transferred at a fixed or nominal value or by reference to a closed market, will not prevent an open market value being required for tax valuation purposes, although such restrictions may in some cases have an impact on the open market value — see 2.101 *et seq*. The use of the word 'fair' with 'market value' or 'open market value' can only be taken to be an unnecessary embellishment, but does 'fair value' differ from 'open market value'?

2.64   Some assistance can be found in the ordinary dictionary meaning. The first definition of the word 'fair' (as a noun) in the *Shorter Oxford Dictionary* is: 'A periodical gathering of buyers and sellers, in a place and at a time ordained by charter or statute or by ancient custom'. On that basis fair value would surely be no different from, and indeed would in fact be, open market value. However, the usage of the word suggests another dictionary definition: 'Free from bias, fraud or injustice; equitable, legitimate'. How then is this definition different, if at all, from 'open market value'? Further assistance can be found in Walker LJ's comment in *A-G v Jameson* that an open market price was not limited to the fair value; see 2.42.

2.65   In the author's opinion, in determining a fair value, it may be presumed that the value must be fair *as between the parties*. One is not being asked to take the open or closed market value; or to take a tax value or a compulsory purchase value; or to take the side of the vendor or of the purchaser. What one is being asked to do is to examine the range of values that either party might argue for himself and then, looking at all the circumstances, even-handedly determine a value that reflects those circumstances fairly as between the parties.

2.66   Open market price is certainly a starting point, but, for example, it may be decided that excessive restrictions in the Articles of Association on the transfer of shares, which may artificially depress the value of a share, should not be given full weight; on the other hand if the acquirer cannot turn his newly acquired shares to account because those same restrictions now apply to him and he cannot alter them, the valuer may regard those restrictions as having some effect on the value. If the acquirer of a minority shareholding thereby becomes a majority shareholder and able to deal freely with the shares, whereas before the transfer he could not, it may be considered that a fair price would be something above the minority value, but not so that it becomes a hostage value. Indeed, a fair value may well be considered to be a value that is not discounted to the same extent as open market value minority shareholdings.

2.67   Since 1981, when it was made possible for companies to purchase their own shares, it has become common for pre-emption clauses to include the company itself, as well as the other shareholders, amongst the potential purchasers. If fair value has to be determined in these circumstances it is suggested that it is necessary to consider the position of the other shareholders after the buy-back. If there is only a small number of shareholders it may be that as a result of a purchase by the company a minority shareholder is elevated to a majority shareholder. The position is then similar (subject to one critical issue) to the straightforward acquisition of a majority holding by a former minority shareholder, and a fair price would be something above the minority value or even a *pro rata value*. On the other hand, if there is a wide spread of shareholders who remain with minority holdings after the buy-back, a minority value might be more appropriate.

2.68   The critical issue mentioned above is that in a company buy-back situation the consideration for the shares is paid by the company itself rather than by the shareholders. The immediate result is that the assets of the company are reduced accordingly. There will also be a tax consequence which requires careful assessment. The net result is a disparity in pre-transaction and post-transaction values that may be particularly pointed where the shareholding of one or more remaining shareholders jumps one of the watershed levels of 10%, 25%, 50% (particularly), 75% and 90% (see 3.76 *et seq*).

2.69   A fair value may also take more account of pre- and post-valuation day events than open market value principles would normally allow, unless it seems unfair to one of the parties to do so.

2.70   The fair value approach cannot ignore the circumstances surrounding the valuation; but perhaps it can ignore some of the extremes that may be associated with an open market value but its principal purpose is usually to reduce bargaining and avoid hostage values. It certainly does not mean that the fundamental valuation bases can be ignored; having said that, a number of cases have supported, in special circumstances, a valuation of minority interests on a *pro rata* basis. These cases are mentioned below.

2.71   In *Dean v Prince* Denning LJ said:

'Suppose it had been Mr Prince who had died, leaving only thirty shares. Those thirty shares, being a minority holding, would fetch nothing in the open market. But does that mean that the other directors would be entitled to take his shares for nothing? Surely not. No matter which director it was who happened to die his widow should be entitled to the same price per share, irrespective of whether her husband's holding was large or small. It seems to me that the fair thing to do would be to take the whole two hundred shares of the company and see what they were worth, and then pay the widow a sum appropriate to her husband's holding. At any rate if the auditor was of the opinion that that was a fair method, no-one can say that he was wrong.'

2.72   In connection with the special purchaser concept (see 2.77 *et seq*) he said:

'I am prepared to concede that the shares might realise an enhanced value on that account, but I do not think it would be a fair price to ask the directors to pay. They were buying these shares — under a compulsory sale and purchase — on the assumption that they would continue in the business as working directors. It would be unfair to make them pay a price based on the assumption that they would be turned out (of their own factory). If the auditor never took that possibility into account, he cannot be blamed for he was only asked to certify the fair value of the shares. The only fair value would be to take a hypothetical purchaser who was prepared to carry on the business if it was worth while so to do, or otherwise to put it into liquidation. At any rate if that was the auditor's opinion, no-one can say he was wrong.'

2.73   Denning's thoughts in relation to a *pro rata* valuation were echoed by Mr Justice Nourse in *Re Company No. 003420* (a case concerning oppression of minority interests — see 2.110), where he said:

'In the majority of cases of purchase orders under *section 75* (*Companies Act 1980* — but see now *Companies Act 1985, s 461(2)(d)*) the vendor would be unwilling in the sense that the sale would have been forced upon him. He would usually be a minority shareholder whose interests had been unfairly prejudiced by the manner in which the majority had conducted the company's affairs.

On the assumption that unfair prejudice had made it intolerable for him to retain his interest in the company, a sale would invariably be the only practical way out, short of winding-up. In such a case it would not merely not be fair, but most unfair, that he should be bought out on the fictional basis applicable to a free election to sell his shares in accordance with the company's Articles of Association, or on any other basis which involved a discounted price.

The correct course would be to fix the price *pro rata* according to the value of the company's shares as a whole, as being the only fair method of compensating an unwilling vendor of the equivalent of a partnership share.

Equally, if the order provided for the purchase of the shares of the delinquent majority, it would not receive a price which involved an element of premium.'

2.74   Denning's views in *Dean v Prince* were distinguished in *Re Castleburn Ltd* where it was found correct that a 44% shareholding should be subject to a minority discount where the Articles of Association required the auditors to determine 'fair value . . . on a sale by a willing vendor to a willing purchaser'. In *Dean v Prince* the Articles stated that 'fair value shall be the auditors' valuation of the current worth of the company's shares . . .' which was taken as meaning that the auditors were expressly required to value the whole of the company's shares in order to arrive at the value of the shares in question.

2.75   Further evidence that fair value could involve a minority discount is contained in the case of *Re Abbey Leisure Ltd* where the shareholder was granted a winding-up order under the *Insolvency Act 1986, s 125(2)* on the grounds that it was just and equitable to do so, since a sale at fair value under the terms of the company's Articles of Association might well be subject to a discount as being a minority holding. The particular facts of that case lent themselves to that decision since the company in question had been set up to carry out one venture, which had been completed, and its assets consisted solely of the profits achieved.

2.76   A *pro rata* basis may be worth considering in determining the fair value of the shares, but the only technical support the valuer would have in choosing such a basis would be in cases of oppression of minorities (see 2.107 *et seq*); in companies that could be described as quasi-partnerships; and where 'fair value' is defined in such a way that a valuation of the whole company is required. It is strongly arguable in a 50:50 'dead-lock' ownership situation.

Special purchaser

General

2.77   In viewing the hypothetical open market the valuer must consider whether the existence of a 'special purchaser' in that market would affect the price obtainable for the property (whether shares or other assets). The special purchaser is a person for whom the property for sale would have a greater value than it has for anyone else in the market, although it is not necessary to suppose that he would definitely be in the market at the time of valuation.

2.78   A number of cases have considered such a purchaser, and the main principle that has emerged is that if the existence of the special purchaser in the market place is or would be known at the date for the valuation the price of the property may be greater than it would be otherwise; if the existence of such a special purchaser is not known then, whether or not there actually might be one, the price would not be affected.

2.79   The special purchaser must be an identified person (or possibly class of person) and must be in a special position in relation to the property in question. It is not correct to postulate a special purchaser. The open market is just that — open.

Intermediary purchaser

2.80   In certain cases involving land, it has been held that the circumstances or value of surrounding land should not be ignored. In the land value duty case of *IRC v Buchanan*, for example, Cozens-Hardy MR said that:

'to say that a small farm in the middle of a wealthy landowner's estate is to be valued without reference to the fact that he will probably be willing to pay a large price, seems to me to be absurd. If the landowner does not at that moment buy, landbrokers and speculators will give more than its pure agricultural value with a view to re-selling it at a profit to the landowner.'

2.81   Also, in the *Buchanan* case, Swinfen Eady LJ suggested that the knowledge that a special purchaser was interested would affect the market price of the property and other potential purchasers would join in competing for it with a view to obtaining it at a price less than that which they believe the special purchaser would pay. To ascertain how the open market value is actually affected by this, we might take the price the special purchaser would pay and then discount it by a 'dealing' profit; alternatively, the ordinary open market price could be used and increased by an amount beyond which the intermediary purchaser would not go for fear of not making his profit on the deal.

2.82   It has already been said that if the existence of a special purchaser in the market is not known to other bidders, his existence cannot affect the value of the shares. This is because the unknown special purchaser would need only to make an additional bid above the normal buyer to clinch the deal, and perhaps the additional bid would in fact be no more than £1 or, for example, an offer to meet legal costs of both parties. So the additional bid is unlikely to be material in relation to the maximum open market price. It may be suggested that if this additional bid were made in public (i.e. at an auction) it might have the effect of putting up the market value; but there is no reason to suppose that the shares would be bid for at auction. An auction sale is not a required element in valuation; but it will take its proper place in the open market. Thus, we can assume an auction market where it is usual and appropriate to do so (see *IRC v Buchanan* and 2.21).

2.83   It is also true that even if the existence of a special purchaser is known the ordinary market value may not be materially affected. First, the maximum price he is prepared to pay may be impossible to determine and therefore the speculator wishing to take advantage of the special purchaser would be in a considerable dilemma. It does not seem at all reasonable to suppose that bull-headed speculators are in the open market, and indeed such types appear more properly to fall into the category of special purchaser with personal reasons for investing (dealt with below). The dilemma would arise out of knowing that some profit can be made but not knowing how much and therefore not being able to quantify the risk attaching to a speculative buy. The speculator would only buy the shares if he was confident of being able to sell on at a profit. Indeed, the special purchaser can only have a marked effect on the open market value if the intermediary purchaser will be able to sell on to that special purchaser at a profit.

2.84   Two other reasons why the share price might not be affected even though a special purchaser is known to exist and that a profit, whether or not determinable, could be made, are first, the uncertainty of selling on the shares to the special purchaser within a reasonable period of time, loss of interest, for example, on the money invested may be relevant (but may be answered by company earnings or dividends).

2.85   Secondly, in relation to minority interests, restrictions on transfer of shares may make it unattractive to the speculator to become involved. The fact that shares cannot be transferred or registered in the name of any new shareholder because of restrictions in the Articles of Association does not prevent them being 'deemed' to be transferred for valuation purposes and thereafter held subject to those restrictions (see 2.101 *et seq*). However, it may be difficult to apply this 'deeming' rule to a speculator. Following the *Re Lynall* decision, where it was said that the hypothetical purchaser was deemed to be registered as a shareholder and would thereafter hold the shares subject to the company's Memorandum and Articles of Association, if the Articles of Association carried restrictions on transfer by the new shareholder, the speculator as that new shareholder would be unable to realise his profit. Therefore, although it may be acceptable to apply the deeming rule as between a willing buyer and seller in a hypothetical market it must be questionable to assume that a hypothetical intermediary as a speculator would acquire shares that are subject to restrictions on transfer.

2.86   In *Re Lynall* Widgery LJ said:

> 'It is desirable, in my opinion, that when the Court is constructing the conditions under which the hypothetical sale is deemed to take place it should build upon a foundation of reality, so far as this is possible, but it is even more important that it should not defeat the intention of the section (*Finance Act 1894, s 7(5)*) by an undue concern for reality in what is essentially a hypothetical situation.'

2.87   If we apply this 'foundation of reality' to the speculator it would appear that he could not in fact as a practical proposition enter into the hypothetical market place. However, knowing of the existence of the special purchaser, the vendor might himself be able to negotiate directly a price higher than would otherwise be offered, but less than that required to be paid to an intermediary. Timing may be important, depending on whether or not the special purchaser is in the market for *immediate* purchase.

2.88   Some knowledge of what the special purchaser would pay is necessary and this must be more than pure guesswork. If no value can be estimated on genuine grounds then there is little basis for supposing that the ordinary market value can be increased at all or at best by more than a notional amount.

2.89   There need not be only one special purchaser in the market; there may well be more. If so, presumably the value of the shares for sale will increase because of the possibility of the special purchasers bidding against each other. It is not correct to theorise; it is a question of fact, and therefore evidence, as to whether there is one, two or a hundred special purchasers in the market. Of course, the more special purchasers there are the less 'special' they become; the more they become part of the ordinary open market, and the more likely it is that the price each is prepared to pay is known.

Personal factors

2.90   Lord Johnston in *IRC v Marr's Trustees* held that if the special purchaser's price is based on factors personal to himself that price should not prevail for valuation purposes. The facts in that case were that a bidder was able to increase his bid for cattle wholly because he had found an underwriter who was prepared to insure certain related risk in ignorance of the normal insurance practice relating to such cattle risk.

2.91 There is a distinction between personal factors and self-evident potential for an increase in the value of the asset being sold. In the case of *Robinson Bros (Brewers) Ltd v Houghton and Chester-le-Street Assessment Committee*, Lord MacMillan said: 'the motives which activate buyers in a market may be of all kinds, but it is not their motives, but their bids, that matter'. This case concerned the rating valuation of a public house and the question arose whether the fact that brewers would pay a higher rent for managed houses was a factor that should be taken into account in the rating valuation. Lord MacMillan went on, referring to the brewer:

> 'why should the rent which he is prepared to pay be excluded from consideration in fixing the market value of the tenancy? He is one of the competitors in the market and the figure which he is prepared to pay is an element which ought clearly to be taken into account in arriving at the market price.'

2.92 In *IRC v Crossman*, the Lord Chancellor gave his opinion that the right way in which to arrive at the value in the open market was not to exclude or include anybody in particular but to consider the matter generally. On evidence that a special purchaser was prepared to pay a much higher price than could otherwise be found because of certain particular attractions for the special purchaser, the Lord Chancellor held that the extra sum which could be obtained from that special purchaser was not an element of value in the open market but rather a particular price beyond the ordinary market price, which the special purchaser in this case would give for special reasons of his own.

2.93 In *Re Lynall*, a case concerning a close family-owned and run company, it was held that a director who would give an enhanced price because he would thus obtain control of the company would be left out of account because he had a special personal reason for paying that price. On the other hand, however, that did not preclude directors as such from being in the market place.

2.94 The *Re Lynall* decision is important because it implies that the valuation of a minority interest in a family company would not be inflated by the existence of another family member/director who might wish to acquire the minority interest and thus obtain control, except (as is unlikely) to the extent that his *active* presence in the market would be known to other potential purchasers who might increase their bids accordingly. In the author's opinion the mere fact that a minority shareholder could become a majority shareholder if he acquired the shares that are for sale does not amount to public knowledge about the existence of a special purchaser.

2.95 The Shares Valuation Division have in the past used the argument that where, for example, shares in a company are held equally by three shareholders, the value of a 33% shareholding will be enhanced by the possibility of the hypothetical purchaser selling on to one of the other two, whom will thus gain control. The Shares Valuation Division do not rely on the special purchaser contention, unless of course one of the two other shareholders is known to be in the market for the shares, but simply put forward the possibility of a further sale as an appreciatory factor. How far the value would be enhanced in those circumstances would depend very much on the facts in each case. The rationale can be used in a taxpayer's favour when valuation is required at 31 March 1982 (see Chapter 9).

Special markets

2.96   In the vast majority of private company share valuations a comparison with quoted companies, even in a similar sector, involves so many variable factors that it is at best only a rough and ready guide, and at worst positively misleading. However, the possibility of a public flotation has been considered in *Re Lynall* and in *Re Holt*, and there are circumstances where such a comparison will be made. The matter is considered in some detail in Chapters 4 and 5; see particularly 4.54 *et seq.*

2.97   It would be wrong to say that the concept of a special market exists naturally as something akin to the special purchaser, who is in a particularly 'intimate' position vis-à-vis a specific asset (invariably land) and whose motives are bound by a special relationship between what he owns and what he covets (which is generally known to the world at large). It may be that the closest one might get to identifying a special market would be where a specific market exists for niche industries and our subject company has some special characteristic that makes it naturally and irresistibly attractive to that market. Perhaps (to be a little controversial) the scenario painted by the valuation experts in *Battle v IRC* points the way to a special market: there, 'bull market' conditions were suggested to create an opportunity to sell shares in a private investment company through a share exchange scheme. Balcombe J in fact places the scenario in the open arms of the special purchaser, but a reading of the case may spark other ideas.

2.98   The concept of a special *market* rather than a special purchaser has not been considered by the courts. However, in the years preceding the stock market crash in October 1987 there arose a 'special market' for shares with a growing 'over the counter' trade and new entrants to the Unlisted Securities Market (USM). Following the introduction of the *Financial Services Act* in 1986, however, the over the counter market virtually disappeared. Today the secondary market for shares in the UK is the Alternative Investment Market (AIM). AIM is designed to be considerably more flexible than the USM. Its development may well influence the future approach to valuing unquoted shares and may be particularly interesting in the area of mergers and acquisitions. See Appendix 2 for more detail about AIM. New tax legislation is promoting the Venture Capital Trust (VCT) which, for well organised and profitable unquoted companies offers another avenue to shareholders to capitalise on some of (though rarely all) their shares. Over time, the performance of VCTs will determine whether a viable alternative market exists for some types of unquoted company.

2.99 In relation to public quotations, there are costly and time-consuming pre-flotation procedures, and one of many reasons may prevent a planned flotation at the last minute. A major problem with any public flotation is that the striking price for the shares can rarely be confirmed until immediately before the flotation, when the whole exercise is highly charged with risk. Private placings, offers for sale or subscription and the new VCT investments also carry costly pre-contract expenses (mostly legal fees) and the whole exercise can be very complex. The valuer must be very clear in his mind about what is being valued. Usually, this will be the shares in the shareholder's hands for sale at the date of valuation, and not a new issue of shares on a flotation. Having said that, complications such as a concomitant issue of shares or debentures, or a buy-back or other reorganisation or rationalisation may also be taking place, which may require additional valuations or have some impact on the value of shares already in issue.

2.100 Whenever a forage into the AIM is contemplated or if shareholders consider an approach from a VCT, the promoters will almost certainly be members of the British Venture Capital Association, who publish 'Guidelines for the Valuation and Disclosure of Venture Capital Portfolios'. A summary of these guidelines is given in Appendix 3. Obviously, this is a very serious issue for those involved and the fullest professional assistance is required by shareholders who contemplate taking such steps.

Restrictions on transfer

2.101 The Articles of Association may carry restrictions on the transfer of shares, pre-emption clauses, valuation formulae and so on, each of which may affect the transferability of the shares. In *IRC v Crossman*, Lord Russell of Killowen said:

> 'It may be that owing to provisions in the articles . . . the subject matter of the sale (the shares) cannot be effectively vested in the purchaser, because the directors refuse to and cannot be compelled to register the purchaser as shareholder. The purchaser could then secure the benefit of the sale by the registered shareholder becoming a trustee for him of the rights with an indemnity in respect of the obligations.'

2.102 This illustrates that there is no bar to a valuation of shares, even though there may be a technicality that would prevent the clean-cut transfer of title. Having said that, if such a bar were burdensome on the acquirer of shares, for example, manifested in the problem that the 'beneficial' owner of the shares would have in selling his beneficial rights to another party, one could see a reason for a discount from the valuer to reflect that burden.

2.103 In the estate duty case of *The Trustees of Johan Thomas Salvesen v IRC*, a company's Articles of Association, after allowing transfers of shares between members of the family, provided that 'no share shall be transferred to any person who is not a member of the company so long as any member is willing to purchase the same at its nominal value if fully paid or at a price corresponding to the amount paid up on the same . . .'. The Articles also provided that by extraordinary resolution the company could resolve that any shareholder, other than one holding more than 10% of the shares and other than directors, could be required to transfer his shares. Lord Fleming said that these restrictions were onerous and would depreciate the value of the shares, but that did not necessarily mean the value would be as low as the nominal value contained in the Articles of Association.

2.104   In the case of *A-G v Jameson* the question was raised whether a fair value of a share which was set at a figure by the Articles of Association could be said to override the value which, in the opinion of the Commissioners, the property would fetch if sold in the open market at the time of death of the deceased (*Finance Act 1894, s 7(5)*). The consequence of fixing that value in the Articles was that none but members of the Jameson family would be shareholders of the company. The value was low enough to render unlikely any disposal of shares to prospective purchasers outside the family. Lord Ashbourne could not altogether ignore the Articles. He said:

> 'The argument of the Attorney-General, which seeks to brush aside the articles and to vest in the executors a property which Henry Jameson never possessed, would ascribe to the Finance Act the power of making a new subject matter. The argument of the defendants clings desperately to the Articles, and gives really no adequate significance to the words of the Act requiring the Commissioners to estimate the price which the shares would fetch in the open market. The solution lies between the two. The Attorney-General must give more weight to the Articles, and the defendants to the statute. It requires no tremendous imagination to conceive what a purchaser would give in the open market for Henry Jameson's shares as Henry Jameson himself held them at his death — *for the right to stand in his shoes.*'

2.105   Lord Ashbourne felt that although not so valuable as owning shares absolutely free and unfettered, the shares were worth more than the value attributed by the Articles and he could see no overwhelming difficulty in estimating the price they would fetch if sold in the open market.

2.106   An interesting point was made by Fitzgibbon LJ in the same case, where he said that the pre-emption clauses could be both appreciatory and depreciatory. Although the right of pre-emption against Henry Jameson's shares was a depreciating incident, the corresponding right (of Henry Jameson or any other person standing in his shoes) to acquire shares from other members at the fair value was an appreciating incident. However, in extending this argument, one might say that the appreciating incident arose simply out of being a shareholder, whether of one share or a large number of shares.

Oppression of minorities

2.107   In valuing shares and, in particular, in looking at the rights and expectations of shareholders, the fact that one or more of the shareholders has a dominant power over the others cannot be manipulated so as to remove all rights of minority shareholders. The *Companies Act 1985, ss 459–461* and *1989 Schedule 19 para 11* contains provisions to safeguard the minority shareholders' rights, and thus preserve the value of such shareholdings.

2.108   The non-declaration (or restriction) of dividends may constitute an unfair prejudice if the retention of the monies has no good business purpose. What has to be shown is conduct (whether current or retrospective) which is unfairly prejudicial to the interests of the company's members generally or of some part of its members. Simply not declaring dividends in itself could not be said to constitute such conduct. Often, a company will wish to retain earnings despite excellent cash flow and increasing earnings — for example, to support financially risky trading activities (such as uninsured international contracts, or new projects or long-term contracts, or new joint-venture parties), or uncertainties in the market place or in the financial world which suggest that cash (or investments) be retained for the time being, or perhaps to meet current expected losses. Perhaps there are plans afoot for expansion or the rekindling of a postponed project. On the other hand, if profits have been made why should they not be distributed and the future dealt with by reference to new sources of finance? Now, a bird in the hand is worth two in the bush, and cash in the company's account is worth a lot more than cash that has to brought in from outside. The foregoing might well be one of the matters that must be weighed in the valuation of a control holding or the valuation of a minority interest, but it would be very difficult to apply the legislation (or the threat of it) in a valuation based on the statutory hypothetical open market basis (see 2.8). Yet, the aura of this legislation tests any argument that, solely because of insignificant and impotent voting power, a minority interest has only token value.

2.109   If shareholders who have a dominant power in a company exercise or threaten to exercise that power to procure that something is done or not done in the conduct of the company's affairs, and when that conduct is unfair or, in the words of Viscount Simonds in *Scottish Co-operative Wholesale Society Ltd v Meyer*, 'burdensome, harsh and wrongful' to the minority shareholders and 'lacks that degree of probity which they are entitled to expect in the conduct of the company's affairs', that action may be regarded as oppressive to the minority shareholders. They would then be entitled to petition the court for an appropriate order, for example, to regulate the company's affairs; enforce or prevent some act; authorise civil proceedings; enforce purchase of shares from a member of the company by other members or by the company itself (with subsequent reduction of capital). In such a case the court may in effect vary or override the Memorandum or Articles of the company, or may put the company into compulsory liquidation. This applies to *wrongful* acts. It would not be oppression if, for example, the company refuses to buy out minority shareholdings. On the other hand, a planned campaign to divert the business of a company into another business medium under different control probably would be an oppression of minorities that might be remedied by the court requiring the wrong-doer to purchase the company's shares from the innocent parties.

2.110   *Re Company No. 003420* (see 2.73) was a case concerning an order under the *Companies Act 1980, s 75* (now *Companies Act 1985, s 461(2)(d)*) for the majority shareholders to acquire the minority shareholders' shares. The company was held to fall into the category of a 'quasi-partnership', i.e. it had been incorporated to be the vehicle for the conduct of a business carried on by two or more shareholders which they could have carried on in partnership together. As such, where a shareholder had been unfairly prejudiced resulting in his exclusion from participating in the company's affairs, and he had not acted to justify that exclusion, the price of his shares should be fixed *pro rata* according to the value of the company's shares *as a whole* and not on the basis of a discounted minority interest (see *Re Bird Precision Bellows Ltd*). The same consequence followed in *Quinlan v Essex Hinge Co Ltd*. A quasi-partnership was established between persons effectively acting as junior 'partner' and senior 'partner'. In this case, the evidence showed that a relationship of mutual confidence had been established between the parties and there was an undertaking that the junior partner would participate in the business over and above the terms of a service agreement between the company and the junior partner and the company's Articles of Association. The junior partner's shares were required to be bought back by the company at a *pro rata* value.

2.111   The elements of a quasi-partnership and the application of the 'just and equitable' rule for the making of an order for compulsory winding-up are discussed in *Ebrahimi v Westbourne Galleries Ltd.*

2.112   Also in *Re Company No. 003420*, the *pro rata* valuation basis applied because it was the most fair in all the circumstances. In other circumstances perhaps a different 'fair value' basis (see 2.57 *et seq*) would have been adopted, and if there had not been oppression of a minority interest in the first place, it is unlikely that the *pro rata* basis would have been used at all (see *Re Company No. 004475*).

2.113   If fair value has been determined under the terms of a company's Articles of Association, the fact that a minority discount may have been applied cannot of itself be complained of as unfairly prejudicial conduct (*Re Castleburn* — see also 2.74). A petition under *section 459* cannot be used to attack the basis of such a valuation.

2.114   It should also be noted that an irreperable breakdown of relations between shareholders does not alone imply unfair prejudice by one side or the other. If a company's Articles provide for what is to happen on such a breakdown, the shareholders have to rely on those provisions without recourse to *section 459* (*Re Company No. 004377*).

Actual sales

Present sales

2.115   If an offer has been made for the company as a whole then it is unlikely that the shareholders would sell for less than the bid price, although it is not impossible that a lower price would be accepted. For example, in the case of shareholder managers, they may believe that a better long-term arrangement, perhaps from the point of view of security of employment, may be had from a party who cannot afford to pay the higher price; alternatively, a lower price may be offered by someone who guarantees the continuance of the company as opposed to asset-stripping it. If bids are to be considered as part of a share valuation exercise, it is incumbent upon the valuer to satisfy himself first, that the offer is genuine and from an independent third party, and secondly, that it is not, for example, an artificially low price based on the personal knowledge that the vendor is in extreme need of cash and in an untenable negotiating position, perhaps because of clawing creditors. If upon inspection the offer is *bona fide*, it is suggested that that bid price must constitute the company's value unless some material disparity can be identified through any of the other bases.

2.116   In a fiscal valuation, because a hypothetical purchaser has to be imagined, the value at a date before the takeover has been effected should allow the hypothetical purchaser to make a profit on his subsequent sale to the bidder. The necessary discount from the bid price will have to take into account all the particular circumstances surrounding the proposed sale. Any uncertainty that the deal may not go ahead will of course serve to increase the discount.

Prior sales

2.117   The case of *McNamee v RC*, an Irish estate duty case, may be quoted as authority for prior arm's length sales influencing the value of the shares. There may well be a case for having regard to a prior sale, of course, but care must be taken that it was a sale in a 'real or imaginary open market', and also that it concerned a sale of shares in similar amounts and circumstances to those that are the subject of the current valuation. Further, the longer the time that has elapsed between the prior sale and the current valuation, the more difficult it is to say that the one is an influence on or indicative of the other. While the *McNamee* case clearly indicates that the court can be influenced by evidence of a recent arm's length sale, a careful reading also shows that the more clear evidence there is to support the present valuation, the more likely it is that the court will accept it.

2.118   Some authorities suggest that prior sales can actually be introduced into a hybrid valuation (see Chapter 7) and weighted accordingly. It is suggested that, except where there are regular dealings in the shares such as to constitute a current market, this has the effect of distorting the current share value without contributing in real terms to defining the underlying value. Where a prior sale might be used to influence a share price is in determining any discounts or price to earnings ratio, but great care must be taken, and the full facts surrounding the prior sale must be ascertained. For example, the prior sale may have been entirely at arm's length, but the vendor may have been in exceptional personal need of cash and decided to sell off some of his shares at a bargain price (perhaps to a colleague) to put himself into funds. It is argued that this situation equates with the special purchaser who has personal reasons for investing (see 2.77 *et seq*) and so this sale value might be ignored for determining a current market value.

2.119   Subsequent to a private sale of part of a shareholding, a vendor might transfer shares into a trust, possibly contemplating a flotation of his company. The value on the flotation could be considerably more than the first sale and bear no relationship to it. The other side of the coin might be that the company simply is no longer as valuable as it was — for whatever reason — and no previous sale can change that. Another case is where 100% of the shares of a company are bought and shortly afterwards a small proportion given to employees of the company. The first transaction (a 100% acquisition valued on prospects prior to acquisition) is likely to be valued on an entirely different basis from the interest given to employees.

2.120   What is now clear, however, following *IRC v Stenhouse's Trustees* is that prices at which shares in an unquoted family company had changed hands between members of the family and associated trusts are admissible as evidence in hearings before the Special Commissioners. So too are values agreed with the Revenue on earlier taxable occasions.

2.121   The Scottish Court of Session emphasised that valuations were a matter of fact and expert opinion which could be made after employing more than one measure, each legitimate but none necessarily conclusive by itself.

2.122   The question of the extent to which previous agreements should be taken into account is often a problem when negotiating values for capital gains tax re-basing purposes at 31 March 1982. This case shows that although such agreements are admissible as evidence, the particular circumstances surrounding them can be examined and if appropriate used to explain why the value agreed should or should not be followed.

Subsequent sales

2.123   Where there is a sale shortly following the date of valuation, at a price materially different from the value given, and the matter is still in dispute with the Shares Valuation Division, the sale price on the second transaction (if it relates to a similar number of shares in similar circumstances) may have a considerable bearing on the outcome of any negotiated agreement. It would be wise to review the valuation to identitfy the elements which differentiate the two prices, such as market interest, profit or asset variance, share reorganisations or shareholding changes. Following the case of *IRC v Marr's Trustees*, however, the mere fact that a higher price could be had if the sale were delayed until better market conditions existed, should not of itself influence the value of the asset at the date for which valuation is required.

Discount for lack of marketability

2.124   The discount for lack of marketability is discussed at 5.37. It comes into play principally when the share valuation is based on a comparison with quoted company shares. The price earnings ratio will be smaller, or the purchaser's required dividend yield will be greater, for a private company because its shares are not so readily marketable as quoted company shares and particularly because private company shares are usually subject to restrictions on transfer in the Articles of Association (see 2.101 *et seq*) — a problem accentuated for the minority shareholder. The discount might also be applicable where the share valuation is based on estimated price earnings ratios or estimated open market unquoted dividend yields (where no restrictions on transfer apply), or on freely marketable alternative investment yields. This discount is for the size and marketability of the *shareholding* that is being valued, it is not in respect of the differences that exist between the subject company as a private company and its comparable quoted companies, and other adjustments should be made to compensate for those factors (see 5.32).

Chapter 3

Shares

Shares and shareholdings

3.1   Not surprisingly, a share valuation starts with the shares themselves. It is necessary to understand precisely what a 'share' is and what it means to the person who possesses it. In the *Companies Act 1985, s 744*, 'share' is defined as a 'share in the share capital of a company, and includes stock (except where a distinction between shares and stock is express or implied)'. Perhaps the most important gloss on this definition can be found in the case of *Borland's Trustees v Steel Bros & Co Ltd* in which Farwell J said:

> 'A share is the interest of the shareholder in the company measured by a sum of money, for the purpose of liability in the first place, and of interest in the second, but also consisting of a series of mutual covenants entered into by all the shareholders inter se in accordance with [the Companies Acts]. The contract contained in the Articles of Association is one of the original incidents of the share.'

3.2   He went on to say that 'A share is not a sum of money but is an interest measured by a sum of money and made up of various rights contained in the contract, including the right to a sum of money of a more or less amount'.

3.3   The *Borland* case was considered in the estate duty case of *A-G v Jameson*, in which Kenny J said:

> 'No shareholder has a right to any specific portion of the company's property and save by, and to the extent of, his voting power at a general meeting of the company, cannot curtail the free and proper disposition of it. He is entitled to a share of the company's capital and profits . . . If the company disposes of its assets, or if the latter be realised in a liquidation, he has a right to a proportion of the amount received after the discharge of the company's debts and liabilities. In applying these rights — that is, in becoming a member of the company — he is deemed to have simultaneously entered into a contract under seal to conform to the regulations contained in the Articles of Association [*Companies Act 1985, ss 14* and *22*]. Whatever obligations are contained in these Articles . . . they are inseparable incidents attached to his rights and the idea of a share cannot . . . be complete without their inclusion.'

3.4   In the estate duty case of *IRC v Crossman*, Lord Russell of Killowen said of a share:

> 'it is the interest of a person in the company, that interest being composed of rights and obligations which are defined by the Companies Act and by the Memorandum and Articles of Association of the company.'

3.5   These cases show that a share comprises a bundle of rights, but that the shareholder has no right to any specific part of the underlying assets of the company per se.

3.6   In the case of *Short v Treasury Commissioners*, concerning the nationalisation of Short Brothers, Evershed LJ said that 'Shareholders are not, in the eye of the law, part owners of the undertaking. The undertaking is something different from the totality of the shareholding'. This is a major principle, and later on in the case Evershed took the point that the Crown was acquiring all the shares of the company and thereby, of course, had full control, but pointed out that the Crown was acquiring shares from a number of individual shareholders. He said:

> 'Prima facie, as it seems to us . . . each shareholder is entitled to get, and to get only the value of what he possesses; that is all that he has to sell or transfer. If an individual shareholder . . . owns such a number of shares . . . as gives him effective control . . . it may well be that the value to be attributed to that holding . . . is a figure greater than the sum arrived at by multiplying the number of his shares by the market value for the time being of a single share. In such a case, the shareholder . . . has and is able to sell something more than a mere parcel of shares, each having the rights as to dividend and otherwise conferred upon it by the company's regulations.'

3.7   On the facts as found in *Short v Treasury Commissioners*, the vendor minority shareholder could have got 29/3d for each of his ordinary shares from a willing buyer; for nationalisation compensation however he claimed a larger sum to reflect the fact that there was added or control value which was also being acquired by the Crown. Evershed summed up his view by saying that he could see no reason in principle why the claimant should receive more than the value of what he had to sell. However, Evershed had not considered the problem of oppression of minority interests where the principle is complicated by minority shareholders being put in an untenable position, especially in cases of 'quasi-partnerships'; see 2.107 *et seq.*

Memorandum and Articles of Association

3.8   It will be appreciated from the foregoing that, early in the valuation, the valuer should inspect the company's own Memorandum and Articles of Association; and, so far as relevant, Tables A, D or E (the latter relating to special classes of company limited by guarantee or unlimited) as published by the Secretary of State (see *Companies Act 1985, ss 7–21*).

3.9 *Shares*

Companies Act 1985, s 14 states:

'Subject to the provisions of this Act, the Memorandum and Articles, when registered, bind the company and its members to the same extent as if they respectively had been signed and sealed by each member, and contained covenants on the part of each member to observe all the provisions of the Memorandum and of the Articles.'

3.9 These documents as originated and properly amended set forth the full rights, entitlements, constraints and limitations relating to the shares of the company and they can be investigated at the company's registered office or through a search at Companies House. This latter course of action is rather unsatisfactory but should be taken if there is any possibility that the statutory affairs of the company are incomplete or not up to date. This matter and the problems relating to information generally are discussed at 2.24 *et seq.*

3.10 Apart from the Memorandum and Articles of Association there is always the possibility that a shareholders' agreement exists (see 3.18 *et seq*), and, unfortunately, there are also circumstances for which the Memorandum and Articles and shareholders' agreement do not cater. An example is the case of an exact balance of power over the control of the company: e.g. two shareholders each having 50% of the voting power and neither having a casting vote.

Dead-lock ownership/control

3.11 The problem of balance of power was examined in the case of *B W Noble Ltd v IRC*, in which case a shareholder held 50% of the ordinary shares. In normal circumstances of course that would not bestow control upon that particular shareholder. However, in this case the shareholder was also chairman of the company. Rowlatt J said that a controlling interest is with the shareholder whose holding in the company is such that he is more powerful than all the other shareholders put together in general meeting. In this case, the shares held by the chairman were reinforced by the position that he occupied as chairman:

'A position which he occupies not merely by the votes of the other shareholders or of his directors elected by the shareholders, but by contract; and, so reinforced, inasmuch as he has a casting vote, he does control the general meetings, there is no question about that, and inasmuch as he does possess at least half of the shares, he can prevent any modifications taking place in the constitution of the company which would undermine his position as chairman.'

3.12 In situations such as these, thought should be given to precisely what is being valued and placed in the hypothetical market to be sold — and acquired. In a situation as in *Noble* above, the chairman has control whilst he has the two elements — the shares and the contract as chairman which gives him the casting vote. If he could in law sell both the shares, and the chairman's contract of employment with the casting vote, as one package, he would have the ability to sell a controlling interest; but if he cannot sell this package, at the best, he is selling a dead-locked holding. Indeed it may even be a minority interest if the chairman's casting vote remains with or is transferred to another.

3.13 If the casting vote or the chairmanship rotates between board members at general meeting, it is unlikely that on a valuation for inheritance tax and capital gains tax purposes the dead-locked shareholding could be valued as a controlling interest because the casting vote is a mere transient power and not unfettered. Where there are no specific powers in the Articles of Association to remove a chairman who has a permanent office and casting vote the *Noble* principle will apply and the problem that could arise for IHT purposes is that the holding might be valued as a controlling interest even though it may not be possible to transfer the casting vote, and any actual sale would be of a dead-locked holding only. One could, of course, argue that the open market value of the 'controlling interest' would only equate with a 'dead-lock' value because in the open market that is all that would be actually sold and purchased — unless the fact is that the casting vote was capable of travelling with the shares, perhaps because of provisions in the Articles of Association.

3.14 A tax problem would arise if a permanent casting vote was transferred, perhaps to a connected party, as this could be regarded as a diminution in value of the transferor's estate (*Inheritance Tax Act 1984, s 3*) and unless it could be argued that the disposition was not intended to confer a gratuitous benefit on the recipient (*Inheritance Tax Act 1984, s 10*) a potential IHT exposure could follow. Also, a capital gains tax problem might ensue on the basis that a permanent casting vote could be regarded as an asset (and particularly the provisions of *TCGA 1992, s 19* relating to the disposal of assets in a series of transactions could be in point). Certainly, a contract of employment is an asset although not capable of being assigned (see *Benson's Hosiery (Holdings) Ltd v O'Brien*).

3.15 Consider the other 50% shareholder. If the controlling chairman has no intention of selling his shares, the other 50% shareholder has only a large minority shareholding to sell, whose value may be influenced by matters such as the terms of the chairman's contract or the age of the chairman.

3.16 The concept of quasi-partnership may be relevant to deadlock situations (see 2.107 *et seq*) but only for purposes of compulsory winding up (see *Re Yenidje Tobacco Co Ltd*). It may also have some relevance to share valuations in divorce cases where husband and wife are shareholders in a quasi-partnership company, with the result that a valuation may be on the basis of a *pro rata* share of the value of the business as a whole rather than on a discounted minority interest basis.

3.17 In the case of *IRC v J Bibby & Sons Ltd* it was held that control must be ascertained by reference to the company's constitution and that it is irrelevant that a shareholder who has apparent control may himself be amenable to some external control. In the case of *Barclays Bank v IRC* it was found that where a shareholder held 1,100 ordinary shares in his own right and 3,650 shares as trustee, because *under the constitution of the company* he was entitled to vote in respect of both of the holdings and together they constituted more than 50% of the shares in issue, the shareholder had control of the company. Viscount Simmons in that case said that he could see no difference between the natural meaning of the two phrases 'having a controlling interest in the company' and 'having control of the company', although he felt it might be desirable in the latter case to give an extended meaning to those words. Although under *Finance Act 1940, s 55* (estate duty provisions) fiduciary holdings were not to be aggregated with other shareholdings by the same person for estate duty valuation purposes, it was held that this exclusion was not to apply where the fiduciary holding was held by a trustee who was also the settlor. In other words, it was not possible to fragment value by settling shares on oneself to hold some in a fiduciary capacity and some in a personal capacity.

Shareholders' agreements

3.18　Usually, such an agreement concerns the division between the parties of profits or assets on a liquidation, or pre-emption rights and restrictions on transfer. The division of profits or assets may be in proportions that differ from the respective shareholdings of those parties and may be calculated by reference to remuneration or management fees drawn by one or other of the parties. In some cases the agreement may provide for a specific profit division for a determinable period and thereafter a different division may apply; in other cases the 'rights' attaching to different classes of share ('A' ordinary and 'B' ordinary) may be specified or qualified.

3.19　The agreement might constitute an agreement to purchase shares or an option to buy or sell; on the other hand, it may in effect be no more than a service contract or management contract. In some cases, it may be a document that evidences the holding of shares in trust for another party: this may be as bare trustee or the shares may be held on trust for sale. The possibilities are just short of endless.

3.20　The first step is to ascertain whether the agreement constitutes an enforceable contract, whether standing alone or in conjunction with other document(s), including the company's Memorandum and Articles of Association. If it does not, it is unlikely to have any serious effect on the value of the shares in point, but nevertheless it may be clear evidence of some management style, third-party influence over the conduct of the business (but note the *IRC v J Bibby & Sons Ltd* case at 3.17), or other relevant matter.

3.21　If it does constitute an enforceable contract it is necessary to determine whether it is in effect an 'appendix' to the Memorandum and Articles of Association, in which case it may have an effect on the value of the shares in point and must be read in conjunction with the Memorandum and Articles (see 2.101), or whether it constitutes a personal arrangement that has no intrinsic effect on the shares themselves or on their transferability. If there is some effect, does the agreement continue in force after a transfer or after the death of the shareholder, and is the agreement assignable?

3.22   If it is discovered that the shares are simply held on trust or that an option to purchase (or sell) is in existence, it may be necessary to reconsider whether the share valuation exercise being carried out is actually relevant. In the case of the shares held on bare trust or trust for sale, the person in whose name the shares are registered will have no beneficial interest in them (but note the case of *Barclays Bank Ltd v IRC*, at 3.17) and is not entitled to benefit personally from any rights that the shares may have. If the shares are being valued for the person who does have the ultimate beneficial interest then no problem arises, provided the beneficial interest is unequivocal. If that is not the case, the document must be scrutinised to see from when it took effect, and other enquiries made to determine whether an earlier transfer by the registered owner had taken place. This will be particularly important in any tax related valuation.

3.23   In the case of an option to buy or sell where an option price is fixed there will be no valuation requirement (subject to tax considerations). However, the option price may, of course, be 'market value' (see 2.4) or some other basis such as 'fair value' (see 2.57).

3.24   A shareholders' agreement may not actually be in writing but without any admission by the shareholders of such agreement or practice and evidence of it, it would be rash to make any valuation adjustment.

The subject of the valuation

3.25   Shares are valued according to their entitlement to:

- earnings;
- dividends;
- assets;
- a combination of these factors.

3.26   A valuation of shares is concerned with determining the extent of such entitlement, each of which is discussed in detail in the following chapters. It must also be ascertained whether the issued shares are fully or partly paid.

3.27   The next step is to identify what entitlement or 'right' attaches to the particular shares which are the subject of the valuation. A number of different types of share may be authorised by a company's Articles of Association, and, as has been seen, the Articles contain regulations governing the allotment and issue of the shares that are so authorised. If a new class of share is to be issued by the company and the Articles do not authorise the issue of such shares, it will be necessary to alter the Articles in accordance with company law. This will require a special resolution and will be minuted. Other relevant matters — such as dividend policy — may be minuted and therefore a share valuation should include inspection of the company's Memorandum and Articles and might require a company search and inspection of the statutory books, share register and minute book (see 2.20).

3.28   In any valuation of shares it will be necessary to identify the different classes of share that a company has in issue, their respective entitlements, the number of shares in issue and who owns them beneficially, whether 'family' or third parties. Certainly, for tax valuation purposes, if not for other commercial purposes, the relationship between shareholders may be of crucial importance (see, e.g. 9.4 *et seq*).

3.29   Some of the classes and types of share that may be issued by a company are:

Ordinary shares:

- A, B or C, etc., ordinary shares;
- preferred ordinary shares;
- deferred shares;
- ordinary shares with weighted voting rights.

Preference shares:

- fixed preference shares;
- redeemable shares;
- participating preference shares;
- cumulative preference shares.

There may also be:

- founder (or management) shares;
- share options and warrants;
- employee shares;
- phantom shares;

and other 'designer' shares.

Ordinary shares

3.30   The 'ordinary' share is the class of share most commonly met in practice. Such shares usually carry unfettered voting rights for use at shareholders' meetings, most usually the company's Annual General Meeting. They constitute the risk capital put up by the owners of the company and typically are entitled to all of the dividends declared by the directors out of the profits (or accumulated profits) of the company. Should the company be dissolved then its net assets would be distributed to the ordinary shareholders in proportion to their shareholdings. Such distribution may be in cash and/or *in specie* (e.g. where a shareholder takes a car or a property or some other asset in full or partial satisfaction of his rights to a liquidation distribution).

3.31   However, this assumes that there are no shares other than ordinary shares. If there are, the terms of the other shares may affect the rights of the ordinary shareholder to receive dividends or liquidation distributions.

3.32   For example, where there are 'A' ordinary shares and 'B' ordinary shares, both carrying voting rights, the 'A' ordinary shares may carry equal rights to dividends with the 'B' shares, but the 'B' shares may carry no rights to a liquidation distribution. It is possible that in such a case there will be a shareholders' agreement which requires the 'A' shareholders to vote for a good proportion of the annual profits to be paid out as dividends because the 'B' shareholders' only right is to income, not to net assets and reserves, and if they missed a year's profits because no dividend was declared they might lose the right to that income forever. Alternatively the 'B' shares may be entitled to receive a proportion of the accumulated profits on a distribution.

3.33   The rights attaching to any class of share can be simple or complex and it is important to identify them. In the above case, clearly the value of the 'A' shares would be greater than the 'B' shares, because in addition to the income entitlement that the 'A' shareholders share with the 'B' shareholders, the 'A' shareholders have the sole right to receive any assets of the company on a liquidation.

3.34   Yet another possibility frequently met in practice is that some ordinary shares have no voting rights but otherwise rank *pari passu* with the other ordinary shares, so they would be equally entitled to dividends and a liquidation distribution but would have no ability through voting power to influence the activities of the company, including the dividend policy and special resolution required to put the company into liquidation. Similarly, one might find 'C' ordinary shares, or 'D' ordinary shares and so on. In valuing such shares it will be necessary to have regard to any shareholders' agreement — including possibly an unwritten agreement where it appears that a definable practice has been followed; this may be construed as an established dividend policy, and dividend policies do play an important part when valuing shares on a dividend basis (see Chapter 4).

3.35   A further variation on this theme is the weighting of voting rights between two (or more) classes of ordinary share. In *Holt v Holt* a company had issued share capital of 1,000 NZ$1 ordinary shares divided into 1 $1 A share and 999 $1 B shares. All shares ranked equally in terms of dividend payments and the right to participate in surplus assets on a liquidation, but the A share carried 10,000 votes whereas B shares carried 1 vote each. The Privy Council decided that the value of the A share to a hypothetical vendor was considerably greater than its value either on an earnings or an assets basis, since the purchaser could either continue to run the business (which in this case was farming) or negotiate with the holders of the B shares for a sale to their mutual advantage. The valuation was for the purposes of a matrimonial dispute but the terms of the Privy Council's decision indicate that it would also be effective if the valuation was required for fiscal purposes.

3.36   Shares of this type have typically been used for family farming companies where the intention has been to retain control in the hands of an older generation whilst at the same time concentrating value in the hands of younger members of the family. The decision in *Holt v Holt* to some extent reinforces the Revenue's view that shares with voting control but limited other rights can have considerable value, but each case will have its own peculiarities. The precise rights attaching to the shares and the circumstances surrounding the company will, as ever, be paramount. As *Holt v Holt* did not contain any guidance on the method of valuation there remains considerable scope for discussion on the exact distribution of value between two classes of share with weighted voting rights.

3.37   The value of the B shares was not considered, but as voting control was wielded by the A shareholder it is suggested that any holding of B shares would be treated as an uninfluential (minority) holding.

Preferred ordinary shares

3.38   These are shares with special rights attaching to them which differentiate them from the other shares in issue. It may be that such shares are entitled to the company's dividends up to some specified limit before the ordinary shareholders can take their dividends, or they may be entitled to some share in the assets on a liquidation. It does not necessarily mean that they are more valuable than the ordinary shares in issue and it is not unusual to find that the right is limited to a fixed rate of dividend, taken before the ordinary dividend, but without the unlimited potential of the ordinary shares — see 3.46. In valuing preferred shares, a proper measure of value must be ascribed to each element of preferential treatment which should be identifiable from the Articles of Association or in a document appended to or forming part of the minutes of the shareholders' or directors' meetings.

Deferred shares

3.39   There are two principal types of share having deferred rights: first, there are shares that have no rights to dividends or assets on a winding-up until a specified time or event in the future, and secondly there are shares whose entitlement to dividends or assets may be subordinate to limited prior rights of other shares. The Inland Revenue Shares Valuation Division officers are required to notify their seniors of the existence of deferred shares. This is because of the potential tax saving characteristics of such shares.

3.40   In the first case the holder of deferred shares will have to wait a specified number of years (say, 20 years) from the date of issue before the shares become entitled to participate at all in dividends or assets, and it would be usual to find that they have no voting rights on any issues except in relation to the creation of other shares. Of course it is almost impossible to determine the state of a company so far into the future. The degree of uncertainty is very great, and what one is valuing in shares that will one day rank *pari passu* with all the then existing ordinary shares, is today's value of that future promise.

3.41   One method of valuation is to take the present day value of the ordinary shares, dilute that value by bringing in the number of deferred shares to rank *pari passu* and then discount that diluted value by the appropriate rate over the period of deferral. The appropriate rate may be the real current rate of inflation. So, if 10,000 shares are in issue, valued at £12 each, and there are 5,000 deferred shares which will rank *pari passu* in 20 years, the diluted value is:

$$\frac{10,000}{10,000 + 5,000} \times £12 = £8$$

Discounted at, say, 7% over 20 years, this becomes *£1.87* (subject to any 'risk' discount that may be appropriate). This value might be appropriate for a disposal of deferred shares for capital gains tax purposes.

3.42   For inheritance tax purposes, where the loss to a transferor's estate has to be measured (see 9.34 *et seq*), it is important to note the effect of separating the ownership of ordinary and deferred shares.

3.43   If a shareholder with 30% of a company's issued ordinary share capital is entitled to a 'one for one' bonus issue of 20-year deferred shares, which he renounces in favour of a third party, for capital gains tax purposes valuation is of the deferred shares in isolation. For inheritance tax, however, the shareholder's position both before and after the renunciation will have to be considered. If the renunciation is a chargeable transfer, or becomes chargeable on the death of the transferor within seven years (see 9.34 *et seq*), the Shares Valuation Division will argue, particularly if the company pays no dividend and there is no short-term prospect of a winding-up, that following the renunciation the holding of 30% of the ordinary share is in effect worth little more than a 15% holding, which is what it will become at the end of 20 years. Compared with what might be a fairly small value for the disposal for capital gains tax purposes, the loss to the transferor's estate for inheritance tax could, in the Revenue's view, extend almost to the full difference in value between a 30% holding of ordinary shares and a 15% holding. The particular instance is not common but the principal is important.

3.44   The value transferred for IHT purposes will depend on the circumstances of the company and the precise rights of the deferred shares. If a transfer of deferred shares is to take place as part of a tax planning exercise, with a view to passing the future worth (if any) of a company to future generations at a low value, it will always be worthwhile to bear in mind the attitude the Shares Valuation Division are likely to have. In particular, they are now taking a view that when deferred shares come to rank *pari passu* with other shares there is an alteration in the rights attaching to the shares. This is an important point considered at 9.44.

3.45   The second type of deferred share is that where they carry rights to dividends only after the preferred and the ordinary shareholders have received their dividends by reference to some specified limit, after which the deferred shares may have equal rights with the ordinary shares to the residual distributable profits. The valuation exercise in this case will be concerned principally with the capitalisation of the residual rights.

Fixed preference shares

3.46   Fixed preference shares are usually entitled to a fixed 'coupon', or rate of dividend which will be payable out of distributable profits before the ordinary shareholders can take the balance. The dividend rate will be whatever is commercial in relation to the funds injected into the company, the need for the funds, the timing and so on, and may be variable. On the liquidation of the company, preference shareholders will usually be entitled to receive back their original capital before the ordinary shareholders can participate in the surplus net assets. It is unlikely that such preference shareholders will have voting rights, although this is not unknown. What can be found is that preference shareholders have votes concerning the declaration of dividends (to ensure they get some annual return, although unless the company's Articles of Association provide otherwise it is established company law that the dividend on preference shares is cumulative). Such shares would not usually carry rights to vote on any other matter.

Redeemable shares

3.47   If shares are redeemable the company can repay the capital at some future time without having to go into liquidation. Depending on the precise terms of the share issue, there may be a specified date on which, or a specified period during which, the redemption can take place — or there may be no such date. The redemption price may be stated or it may be open. Usually the redemption will be at par (i.e. the value when issued), but it may be at a premium or a discount — the first to reflect a low income return during the period of ownership, the latter to reflect a high income return. The Articles of Association may allow preference shares to participate in liquidation surpluses. Usually on a liquidation, repayment of preference shares takes priority over the repayment of ordinary shares but not over mortgages or debentures.

The normal valuation basis of such shares is the dividend yield (subject, as always, to ascertaining the full rights attaching to the shares). It is usual to identify the yield from quoted preference shares of a similar character. This is discussed in more detail at 3.66 *et seq*.

Participating preference shares

3.48   Subject to the precise rights, which will be found in the company's Articles of Association, these preference shares would normally be entitled to participate in distributions relating to the ordinary share capital — i.e. after fixed and non-participating preference shareholders etc. have been paid out. There may be no right to vote attached to these shares, but if there are voting rights the shares would be valued on the same basis as ordinary shares.

Cumulative preference shares

3.49   Under the rights attaching to these shares, where in any year a company has been unable to pay a dividend on its preference shares, because of lack of profits, the dividend that would have been paid is effectively reserved until the company has the funds to enable it to distribute the backlog and to continue the payment of dividends on the preference shares. This accumulated reserve must be paid to the preference shareholders before the ordinary shareholders are entitled to receive the dividend. Preference shares are usually cumulative automatically unless specific provision otherwise is made, either in the terms of the issue or under the Articles.

Management or founder shares

3.50   These types of share are usually found in a company start-up, or management buy-out or buy-in financed by a financial institution. They may carry tortuous rights and provisions and are usually issued in tandem with shareholder agreements and options to purchase or sell shares or convert loan stock. Typically, even though they actually constitute a minority of the shares in issue, they will carry voting control (perhaps subject to conversion terms); there may be a variable dividend entitlement changing over time and profit (defined) levels. The valuation exercise requires a very careful scrutiny of the financing and debt and the 'dilution' effect on issued share capital of conversion rights and options, warrants and so on. The tax issue whether the shares are true 'founder' shares or constitute an employee incentive arrangement is another matter.

Share options and warrants

3.51   Share options or share warrants are basically rights to acquire or subscribe for specified shares in a company, usually at a stated price at some future date. The option/warrant would in almost all cases have some value at the time it is acquired, the major factors being:

(*a*)   the present-day value of the same 'class' of shares that would be purchased if the option/warrant was to be exercised in due course;

(*b*)   the time-lapse between the present-day value and the first occasion when the option/warrant can be exercised;

(*c*)   any dilution in the then value of the issued shares that the exercise of the option/warrant would cause; and

(*d*)   the 'tradeability' of the options/warrants in the meantime.

3.52   These principles apply to both private company and quoted 'traded' options. The latter tend to be for short periods (usually reckoned in months). Options (other than traded options) are most often found to be used in employee incentive scheme arrangements where restrictions on transfer are considerable, but founder-shareholder arrangements with financiers may also include some form of share options.

3.53   In valuing an option/warrant, the present-day value of the related class shares would be the starting point to determine an estimated value of the shares (duly diluted by any other share issues and options exercised up to and on the first possible date of exercise of the subject matter options) at the future exercise date. That future value would then be discounted to a present-day value, having regard to the combined effect of inflation over the period and the interest foregone over the period (because the option would not generate income during its dormant period).

3.54   If (as is likely) the option is not transferable, a future discount to reflect this lack of marketability would be appropriate. The level of this discount may depend upon the time period involved and the underlying 'strength' supporting the related class of shares. In this case, 'strength' means longevity of the company. Any period in excess of five years carries real uncertainties.

Employee shares

3.55   Under various incentive schemes, whether devised by individual companies or which follow the rules laid down in share scheme tax legislation, a growing number of organisations give their employees shares or options to acquire shares in the company. These may be non-voting shares and may be required to be surrendered to other employees or shareholders if the holder leaves employment. In some cases there will be restrictions on disposal and the shares may be held by trustees on behalf of the individual employees. In certain arrangements involving employee trusts, the 'dividends' paid to the employee may be treated not as investment income but as emoluments from the employment (see Chapter 9).

3.56   If the employee shares are special shares then clearly the terms on which they have been — or are to be — issued must be considered. If there are any options in existence in the hands of employees the terms on which the options were given must be examined; the timing of the exercise of the option, the price and from whom the shares are to come (company or shareholder) are all relevant (see Chapter 9). The effect of such shares on the other shares of the company will usually be minimal but clearly this depends upon the number of shares in issue and the number of 'new' shares that may be issued on the exercise of the option(s).

3.57 If the shares are ordinary shares or otherwise rank *pari passu*, the normal criteria apply for valuation, subject to the subtle differences that exist between valuations for income tax and for capital gains or inheritance tax.

Phantom shares

3.58 The phantom share concept developed to reward employees for their special contribution to the growth in asset value or earnings of the employing company by giving them a direct interest in profits or capital growth without involving them in real terms in the equity of the company.

3.59 In tax terms this is a most uncertain area and the tax consequences — for both individual and company — will depend upon the circumstances. An income tax charge normally accrues in respect of any receipts by the individual arising from 'ownership' of or entitlement to the phantom stock, but, given the right circumstances the 'share' might be regarded as a 'chose in action' with capital gains tax as well as income tax consequences.

3.60 Although the existence of such shares may not affect the rights attaching to equity share capital it may very well have an effect on the company's own obligations and on net distributable profits and assets available for distribution on a liquidation, and thereby could affect the value of the equity shares.

3.61 Phantom stock would not usually be regarded as part of the company's capital structure although, by virtue of the phantom stock, there may be arrangements in force which restrict the directors' (or shareholders') actions in some areas, such as declaring dividends, voluntary liquidation of the company or disposal of shares.

Convertible shares

3.62 Where loan stock or shares carry rights of conversion to other classes of share, in valuing the stock, apart from the basic value of the stock itself, the rights of conversion should also be taken into account if there is a measure of value. An appropriate approach to the valuation is to calculate the value of the shares as if the conversion took place at the date of valuation, and then apply the discount factor which would have to be brought into effect as explained for deferred shares (taking into account any cost of conversion in terms of monetary contribution, or the loss (or gain) of other rights).

Loan capital — debentures

3.63   Debentures carry their own terms and it should normally be possible to value a debenture by looking at the terms under which it is issued. It is unlikely that terms would be found in the Articles of Association but they may be found in the directors or shareholders' minutes or under a deed. If unsecured the loan may have to be valued for the purposes of the loan creditor on a hope-value basis that may well take into account the company's previous dealings with loans and debentures, the personal standing of the individuals involved, even perhaps the relationship between the lender and borrower. It may also be relevant to look for side agreements which may be actionable in law even if not evident on a shallow inspection of the affairs of a company. The hope-value approach would not be appropriate, however, if a commercial rate of interest is being paid.

3.64   Most debentures are entitled to a fixed or determinable rate of interest (rather than a dividend) paid under deduction of income tax. The redemption date (i.e. the date on which the loan is repayable) may also have some bearing on the matter, as may the terms for repayment, for example, the repayment may carry a premium.

3.65   Debenture stock and loan stock consist of a number of negotiable units which are marketable in their own right. A large commitment to such stock by a company must be considered very carefully indeed for it is possible for a large stockholding to carry effective control of the company, depending upon the terms of the issue and of the other shareholdings. For example, a minority ordinary shareholding when combined with high coupon loan stock might give effective control over the affairs of the company, including its dividend policy.

Valuing fixed interest securities

3.66   To value any fixed-interest stock, a number of factors need to be determined. First, the actual or probable date of redemption of the stock must be known. This may be a fixed date or floating. The terms of the redemption — at par, at a premium or at a discount — must also be ascertained. Naturally, the coupon (i.e. the nominal rate of interest payable on the debenture) must be taken into account, as must the timing of interest payments — usually half-yearly on gilt edged securities. The coupon itself usually remains constant through to redemption.

3.67   If there is no ascertainable redemption date, what is to be valued is the infinite stream of interest payments. Otherwise, the value to be determined is the current market value of the right to receive the fixed interest payments through to redemption plus the redemption monies in due course. Here, the current market value is computed by discounting all future payments to a present day value. This is done by identifying a required rate of return (otherwise known as the redemption yield) and discounting by that rate. This can be readily achieved by adopting mathematical formulae as follows.

Example

To value, at 1 January 1996, 1000 × £1 (6%) debentures redeemable on 31 July 2003 at a premium of 15%. Interest is payable half-yearly. The required redemption yield at 1 January 1996 is, say, 16% p.a.*, or 8% per half year. There are 7.5 years to redemption which comprises 15 half-yearly periods.

The formula to use is:

$$\text{Value} = \frac{r}{y} + \frac{R - r/y}{(1 + y)t}$$

where:

r   is the nominal rate of interest expressed as a decimal
(per half year is 3%) = 0.03
y   is the required redemption yield expressed as a
decimal (per half year is 8%) = 0.08
R   is the redemption value of the security where par is 1
(at a 15% premium) = 1.15
t   is the number of years (or half years) to redemption =15

So:
$$\frac{.03}{.08} + \frac{1.15 - \frac{.03}{.08}}{(1 + .08)^{15}}$$

$$= 0.375 + \frac{0.775}{3.172}$$

=0.619 or (say) 62%.

Therefore each £1 of stock is worth *62p*.

* In this example we assume a private company in a high-risk business sector. Assume a short-medium term average redemption yield quoted in the Financial Times is around 11% — add 20% for non-quoted debentures plus a further 20% for the additional commercial risk — say 16% in total.

3.68   The required (gross) redemption yield can be identified from lists of yields for quoted corporation stock prepared by firms of stockbrokers. Alternatively, average gross redemption yields can be taken from the Financial Times Actuaries Equity Indices which give yields for low, medium and high coupons for each of short-, medium- and long-dated gilts as well as irredeemables, and give average yields for short-, medium- and long-dated debentures and loans.

3.69   Because of the problems associated with quoted share comparisons (see 4.46 *et seq* and 5.22 *et seq*), it is perfectly in order to consider increasing the quoted yield for private company purposes. On the assumption that the private company is secure and there is no fundamental problem in this area, the required yield for private company fixed-interest stock could be taken at around 20% greater than the average yield for debentures or perhaps 25% greater than the average yield for gilts. If a comparable quoted corporation debenture can be found an uplift of around 10% to 15% may be appropriate — it is primarily a question of security. Unlike ordinary and other shares, debentures do not usually carry restrictions on the right to transfer to new ownership, but they are less readily marketable than their quoted cousins. Also, it has to be said that the financial controls on quoted company gearing are likely to be more stringent than for the private company, and while it might not be too difficult for a public company to meet its continuing debt obligations — and particularly the full redemption cost — by the issue of new stock, this may not be the same for the private company. Therefore the debt/equity gearing should be checked. The interest 'cover' by income and assets, i.e. the amount of the interest obligation covered by the company's profits and/or net assets, must be satisfactory. The rights attaching to the loan stock on a liquidation or on a failure to meet interest payments should also be investigated. Any unsatisfactory elements would naturally affect the required yield.

Capitalisation

3.70   The specific rights attaching to shares issued by a company will be specified in the company's Articles of Association. Those rights may not be altered without a special resolution being passed either at the annual shareholders' meeting or by an extraordinary shareholders' meeting. Where rights are altered or where a new class of share is to be issued the company's Articles of Association may have to be altered, and this, too, requires a special resolution. It may be that under the Articles, the directors do have power to issue new shares and to determine the rights attaching to those shares.

3.71   A company may revise its capital structure from time to time by making bonus or scrip issues of shares or by offering new shares for subscription. This is done to help keep the balance between capital employed, current earnings and dividends on an even commercial keel. For example, in its early years of trading a company may have an issued share capital of 10,000 £1 ordinary shares and assets of £10,000, earning £5,000 per year; from these earnings a dividend payment of (say) 10% of £10,000 (£1,000) could be made.

3.72   Some years later, the company's assets may have grown to £200,000 and its earnings to £50,000. It might be that its annual dividends now are £10,000, i.e. 100% of the issued share capital. A bonus of 9:1 would improve the ratios, making the issued share capital (after the bonus) £100,000 and the dividend yield would be 10% rather than 100%. The value of the shares as a whole remains the same, although each share is a smaller proportionate amount of the entire share capital. This may also make it easier to dispose of small parcels of shares either by gift or sale.

3.73   Often, such a bonus issue would be followed by a declaration that future dividend rates are to increase (from 10% say, to 12%). Such announcements may be very relevant in a share valuation exercise. In fact any statement as to future dividend policy is obviously of some interest.

3.74 A *rights issue* is made when a company wishes to attract more capital, maybe as working capital or for some specific expansion purpose. In such cases, existing shareholders are circularised with details of the issue and are usually offered favourable terms if they take up some of the additional shares before a specified date.

3.75 At the end of the exercise — when the share capital becomes 'ex rights', the par value of the new share capital will equal the par value of the old shares plus the new money attracted by the rights issue. If new shares were issued 'at a premium' this means that the shares have been subscribed for at a price higher than the par value. In this case the company's balance sheet will include a 'share premium' reserve as part of the shareholders' capital. The premium will belong to the company and thereby be for the benefit of all the shareholders, not just those who paid the premium. There are many variations on a theme and novel ways of raising new capital by the variation or creation of share rights and interests.

3.76 It will be appreciated that one of the first steps is to ascertain the types of share in issue, and the rights attaching to those shares whether specified in the company's Articles of Association, an agreement or other arrangements. Then it is necessary to identify the history of issues, dividends and redemption, and to ascertain what policy decisions have been taken concerning future redemption, issues or dividends.

3.77 This forms the basic information necessary to identify what is to be valued, and it also provides the full background to the 'environment' within which the subject of the valuation lies.

3.78 The standard bases for valuing company shares are:

● the dividend basis (Chapter 4);

● the dividend growth model basis (Chapter 8);

● the earnings basis (Chapter 5);

● the asset basis (Chapter 6);

● the hybrid basis (Chapter 7);

● the discounted cash flow basis (Chapter 8).

3.79 Whichever basis should be adopted in any particular case depends upon the circumstances. The first indication of the appropriate basis will be found from the size of the shareholding that is being valued, as explained below.

3.80 Having identified the 'rights' attaching to the shares in issue, it is necessary to ascertain the total value attributable to each class of share. The next step is to consider that value in relation to the total number of shares held by any one shareholder, either directly or perhaps through a trustee or nominee. An important point here is that for tax purposes the number of shares to be valued on any particular occasion will depend on the specific rules of the tax involved. For a discussion of the position concerning 'connected' persons for capital gains tax and related property for inheritance tax, see 9.4 and 9.34.

3.81   In the case of fixed-interest stocks and bonds, debentures and so on, it should be possible to determine their value without great difficulty because the terms on which they were issued would normally contain all the information necessary for determining their value at any time. A problem is encountered, however, in establishing the value of shares carrying voting rights, as the value of such a shareholding will not necessarily be a direct proportionate share of the total value of the company. There are certain levels of shareholding at which the value of the shares in the holding will be influenced considerably by force of numbers. This 'critical mass' concept is fundamental to choosing the correct valuation basis, but is not the end of the matter. The circumstances surrounding the valuation may require a hybrid basis of valuation to be adopted (see Chapter 7); a non-going concern will invariably require a net assets valuation on a break-up basis; an asset-rich company may require a straight net-assets basis; and tax rules (especially IHT) may require a basis different from that which would be expected (e.g. a disposal of a minority interest out of a controlling interest — see 9.34).

Shareholdings

90% shareholdings

3.82   By virtue of the *Companies Act 1985, ss 428* and *429*, the holder of 90% or more of the shares in a company has not only an unfettered right to sell his shares but he can, if the correct procedures are followed, give a corporate purchaser of the shares compulsory powers to acquire the remaining issued shares whether or not the other shareholders wish to sell. The holder of 90% or more shares has total control over the direction of the company, its dividend policies and so on.

75% shareholder

3.83   The holder of 75% or more of the shares has sufficient power to pass a special resolution to wind up the company or to sell the business as a going concern. Although he cannot engineer the sale of 100% of the shares of the company to a single purchaser, in other respects he has effective control over the company.

50% shareholder

3.84   The shareholder with more than 50% of the voting shares has the day-to-day control of the company. This shareholding gives effective control as the shareholder can appoint himself or his nominees as directors in charge of the company's business (albeit, possibly, at a cost if the consequences of so doing would be to effect a constructive dismissal of an existing director or employee).

50% shareholder

3.85 A 50% shareholder does not have absolute control, but then neither does any other party unless additional factors provide that shareholder with the effective control over the company, such as a casting vote at meetings (see 3.11). However, if all other shareholders do not vote together as a matter of course the 50% shareholder would have effective control in those circumstances.

3.86 If effective shareholder control can be shown then the shares might be valued as though the holder owned more than 50% of the issued shares, and the valuation would then usually be on an earnings basis. If there is no effective control, however, the value of the shares will probably be based on the dividend yield, and this depends on the dividend policy of the company. All the factors are looked at with an eye to determining the future direction of dividend policies.

3.87 It may be useful to see whether the shareholder has a contract of employment with the company under which he or she receives remuneration. If it can be shown that the employment would cease upon a sale of shares and no-one would take the place of that individual and take the remuneration, then it may be reasonable to expect an increased dividend payment. Indeed, it would be perfectly reasonable to proceed in valuing the shareholding on the basis of the payment of notional dividends where the policy is not to take dividends but to accrue profits or pay them all in remuneration and benefits to shareholders. This approach is fraught with difficulties and there must be evidence that the transmutation of remuneration into dividend income is a reasonable possibility. One would have to view the decisions of the board of directors as being rational and assume that dividends would be paid according to the company's trading results and business requirements. A starting point for estimating a notional dividend (and it is no more than a starting point) would be to take one-sixth of the available profit after corporation tax and discount it on the grounds that the dividend is only notional. The rate of discount would reflect the degree of certainty of real dividends reaching the new shareholders. For a fuller discussion, see 4.31 and 4.46.

25% shareholder

3.88 A shareholder having greater than 25% of the shares in the company can block a special resolution — particularly for the liquidation or disposal of the company. A shareholding of anything from 33% upwards may be in the area of effective control, depending upon the full circumstances. The Shares Valuation Division regard any 25%+ shareholding as an 'influential minority shareholding' which means that they would expect the value of each share to be greater than a share in a 'small minority shareholding' — i.e. 25% or less. However, it should also be realised that a shareholding as high as 49% may be totally without influence if 51% is owned by a single party.

25% shareholders

3.89   This is a small minority shareholding and would normally be valued on a dividend yield basis. In normal investment terms no-one would acquire such a shareholding unless:

(*a*)   a high yield is available to compensate for the vulnerability of the shareholding to special resolutions against which it would not be effective; or

(*b*)   it was to be added to other shares in the company to create a majority shareholding and thereby give control (the 'special purchaser' concept and the 'intermediary purchaser' concept may be relevant in this situation, see 2.77 *et seq*).

3.90   As a further consideration, where all the shareholders are minority shareholders it may not be appropriate to discount the value of the shares to the same extent as when a controlling shareholder does exist. Their marketability would be greater, all other things being equal.

10% or less shareholders

3.91   Such holdings can be subject to the limited compulsory acquisition powers under the *Companies Act 1985, ss 428* and *429* and the dividend yield required from such a shareholding would be greater than that for the larger shareholding which protects the shareholder's position.

Chapter 4

The Dividend Basis

Shareholding influence

4.1   The dividend basis of valuation is adopted for a shareholding in a company that is not in danger of being liquidated, where the benefit of holding the shares is manifested principally in the right to receive dividends that flow or may flow from the shareholding.

4.2   It is usually found that small minority shareholdings (i.e. 25% or under) have very little prospect of income returns except through the operation of dividend policies of others (i.e. those having control of the company or the directors), and therefore any value will only be found in the established dividend policies of the company or, in some cases, in 'deemed' dividend flows (see below). In cases where the shareholdings are held widely and the company's dividend policy is solid, a more sophisticated valuation model may be appropriate. The 'dividend growth model' is dealt with at 8.13 and at 4.21 *et seq.*

4.3   For shareholdings between 25% and 50% (influential minority shareholdings), there may be an argument for the earnings basis of valuation rather than the dividend basis, but probably only if it can be shown that through some other identifiable power or circumstance (perhaps a shareholders' agreement) the shareholding exerts influence over the way the profits of the company are applied, or over the realisation of assets.

4.4   For certain tax purposes, 'control' exists if a shareholding exceeds 30% (see 9.85; *ICTA 1988, s 298(1)*). The context in which that is applicable is very special and ties in with other tax rules, but it illustrates the belief that a shareholding above 30% can exert a special influence, and this would especially be the case where all the other shareholdings are small in comparison.

A shareholding of more than 25% gives the holder power to block a special resolution (see 3.88) and would usually give the shareholder the expectation of a seat on the board of directors. This opportunity to exert influence must count for something, although the power to block a special resolution can be regarded more as a power to maintain the status quo than a power to positively influence company policies. The Shares Valuation Division regards holdings between 25% and 50% as 'influential minority shareholdings' and in these cases they would normally expect a valuation to be biased towards the price/earnings ratio (see Chapter 5). Whether the assets basis is appropriate will depend largely upon the size of the shareholding and the likelihood of an early liquidation, and this is discussed below in more detail.

4.5   The influence of a shareholding per se should not be confused with the personal influence exerted by an individual through common sense or personal persuasive attributes, neither of which can be a factor for tax valuation purposes. However, the Articles of Association or a shareholders' agreement may give a casting vote to a particular shareholding or to the chairman of a meeting of the members of the company.

Liquidation

4.6   Because its shareholding does not exert any intrinsic influence over the management or policy-making machinery of the company, the minority shareholder will find that the only benefit that can arise from holding the shares will be the flow of dividends, and the right to receive a liquidation distribution should the company be wound up. There is also the ability to sell the shares (subject to restrictions on transfer and/or pre-emption rights, shareholder's agreements, or options), but the market for such shares is hardly as immediate as that for quoted shares. One might speculate that the investment is best considered as tied up for a number of years and, subject to the facts, equate the holding to fixed interest or zero-coupon long-dated stock (see 3.66).

4.7   The right to receive a liquidation distribution derives its value from the likelihood that the net asset value of the company will be realised in the *foreseeable* future through a liquidation, or through a reorganisation or acquisition of the company's shares.

4.8   If liquidation (whether voluntary or otherwise) is a strong possibility, or a takeover is likely, and/or if the character of the asset-backing is substantial (e.g. land, buildings, intellectual property or substantial reserves), then it may be necessary to consider an asset basis valuation in addition to the dividend basis valuation, or as an alternative to it. This would depend largely upon how soon such a realisation of value might be expected or how 'solid' the asset-backing. In the case of a court order for the compulsory winding up of the company under the *Companies Act 1985, s 461*, a *pro rata* valuation basis may apply even though the shareholding is a minority shareholding (see also 2.107).

4.9   Dividends emanating from a company with solid asset-backing are assumed more likely to be maintained or to grow than dividends depending upon, for example, a seasonal or a 'fashionable' trade. On the other hand, it may be argued that in the immediate or foreseeable future the dividends expected to be earned from a fashionable trade would easily outstrip any dividends backed by traditional assets such as property.

4.10 Where a liquidation of a company is expected, the dividend basis is not applicable. The only benefit to be had from the shareholding would be the eventual pay-out from the disposal of the company's assets. For this purpose, the likely date of liquidation should be ascertained and the projected asset value given a present day value by discounting over the period of time by the required rate of return (see below); but, of course, the circumstances must be investigated fully before any final decision is made as to which basis is applicable.

4.11 If losses are being made but no liquidation is foreseen and no dividends are being paid, the first question to be resolved is 'will the company make profits in the future?'. If the answer is that profits will be made, it should be possible to quantify the expected profits, dividends and earnings yield, and having done so, to determine a share value on the basis of expecting those dividends — see 4.31, where this matter and the question of a discount for uncertainty are discussed.

Expectation of future dividends

4.12 If the company is not about to be liquidated, and the asset-backing comprises only fixed assets of no special value, trade debtors and some cash, the shareholder's only expectation from holding the shares is to receive dividends such as he has done in the past. It is this expectation that is valued under the dividend basis.

4.13 The first stage is to look at the past dividends (say in the preceding three to five years) and take note of any actual dividend policy. There are four possibilities:

- the dividends are constant year by year;
- the dividends show a steady growth or reduction;
- the dividends fluctuate;
- no dividends (see 4.25 *et seq*).

Constant dividend

4.14 Taking the first case, let us assume that a dividend of 50p per share is paid each year. Assume also that the current *required rate of return* (see 4.18) from an investment of similar character and risk is 10%. The value of such a share would be that amount which, if yielding 10% per annum, would give 50p. Arithmetically this is calculated quite simply by grossing up 50p as follows:

$$\frac{50p}{10\%} \times 100\% = £5$$

(i.e. Value £5 at 10% = yield of 50p per share).

4.15 Often, a dividend is declared as a rate per share (e.g. 20% per 25p share = 5p dividend). Note that the 25p is the nominal or par value, not the current market value. The current market value of this share, if we continue to assume a required rate of return of 10%, would be that amount which, if yielding 10% per annum, would give 5p (i.e. 20% of 25p). The actual value of the share is therefore:

$$\frac{5p}{10\%} \times 100\% = £0.50$$

(i.e. Value 50p @ 10% = yield of 5p per share; 25p @ 20% = 5p).

Dividend growth

4.16 Suppose that a dividend has been shown to increase each year by an average of 20% gross (of the previous dividend), and that this growth is expected to continue into the foreseeable future. The last dividend declared was 10p which represented a return of 20% on the nominal value of the share which is 50p. Assume that a respectable required rate of return from any investment on similar risk is 12.5% (without reflecting the in-built growth factor). A naive valuation would be simply to take the current dividend and gross it up by the required return. This would give:

$$\frac{10p}{12.5\%} \times 100\% = £0.80$$

(i.e. Value 80p @ 12.5% = yield of 10p per share).

4.17 However, the return from the investment made today will be the next dividend, and that will be 20% up on the last dividend. This means the expected dividend will increase by 2p (10p @ 20%). Thus:

$$\frac{10p + 2p}{12.5\%} \times 100\% = 96p$$

(i.e. Value 96p @ 12.5% = yield of 12p per share).

If we had not increased the value of the share to reflect the expected dividend increase, the actual return received on 80p would have been 12p (that is 15% — much greater than the required return of 12.5%).

4.18 This calculation takes into account the next following dividend but does not reflect the benefit of the constant growth expected. There should be weighting to take this growth factor into account, except to the extent that the *required rate of return* itself includes any growth expectation, for example, if it is derived from dividend yields based on quoted share prices which themselves reflect dividend growth in their quoted company. The growth factor should only be entertained if it is certain that the dividend growth will continue — again, this will depend upon a thorough-going review of the performance of the company.

4.19   Such a review would be undertaken to ensure that a recent high or steady dividend record is not being met solely out of retained earnings (which will eventually dry up), and does not arise out of a ploy to defeat an unwelcome takeover bid, but arises out of sound trading results (going back three to five or more years), and all economic and commercial forecasts for the particular business and the industry in general indicate that the growth will continue. It is quite common for dividend payments to be smoothly progressive so far as dividend growth is concerned but for the underlying profits of the company to be more volatile. This is perfectly in order provided that the company's profit velocity is satisfactory i.e. that the overall level of profits is increasing against inflation despite *occasional* set-backs whether manifested in a loss or a weaker growth rate one year.

4.20   In the case of constant growth the exercise is to ascertain for each share such a value as will provide the required rate of return allowing for the fact that there is an in-built growth in the dividends that are being received. The difficulty is that where there is such in-built dividend growth it is not possible to give a simple valuation that can be stated in terms of an amount which will earn a fixed x% every year.

Constant growth formula

4.21   The simplest 'constant growth' value formula is as follows:

$$\frac{\text{first } projected \text{ dividend}}{\text{required rate of return} - \text{dividend growth rate}} \times 100 = \text{value}$$

4.22   Suppose the nominal value of each share is £1. The latest dividend to be declared was 20p, and over the last five years the dividends have grown at a compound rate of 4% each year (that is 4% of each previous dividend). This growth is fully expected to continue and the required rate of return in an investment of similar risk but without the promise of an annual 4% income growth in addition to capital growth is 11%.

Applying the formula:

$$\frac{20p + (4\% \times 20p)}{11\% - 4\%} = \frac{20p + 0.8p}{7\%} \times 100 = £2.97$$

4.23   However, £2.97 at the required rate of return of 11% should surely yield 32.67p, not 20.8p! This illustrates the problem with this formula: that the required rate of return will only be achieved after a long period (above twelve years) and even then includes the gain made on a future sale at the then value which is calculated using the same formula. This seems to be an excessive risk period. However, this risk may be more apparent than real. If the proper elements, including the risk factors, were taken into account in the first place in determining the required rate of return on the investment then the formula works fine. If the investor's primary requirement is a regular annual dividend at a fixed required rate of return, investing in ordinary shares in a private company may not be the appropriate move!

Fluctuating yields

4.24   In this case it is a question of determining the minimum level of maintainable dividends and to add to that what (if anything) is reasonably certain of being achieved in the future in terms of growth. If the company is large enough and well established, it might be helpful to apply the linear trend analysis formula set out at 5.56. Alternatively, the possibilities set out in the following sections of this chapter may be of assistance in finding future dividends.

No dividend record

4.25   A company may be profitable yet not pay dividends for a variety of reasons. In these cases it may be appropriate to calculate a notional dividend. One way to compute notional dividends is to divide maintainable earnings (see 5.51) by the proper dividend cover (see 4.77). Dividend cover is the ratio of earnings yield to dividend yield (see 10.61) and if this approach is to be meaningful, it is important that an independent, empirical figure for cover is used, and not one itself derived from the company's own yield figures.

4.26   If the liquidation of the company is in prospect, the notional dividend approach would not apply because the asset basis would be more appropriate (see Chapter 6).

4.27   If there appears to be no chance of future dividends arising and there cannot be said to be an oppression of minorities (see 2.107) then perhaps a hybrid basis (see Chapter 7) is appropriate. The full facts concerning current dividend policies and the possibility of future dividends must be considered carefully and any positive likelihood of dividends should be reflected in the valuation given, either by construction of a notional dividend or by applying a hybrid valuation.

4.28   In deciding what the notional dividend should be, the valuer would effectively be determining a dividend policy for the company where the policy to date had been not to declare dividends. It is almost a contradiction, but this perversity will be recognised in the discount for uncertainty that must ultimately be applied to the share value determined under the 'notional' dividend basis valuation.

4.29   The valuer must have regard to everything concerning the business and its standing, and the structure of the company, its management and ownership. Is it working at full extent? Are all its profits (now and in the future) taken up in meeting bank interest or on other borrowings or debentures, preference stock etc.? What about cash flow requirements, and capital investment commitments in the past, present and future? What are the levels of wages, salaries and fees — are any such payments being made to current shareholders and would such payments cease if the shareholder ceased to be a shareholder? Is the business improving or not? What retentions are necessary for continuing or future business development? Are current reserves sufficient to meet all these real or contingent liabilities? Are current reserves excessive and will they continue to be so?

4.30   When, at last, a notional dividend policy which recommends a notional dividend has been determined — why have the directors not so recommended? Could there be a reason that has not been considered?

4.31   An artificial dividend policy being assumed and a value for the shares being determined, what rate of discount for uncertainty should be applied? Perhaps the discount to be considered is really a discount for certainty that the proposed dividends will *not* be declared. After the painstaking effort of arriving at a perfectly reasonable dividend policy on the evidence of past performance, the valuer may well feel that there is a high degree of certainty that future dividends will *not* be declared. If that is not his opinion there is a presumption that the current directors have not been doing their job properly because they had not come to the same conclusion.

4.32   As a matter of practice, the Shares Valuation Division may allow a notional dividend discount of 50% in respect of a 10% shareholding. In theory, discount at a much higher level would be justified in some cases, but one would be mistaken not to expect some resistance to this. Of course, the Shares Valuation Division might agree the higher discount but then take issue with the pre-discount price, questioning the amount of the dividend or the rate of return adopted to determine the value. Nothing would be agreed in isolation and all the facts may have to be aired before the final discounted value is arrived at.

Irregular dividend record

4.33   A company's dividend record may not have shown smooth growth over the years, but may have been irregular and intermittent. In such a case a careful appraisal of the past performance of the company should be undertaken. The dividend policy criteria should be investigated to discover the underlying reasons for the way in which dividends have been declared.

4.34   The valuer might find himself undertaking a full review of the company's dividend policy, even constructing a new one on the bases of the known earnings of the company and development of the business. Alternatively (and much more simply), the past dividends can be extrapolated using the linear trend analysis formula set out at 5.56 *et seq.*

4.35   Whatever approach is adopted the valuer must continuously remind himself that it is the future maintainable dividends that need to be determined — a future policy that it would be reasonable to suppose will be followed and future level of earnings out of which those dividends would be paid. One is using past performance to help identify the dividend growth factor to apply to the future.

Long established companies

4.36   There are some companies whose performance can be gauged over a very long period indeed — much longer than the normal three to ten year spread — and there may well be cases where there are 'cycles' in the trading history that can be illustrated over such a period. A long established fixed growth rate — whether or not adjusted for inflation — may form the mainstay of a share valuation provided it is expected that the growth will continue at that rate. In the *Salvesen* and *Holt* cases, the performance of companies over very long periods indeed were considered in the valuation exercise.

4.37   However, the smoothest of progressions can be interrupted and it really is impossible to say with certainty even for the largest of companies that a fixed growth rate or a particular level of profitability or cash flow will continue uninterrupted into the future. This is one of the major problem areas in applying this discounted cash-flow basis to valuation exercises — see Chapter 8.

4.38   The long-established company can be considered with less scepticism than other companies, but it would be naive to ignore clouds on the horizon. For example, a major research programme which is not 100% funded cannot be said to be a safe bet for the future prosperity of the company. Indeed if the very survival of the company depended upon such a project, the valuer would be well advised to adopt a sceptical position.

The required rate of return — the quoted company comparison and the alternative

4.39   In calculating a share value on the dividend basis, it is necessary to identify a required rate of return that the purchaser of the share (or the deemed purchaser) would have in mind. This is the real return he expects to get for risking his money. Thus, shares with a nominal value of £1 each may be yielding a dividend of 30p per share. If each of those shares were for sale at £3, the dividend of 30p would represent a dividend yield and a rate of return of 10%: the dividend yield is a function of the share value. If the yield is less than the market place requires, the share price is overvalued.

4.40   The correct formula for determining the *dividend yield* is:

$$\frac{\text{nominal value of share}}{\text{share value}} \times \frac{\text{dividend as a percentage}}{\text{of nominal value}} = \text{dividend yield}$$

substituting the figures from 4.39:

$$\frac{100p}{300p} \times 30p = 10\%$$

4.41   If the value of the shares is unknown, the calculation becomes:

$$\frac{\text{dividend as a percentage of nominal value}}{\text{dividend yield}} \times \text{nominal value of share} = \text{share value}$$

4.42   How do we identify the yield that is required by the market place for the shares? Theoretically, the return that the investor will require is the same return that he would get if he invested his capital elsewhere on similar risk with similar growth prospects and with the same ease (or difficulty) of conversion to cash. If no such alternative investment can be identified, it becomes a question of looking at what other investments are available and making appropriate adjustments to the yield to compensate for the intrinsic differences between the minority shareholding on the one hand and the alternative investment on the other.

4.43   If it is not possible to identify an alternative comparable investment that carries a specified yield, there is little option left but to take all the available evidence (including quoted company data) and determine where else the money could have gone and at what rate of return.

Comparing the quoted company

4.44   The Shares Valuation Division will almost certainly attempt to compare the unquoted company with an 'equivalent' quoted company yield if it can. In the case of fixed interest securities, the Shares Valuation Division would compare quoted company stocks and gilts (see 3.66). Therefore, if in any particular case one wishes to avoid a direct comparison with quoted company yields, it will be necessary to marshal one's reasons. The matter is discussed below but also from the earnings basis perspective at 5.22.

4.45   Before considering how to make a quoted company comparison, it is fair to point out the courts' displeasure with ill-considered quoted company comparisons. In dismissing the quoted company comparison, some experts will argue that the potential buyers in the quoted company sector are fundamentally different from those in the market for private company shares and this view would be borne out by Danckwerts J in *Re Holt* when he said:

'I think the kind of investor who would purchase shares in a private company of this kind, in circumstances which must preclude him disposing of his shares freely whenever he should wish (because he will when registered as a shareholder, be subject to the provisions of the articles restricting transfer) would be different from any common kind of purchaser of shares on the Stock Exchange, and would be rather the exceptional kind of investor, who had some special reason for putting his money into shares of this kind . . . .'

4.46   That case concerned a minority shareholding of some 6%. The passage was quoted and supported by Lord Pearson in the *Re Lynall* decision.

4.47   In *Re Lynall*, Plowman J in the High Court criticised the quoted company comparison, giving some examples of why the method is unsatisfactory: dividend policies are entirely different; regulations concerning the transfer of shares are entirely different; and, perhaps the most pointed comment of all, 'Moreover, it is in the company . . . and its management and not in the industry that the hypothetical purchaser is likely to be interested'. That case concerned a minority shareholding of some 28%.

4.48   Share valuation principles require the hypothetical market to be fully open to all potential buyers and this must include the corporate speculator, the institutional buyer and the personal investor. Notwithstanding Danckwerts J's statement (above), if the circumstances of the case — particularly the free availability of information about the company and its prospects — are such that the shares in question can be compared fairly with any quoted company shares, then it is unlikely that the courts would upset a valuation that is fully supported by factual evidence. Otherwise, subject to the following comments, for small minority interests a value based on quoted company comparison is of dubious accuracy at best.

4.49   The final word concerning the choice of valuation technique must go to Plowman J in *Re Lynall*. He was considering the various valuation attempts made by expert witnesses in this case which concerned a minority interest in a long-established private company. One witness valued the shares on the basis of a bank injecting money into the company with a view to accelerating expansion and nursing it to the point where the bank itself would be able to float it. The transaction would be one between the board (not an outside shareholder) on the one side and the bank on the other. Plowman J said of this approach 'I propose to disregard it'.

4.50   Assuming that a class of quoted company can be identified, into which can be slotted the subject matter of the valuation, the dividend yields of a number of such companies over a period of, say, three to five years are calculated. The latest dividend yield is calculated by dividing the latest dividend by the latest quoted price (that is, the latest prior to the valuation date) and multiplying by 100; for earlier years one should take the company's year end price.

4.51   In this exercise care should be taken to arrive at yields that have been calculated on exactly the same basis. Financial year ends may be different and it is not satisfactory to take published dividend yields that reflect different bases of calculation. Because the published yields are usually based on a calendar year, there is a considerable danger that companies with different financial year ends will be represented quite differently. One company may have paid an interim and a final dividend in respect of that calendar year, whilst another may have paid in that same year a final dividend in respect of a previous financial year and an interim dividend in respect of a financial year not yet completed.

4.52   This exercise gives us a range of dividends and dividend yields for a range of companies carrying on business of a similar type or within a similar economic framework. Also, the figures will enable us to calculate the dividend *growth* over the period under review, and it may then be possible to arrive at a required rate of return that includes a dividend growth expectation — if such a rate is wanted for the valuation exercise — but see below. Of the various dividend yields the latest is the most relevant, but a comparison with earlier yields is useful to ensure that the latest is not obviously untypical. If yields have varied considerably over the years, it will be necessary to investigate the reasons — and also perhaps compare that volatility with the movement in money market rates or the Financial Times All Stocks Index.

4.53   It is also important to remember that dividend yields published in the *Financial Times* and the average yields used in the Financial Times Actuaries Share Indices are gross yields which allow for advance corporation tax paid by the company on making the distribution.

4.54   If a share value is to be arrived at by reference to a dividend yield derived from quoted yields, the maintainable dividend has to be expressed in gross terms before the yield is applied. The grossing factors are described at 5.9.

4.55   There are two further matters to consider: first, having ascertained the various quoted company dividend yields, can the average of the yields, or any particular one of them, be applied to our private company without any further adjustment; and secondly should the dividend growth record be used to influence the yield that is ultimately to be applied?

4.56   There will be an opportunity later in the valuation exercise to discount the share valuation for lack of marketability (see 5.37) and this discount will depend upon many factors, but should a discount (or a premium) be applied at this preliminary stage? The answer is to take the 'base' yield — i.e. the quoted company yield — and ask whether that return is reasonable, disregarding the fact that the private company shares lack the readily accessible Stock Exchange market. The required yield from the private company share would be increased where any required factor was lacking and reduced where there is a surfeit. Similar considerations apply here as apply in the case of discounts from the P/E Ratio — see 5.32.

4.57   Secondly, as far as dividend growth is concerned, it is unlikely that any quoted company dividend growth pattern can be used. A dividend growth pattern which is determined directly from the performance of the subject matter of the valuation, whether that is an actual performance or through the notional dividend policy may be a far better indicator. The quoted company may be useful for determining the current expected rate of return, but only the specific investment itself, i.e. the private company, can give the promise of future dividends or growth. Therefore, quoted company dividend growth records probably are best used only in establishing a starting point for the current yield, although they may be of some use in making a year-by-year comparison between the quoted company and the private company.

The alternative

4.58   Moving on to the second option, in which quoted securities are ignored altogether, the starting point is to look at the current investment opportunities and consider investment psychology. The purchaser will be someone who has money to invest and is completely free to choose, yet he will choose to acquire the private company shares and these will be purchased not by way of subscription for new shares but by acquisition from the vendor shareholder.

4.59   In terms of investment in quoted securities, one would invest with an expectation of income and capital growth. Of course, the stock market can meet most investment requirements — for example some investors require a low income and high capital growth; others require the opposite; some are in for short-term gains, yet others require average income and growth potential to maintain real value against inflation. Some people enjoy the risk-taking, others prefer safety.

4.60   As interest rates change, so the value of quoted shares may change and money may move to where a better immediate return is available. If economic problems arise, money may be moved into gilts as a safer prospect for the immediate future — the income yield on gilts is generally on the low side, the risk factor however is also very low. The newest breed of gilt — the index-linked bond — has a very low coupon indeed, but the real value of the investment is protected against the ravages of inflation.

4.61   As a general rule the knowing investor will spread his investments for protection and is prepared to take a smaller income yield if his capital is safe — and especially if it is growing. It is unlikely that the average investor will actually risk his capital for a slightly better than average income yield, but he might well put up with inconvenience (such as the inability to convert immediately to cash) to achieve it.

4.62   If shares which are being valued on a dividend basis are to be valued without reference to any publicly quoted companies, it may be necessary not only to make projections of dividends (and the earnings out of which they are paid) and value any non-business assets, but also to determine a 'risk' factor and an 'accessibility' factor.

4.63   A free investor may choose to put his money into gilts (possibly for capital gains tax saving purposes), into one or more building societies, into quoted company debentures, local authority loans, savings certificates, single premium bonds or even endowment policies or property. By choosing to ignore quoted company comparisons, a valuer would be relying on far more subjective criteria in determining his value, effectively entering a much wider and competitive investment market. That market will require a much higher yield from a minority interest in a private company than it would from the traditional forms of investment — except where the private company's asset backing or earnings factor is sufficiently strong to justify a lower yield. The effect of these matters on the required yield can be substantial.

In cases where the asset backing is stronger than is necessary simply to contribute towards maintaining dividends it might be proper not only to look at a dividend yield basis of valuation but also at whether an asset basis valuation would be appropriate. An investment company or property company may be cases where an asset-related value or a hybrid basis is more appropriate than a dividend yield basis. It may still be, of course, that the asset valuation would be heavily discounted for a minority interest. Alternatively, perhaps the earnings of the business are too great to be ignored, and an earnings basis should also be taken into account. The combination of valuation bases is dealt with in Chapter 7.

4.64   If the other valuation bases cannot displace the dividend yield, it is necessary to identify how secure the investment is and how easily accessible it would be. For example, would the bank accept the shares as security for an overdraft facility or other borrowing and upon what terms, and how would that compare with alternative investments. Looking at the company itself and the shareholding in question, how do the prospects for future income and future capital growth compare with the alternative investments available? Does the projected maintainable dividend or earnings yield compare favourably or unfavourably with the current yield on, say, undated gilts, bank deposit interest or more sophisticated money market returns? Do the alternative investment opportunities that equate with the income yield from the shares also equate with the capital growth expectations from the shares, or *vice versa* ? By building up a picture of the comparative pros and cons, a required yield can be determined; and this is where the art of the valuer is tested in the extreme.

4.65   The index-linked gilt provides the investor with a safe, long-term, investment medium. It is not a short-term prospect because so much of the yield is stored up to accrue at maturity and the coupon is extremely low because the value of the capital is protected against inflation. There is also the benefit that capital gains from gilt-edged securities and qualifying corporate bonds, including deep gain securities (see *TCGA 1992, s 115* as amended), are free of tax.

4.66   However, it is unlikely that these securities can be of any direct use in helping to establish a required yield for private company shares. Their average gross redemption yield may be smaller than non-index-linked gilts by a factor of 3 or more and this yield is directly affected by the rate of inflation, which is unlikely in the case of yields from ordinary shares.

4.67   A tool that may be used to identify how secure the dividends are is the dividend cover. This is the number of times that the current dividend could be met out of current net profits. It is not an absolute measure, because there are many factors which can affect the level of dividends, but, for example, a low cover (of 1 or 1.5) would indicate no profit retention in the business. This would be acceptable, for example, if the company was not carrying on a business that requires capital expenditure or cash retention. A high cover, of above 4, would be acceptable if the company does need to invest back into its business.

4.68   A look at the past few years' dividend cover record may prove useful in checking the company's consistency; it may also be helpful in identifying whether the shareholders' dividends are hard-earned or otherwise. Where a comparison is being made with a quoted company, the dividend cover may also be compared, as this is one of the data published in the *Financial Times*.

4.69   Even if a comparison with quoted equity shares is not being made, it may nevertheless be helpful to look at the general level of yields for the particular industry as a whole. The Exchange Telegraph Cards (via the Actuaries Share Indices (FTASI)) will give the yield for some of the larger companies in various industries — but in view of the size and make-up of those companies the yields may be considerably smaller than might be expected from a small or medium-sized private company.

Chapter 5

The Earnings Basis

Shareholding influence

5.1   The earnings basis is used for the valuation of a majority (control) shareholding in a company that will not be liquidated in the foreseeable future — i.e., a going concern. The earnings basis looks at the future profit-generating potential of the company and its profits available for distribution after tax, interest and preference dividends are paid. Thus, the valuer seeks to establish the maintainable profits (which are the profits that, on the evidence, can be maintained in the future, all other things being equal). This profit figure is then capitalised, inflation risk and growth factors being considered, to give the present-day worth of the right to receive those future earnings. The case of *Buckingham v Francis* confirmed this approach.

5.2   The payment of ordinary dividends out of current profits and reserves will depend upon the company's dividend policy. That policy will have the approval of the majority shareholders; but minority shareholders will generally have no power individually to influence the payment of dividends. So a single majority shareholder, because of the power of the shareholding, has power over the distribution of the company's profits, and thereby has a more valuable asset than an equivalent, aggregated, shareholding made up of individual minority shareholdings. That value is not based on a mere 'hope' or 'expectation' of dividends but on the certain ability (subject only to commercial factors) of the majority shareholder to turn current profits and available reserves to personal advantage.

5.3   Thus, a majority (or control) shareholding in a 'going-concern' trading company will normally be valued on an 'earnings' basis, the 'dividend basis' being more appropriate for minority interests (see Chapter 4).

5.4   The assets basis (see Chapter 6) does not normally apply to an ordinary trading company because the value of its business assets is reflected automatically in its earnings. The earnings are the company's distributable profits which are derived from pre-tax net operating profits (before payment of debenture interest and preference dividends). These profits are derived from the employment in the business of the company's *business assets* — whether fixed assets, cash, goodwill or any other asset directly involved in the earning capacity of the business. Provided that the capitalised value of the after-tax profits is at least equal to the after-tax value of the business assets, the value of those assets is reflected in the annual profits.

5.5   It would not be unusual for the valuer to find assets standing to one side of the business assets and in that case a separate valuation of those assets would certainly be necessary. The earnings basis would only deal with part of the story and a separate asset based valuation may be necessary to complete the picture. Again, in the case of impending liquidation, neither an earnings basis nor a dividend basis would be appropriate as there would be no earnings or income distributions in prospect (even if there had previously been a full dividend-paying policy), but only capital distribution of cash or kind. Such an approach is further described in Chapter 7 as the combination basis. In some cases it may be necessary to use a hybrid basis which relies on 'weighted' mixing valuation bases: see Chapter 7.

Earnings

5.6   Although Statement of Standard Accounting Practice No 3 (Earnings per Share) (published by the Institute of Chartered Accountants in England and Wales) is not intended to apply to the majority of unlisted companies, it nevertheless provides assistance. Earnings can be defined by reference to the definition of 'Earnings per share' thus:

> 'the profit-in-pence attributable to each equity share, based on the profit (or in the case of a group the consolidated profit) of the period *after tax*, minority interests and extraordinary items and after deducting preference dividends and other appropriations in respect of preference shares, divided by the number of equity shares in issue and ranking for dividend in respect of the period.'

5.7   It should be noted that the foregoing definition is that as amended by Financial Reporting Standard 3 (FRS3) (effective for accounting periods ending after 21 June 1993). The principal amendment (or *volte face*) was that extraordinary items were previously excluded from the determination of profit but are now to be taken into account. This is for reporting purposes, and indeed, other versions of earnings per share may still be used in the financial statements provided any adjustments to the standard are highlighted. In FRS3 it is stated that extraordinary items are 'extremely rare'. It may therefore still be stated confidently that in determining a year-on-year comparison for determination of earnings per share for the future, extraordinary items may be disregarded if the valuer believes them not to have a definite periodic or cyclical character.

Taxation

5.8   Using the above definition then the annual earnings of the company can be determined from the company's accounts. There remains the question of taxation and there are currently three ways of calculating earnings having regard to the impact of taxation on profit and distributions: the gross basis; the net basis; and the nil basis. The PE ratios quoted in the Financial Times Actuaries Share Index are on the net and the nil bases. The *Investors Chronicle* deducts a notional corporation tax charge at the standard rate, which is intended to iron out fluctuations in tax levels. PE rates quoted in the *Investors Chronicle* may be particularly useful when considering a value at 31 March 1982 for capital gains tax purposes (see Chapter 9).

5.9   The *gross basis* recognises that when a distribution is made out of a company's profits advance corporation tax (ACT) is payable to the Inland Revenue. After 6 April 1994 until 5 April 1999 (after which it is abolished) the ACT payable is one-fourth of the distribution, and, within limits, this ACT is credited against the mainstream corporation tax that the company bears on the profits out of which the distribution is paid. There is also a tax credit at 20% (previously 25%) but reducing to 10% after 5 April 1999 for the UK resident recipient of the distribution. However, for dividends paid after 1 July 1997 pension schemes and UK companies (other than charities) cannot claim repayment of tax. The following example attempts to illustrate this complex picture.

	Before 6.4.93 £	Payments 6.4.93–5.4.94 £	6.4.95–5.4.99 £	from 6.4.99 £
Net dividend of £100				
Dividend payment				
Gross	133	125	125	—
Tax credit	@25% 33	@20% 25	@20% 25	10% 10
(Net) dividend	**100**	**100**	**100**	**100**
Shareholders additional liability				
Lower rate taxpayer (repayment)	(6)	—	—	—
Basic rate taxpayer	—	—	—	20
Higher rate taxpayer	20	25	25	30
Company liability				
Dividend & ACT	133	129	125	100
— ACT × (div & ACT)	@25% 33	@22.5% 25	@20% 25	@nil —
= (Net) dividend	**100**	**100**	**100**	**100**

Gross dividend of £125 — higher-rate taxpayer additional rate on 'net' dividend

Dividend & ACT	125.00	125.00	125.00	125.00
Tax credit	@25% 31.25	@20% 25.00	@20% 25.00	@10% 12.50
(Net) dividend	**93.75**	**100.00**	**100.00**	**125.00**
Tax @ 40%	50.00	50.00	50.00	50.00
— Tax credit	31.25	25.00	25.00	12.50
= Additional tax	**18.75**	**25.00**	**25.00**	**37.50**
Additional rate on 'net' Dividend therefore	20%	25%	25%	30%

So it can be seen that before the April 1999 change the gross earnings can be affected by a change in the tax rate, which, of course, has little or nothing to do with the company's performance. Franked investment income (i.e. dividends having suffered ACT) is not further taxed in the hands of a recipient company and the tax credit can be set against ACT which is payable in respect of distributions made by the recipient company itself.

5.10   It is unlikely that any company would distribute its entire distributable earnings — an estimate of a reasonable annual distribution policy for a private trading company would be 25%–33% of (pre-tax) distributable profits, but this has to be looked at along with the company's remuneration policy.

5.11   On the basis that earnings are valued in net of tax terms, thereby treating tax as an expense, the gross basis is unlikely to be of use in calculating the earnings that are to be capitalised. For the dividend basis, however, because it is the pure income stream with attendant tax credit that is being valued, the tendency is to capitalise the gross dividend yield and that means grossing-up the yield for the ACT/tax credit.

5.12   The *nil basis* is the basis most often used in determining earnings. It is simply the post-mainstream corporation tax profits and as such reflects the net value to the shareholder after net corporation tax plus basic rate tax.

5.13   The *net basis* considers a special problem where the mainstream corporation tax charge is small (because, e.g. the company has a large double tax credit relief), but the ACT charge is high because of a full distribution policy. In this case the 'surplus' ACT that could not be set against mainstream corporation tax liability and the corporation tax liability itself are together deducted from gross profits. This picture radically changes after 5 April 1999 when ACT is abolished.

5.14   Some authorities, including the Inland Revenue Shares Valuation Division, consider that it is preferable (but not essential) to capitalise maintainable *pre-tax* profits rather than *post-tax* earnings. What will be universally agreed is that whatever the preference, it is important not to mix apples and oranges. A common approach in determining future maintainable profits is to list the company's previous three, five or whatever years' profits and (see 5.51 and 5.56) magically extrapolate from the trend of that list the maintainable future profit. This is most easily, consistently and accurately handled if at this stage all profits are pre-tax. We keep it simple and get our future maintainable *pre-tax* profit.

5.15   Now, either we capitalise the maintainable pre-tax profits not troubling ourselves with corporation tax at this stage, or we apply a rate of corporation tax (as known at the date of valuation) and capitalise the post-tax earnings; but what Price to Earnings ratio (PER) do we use in each case?

5.16   Consider the published share price and PER of Superco. On a particular day people are prepared to pay £5 for a share in Superco which has 1 million shares in issue and whose latest published results show a profit of £500,000. The post-tax earnings were £350,000 which produces a *post-tax* PER of 14.286, which is published in the *Financial Times* on the day. The *pre-tax* PER is (£5 × 1,000,000 ÷ 500,000) = 10, but that PER is not published and we have to calculate it from the background information. Either way, 14.286 × £350,000, or 10 × £500,000 gives a capitalised value of £5M. The pre-tax PER (10) is smaller than the post-tax PER (14.286) but it is applied to a larger amount.

5.17 *Does any of this make a difference?* It can do when we put the comparable PER into our valuation. Suppose the company whose shares we are valuing has maintainable *pre-tax* profits of £200,000, a tax charge (estimated or actual) of £40,000 and consequent *post-tax* earnings of £160,000. The comparable *post-tax* PER of 14.286 applied to the post-tax earnings of £160,000 gives a value of £2,285,760, whereas the comparable *pre-tax* PER of 10 applied to pre-tax profits of £200,000 gives £2M. The answers are not the same. The difference of £285,760 can be ascribed to capitalising the difference in the tax charge between the quoted company and our subject company.

5.18 *Why capitalise post-tax earnings?* The capitalisation of private company profits is often by reference to a price-earnings ratio derived from the average of the PERs of several 'comparable' quoted companies (the Inland Revenue Shares Valuation Division preferred option) or from other published information which usually quotes or is based on post-tax earnings – the FTASI, the *Investors Chronicle*, and *Acquisitions Monthly* all go this route. The difference is that the FTASI and *Acquisitions Monthly* takes into account the actual corporation tax suffered whereas the *Investors Chronicle* applies a standard rate of corporation tax. None of this is perfect. The amount of corporation tax (or the effective rate) in any one year can be different for companies with the same profits (quoted or unquoted). The important thing is that when making quoted company comparisons we must research the comparable company results (see 5.26 *et seq*). In that exercise we would look to find all the significant financial differences (including tax charges and the like).

5.19 *Why capitalise pre-tax profits?* If all data is consistent and complementary there will be less room for error in our calculations. However, to get there we will need price-earnings ratios that are derived from pre-tax profits. If we are taking quoted company comparisons, we must get the latest relevant published financial statements from each of the chosen companies, determine the pre-tax profits and adjust the published price-earnings ratio for the appropriate date accordingly. We must do a similar exercise if we are comparing private company sales. So the danger here is the possible error incorporated in the re-engineering of PERs; but if it can be done with sufficient accuracy, the result should be correspondingly more certain.

The valuation approach

5.20 There are two ways of arriving at an earnings-based value of a going-concern private company:

● Price to Earnings ratio basis;

● required yield basis.

One or other basis may be chosen whether because one gives a more 'acceptable' value according to the purpose for which valuation is undertaken; because of a personal preference for that particular method; or because supporting evidence for a valuation is not available to allow the other basis to be used. Either of the bases may be used in exercises comparing the private company with other private companies or with quoted companies. Where there are no satisfactory comparable companies, the valuer is really left with the required yield basis, which basically looks at the returns available from alternative investments to the private company shares on offer — this matter is covered in some detail in Chapter 4.

5.21   The exercise of making comparisons between private companies is difficult but more satisfying (in that it should be more representative of actuality) than using the expedience of quoted company data which abounds but may not be truly comparable. Much the same principles apply to a private company comparison as a quoted company comparison. The comparison must be realistic in all the areas of structure and operation. The major difference is in the removal from the comparison exercise of the macro-economics, and the accompanying discounts, but there are likely to be discounts (or premiums) in comparisons of private companies too, in adjusting for the inevitable differences that will be evident. Some assistance may be found in looking at industry norms (see 12.34) where private company comparisons are being made — but caution should be exercised. Discounts for control holdings (see 5.43) will apply the same as for the quoted company comparison. Other discounting factors can arise also. In the case of *Cash & Carry v Inspector of Taxes* a discount of 66⅔% was offered by the Inland Revenue (who wished for a low value) in respect of uncertainties that a prudent prospective purchaser would have taken into account in respect of the acquisition of minority interest shareholding of 24%. The taxpayer claimed the discount should have been 10%. The Special Commissioner held, amongst other variations of the figures presented, that the discount should be 55%.

Price to Earnings ratio basis — the quoted company comparison

5.22   The PER is basically a capitalisation factor to translate earnings into a current purchase value. It is really another way of expressing the required yield but is determined in a somewhat different fashion. Suppose the PER is 8 and the current earnings (after tax) are £100,000. The value of those earnings in current purchasing terms would be £100,000 multiplied by 8 = £800,000. This capitalised value may be subject to adjustment as explained later in this chapter.

5.23   It would be simple to take the earnings per share as calculated according to the latest Financial Reporting Standard for Earnings Per Share (see 5.7) and apply a PER to give an immediate current valuation of that share. Unfortunately there are one or two practical difficulties.

5.24 The PER is used widely as a tool to compare the 'value' performance of companies against each other or against industry trends. This is particularly true of quoted companies and large private companies which have institutional investors as shareholders. If the PER increases, this is usually an indicator of greater market appeal, but the causes lie hidden and the PER is not an answer, but merely an indicator.

5.25 The Inland Revenue Shares Valuation Division relies heavily on quoted company PERs in its valuation exercises. Typically, the exercise involves choosing several quoted companies whose business can be said to resemble that of the private company whose shares are being valued, and adjust the quoted companies price earnings ratios to bring them more realistically in line with the private company. It will be seen that there are several obstacles to be overcome in the march towards settling on a proper value for a private company when quoted company PERs are used. Notwithstanding misgivings, it is growing practice to follow this approach and it is essential for any share valuer to understand the processes. What the valuer is grappling with is the distinction between the businesses and asset profile of the subject company and the quoted companies and the distinction between quoted company and unquoted company, and the respective markets for their shares.

5.26 The number of companies to be taken is as many as one can practicably justify as being tolerably comparable. Care must be taken to compare like with like. If the private company is in heavy engineering it would not be appropriate to compare it with companies in an industry outside heavy engineering unless some special factor is present. For example, if the main function of the company in question is to provide transport services, even if exclusively within the engineering industry, it may be appropriate to look at quoted transport companies because they might have more comparable underlying economics. Of course, the subject company's fortunes may vary in direct relationship with that of the heavy engineering sector. It may be necessary to compromise between the PER for the heavy engineering sector and that for the transport sector. If the subject company has been in existence for some time there should be information available to the valuer that will suggest the proper course.

Distinguishing elements

5.27 It cannot be right to make a direct financial or business comparison between private and quoted companies without removing the elements that distinguish earning power, asset backing and so on. In fact, there may be many distinguishing factors at play and where a share valuation is to be based on the multiplication of a private company's earnings by a quoted company it is clearly necessary to identify and remove those distinguishing elements. We have of course already taken the first distinguishing steps by selecting a number of quoted companies which can reasonably be said to be in the same sort of business as our subject company and which are not separated from our company by billions of dollars of asset backing.

Fine adjustments

5.28   Between our several chosen quoted comparable companies and our subject company there may be glaring financial or business differences which can be compensated for by fine-tuning the PER or dividend yield of the comparable companies. The adjustment exercise is considered at 5.32. The share valuer will be familiar with the make up of the subject company and should be able to identify such differences. Some indicators are given here. Of course, it may not always be easy or possible to actually make a fine adjustment.

● Geographical factors are certainly important, whether local or international, and may impact not just trade and markets but also assets and cash exchange controls, currency exposure, foreign assets, export markets, import markets, etc.

● Debt/equity ratios or other financial ratios (see 10.61) can be very different between companies and lead to issues such as interest charges, exposure to interest rate changes, etc.

● Asset backing will usually be markedly different, but sometimes can be excessively different impacting the value of the quoted shares in a way that allows fine adjustment with a credible result.

● Market fashion often means short-term favouritism in the market. An otherwise ordinary company may have a special product or special publicity that makes it much more in demand than comparable companies.

Quoted versus Private

5.29   More fundamentally, we have to recognise the differences that distinguish the private company persona from the quoted company persona and adjust the average quoted PER to remove these distinguishing characteristics. This adjustment exercise is discussed at 5.33. The distinguishing elements that need to be considered in that exercise include the following, but some will be more appropriate than others in any given case.

● The quoted company's intrinsic strength and resilience, derived from its capital structure, diversification or trading partners, its track record or its customer and supplier base.

● The size of the quoted company, whether measured by turnover, employees, assets or some other criterion.

● The costs of going on the market and the costs of staying there.

● The financial regulation regime.

● The management skills level of executive boards.

● The institutional recognition and observation of performance.

● The open and aware market place and its readiness to allow almost any share sale or purchase.

- The ease of share transactions.

- The information that is so readily available (whether on the subject company, competitors or customers and suppliers) including professional assessments of current, historic and prospective prices, PERs and yields.

- The freedom that this particular market place offers for the utilisation of the shares themselves (as simple and immediate security for borrowings).

- The 'public' presence and associated marketing advantages and opportunities.

- The regulation and structure of the market safeguards a high degree of integrity in the quoted price.

- The power of the quoted company to attract key employees.

- Management and employee performance incentives through share option schemes will cause minor dilution of the issued share capital of quoted companies and of the larger or more sophisticated private companies. Such incentives are regarded as an essential tool in powering growth but are often missing from private unquoted companies. The impact of dilution is clearly a most important valuation issue. The lack of management performance incentives may be one of the depreciatory factors in the comparison stakes.

- Quoted company shares are not subject to restrictions on transfer or to pre-emption rights (see 2.101), but this difference is dealt with by special discount for lack of marketability, discussed at 5.37.

5.30   There are some other areas that require care and consideration in making choices. Companies in the throes of public discussion (at the date of the valuation) perhaps should be excluded from the exercise. Companies whose shares have been suspended around the time of the valuation perhaps should also be avoided, as should any involved in financial hype. Companies whose shares have been ignored by the market for a prolonged period may have structural problems as may those showing a continuous decline in share price. The published ratio or yield of a quoted company whose latest results are expected but not yet published clearly is a questionable item but the latest price may to some extent reflect analysts' predictions of those results. In the full range of 'comparable' companies the very best and the very worst performers should be removed altogether from the choice of which to take on board to construct an average PER.

5.31   A final point for consideration in making stock market comparisons is the timing of the comparison. The date of valuation of the subject company is one thing, comparable prices of comparable companies at a different time is another. The aim must be to compare like with like and this applies to the dates involved as much as anything else. It is no good blindly taking quoted ratios or yields for the shares of a quoted company in respect of results for a period ending with a date that is months away from the date of valuation of the subject company.

Discounts, premiums and adjustments to the quoted Price Earnings Ratio (or the Required Yield)

First — fine adjustments

5.32   Having identified a number of candidate 'comparable' quoted companies (which will be in the same industry sector as the subject private company or in an appropriately related sector), we consider the PER of each company for the appropriate year. Note also that exactly the same principles apply if the valuation exercise is using the required yield approach, except that where a discount is applied to a PER it will be a premium for required yield purposes and the reciprocal figure is taken (which is given below) — and vice versa.

In either case we consider whether it is necessary (or possible) to finely adjust the ratio or yield to remove the effect of specific peculiarities that distinguish between the business or asset profiles of the comparable company and our subject company (see 5.28). The reasons for making the adjustment should be noted. The adjustment might be up or down and there should be a consistent approach to all comparisons. Of course, a good spread of comparable companies may iron out individual inconsistencies; but the valuer should be alert to this matter even if no adjustments are made. How do we make a fine adjustment? An example (if somewhat arguable), is a quoted company having a very similar profile to our subject company but with greater proportionate earnings derived from a special foreign market: see whether it is possible to recalculate the quoted company's earnings by removing the foreign earnings and related direct costs.

Second — the quoted company adjustment

5.33   The average of the range of finely adjusted PERs gives us a more-or-less comparable ratio *as if our subject company were quoted*. As our subject company is not quoted, however, before we apply this PER to its future maintainable profits we must consider the factors that distinguish the quoted company persona from the private company persona and make a further adjustment so we have a more-or-less absolute comparable PER. The distinguishing elements themselves are discussed at 5.29. The effect of restrictions on the transfer of private company shares and of pre-emption rights are bound up in the discount for lack of marketability which is considered below. For a general discussion of restrictions and pre-emptions, see 2.101.

5.34   Bearing in mind the quoted company distinguishing factors, we now discount the adjusted quoted PER to transport it from the quoted company ether to the private company earth! This discount will depend upon how far the overall profile of the subject company fits in with the public company persona.

The range of adjustment

5.35   The range of this adjustment is generally considered to be anything (in PER discount terms) up to 50%. Most private companies should fit within the 25%–40% adjustment range. The following is a suggested spread of discounts for types of private company.

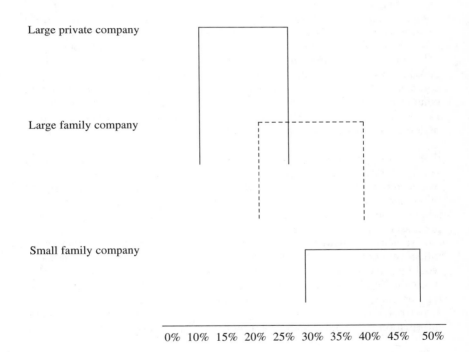

Large private company

Large family company

Small family company

0%	10%	15%	20%	25%	30%	35%	40%	45%	50%
11%	*18%*	*25%*	*33%*	*43%*	*54%*	*67%*	*82%*	*100%*	

PER discount/*Required yield premium*

5.36   After this adjustment we have a PER applicable to a non-quoted company in the same industry sector as our comparable quoted companies. We next make an adjustment basically to reflect the size of the shareholding in the private company that we are valuing, and this adjustment will encompass the discount for lack of marketability.

The discount for lack of marketability

5.37   It is sometimes said about the average 'model' quoted company that its quoted share price is a minority interest price, and that it may jump by anything up to 50% upon a takeover of the company and that that jump represents the control holding value. This may not be the whole story. The transaction, and the emerging final price, can be influenced by factors that simply may not be attributable to our subject company or indeed other quoted company share price movements. A price hike may partly be in sudden realisation of hidden or unutilised value in the target company, or a reflection of the PER of a known predator. It might be a 'synergy premium' where the value of the target company's assets and businesses will be enhanced by a new business environment or team. It may be pure speculation fired by press comment. Or, it may be that the acquirer's future plans for the target company's business have become known. It is not unknown for the share values of an entire industry sector to move because of an expectation of a major takeover possibility somewhere within that sector.

5.38   In a private company valuation for tax purposes we cannot pretend to know the inner mind of the purchaser. That would introduce impossible layers of uncertainty: as to whether our guess was right, as to whether it makes any difference to the share value whatever the purchaser has in mind, and as to whether the purchaser's intentions in any event make sense. Even if the purchaser is prepared to pay much more than the ordinary market value for our subject company's shares, unless this is widely known enough to influence other people's bids we can only assume that the succesful purchaser would pay a nominal amount greater than the market rate or the intrinsic value (the value uninfluenced by extraneous matters) of the shares (see 2.77 etc. as regards the special purchaser). We should ignore the effect of the purchaser's actual plans, yet in this day and age these are often a part of the available information or dis-information in a quoted company takeover bid.

5.39   Even more important than the purchaser's intentions is that the nature of a takeover on the quoted markets is usually a 100% acquisition, not merely any old control holding acquisition, and this is usually driven by a share exchange. The quoted company share price jumps from a minority interest value 'snap' to a 100% ownership value. How can this be true? When one quoted company wishes to acquire another, it aims for a minimum percentage of the target's issued shares. That minimum is not normally 51%. It might be that the shark only closes its jaws at 90%. It would then be at 90% that the 100% value is determined and clicks in for a quoted company. No 90%, no deal! The price falls away! The shark does not want to be stuck with

89.9% — it is too expensive to hold, there are other things to eat! Yes, of course, there are always exceptions, and it may be reasonable to work on the assumption that on average the price 'snap' happens at the magical 75% when no dissenting shareholder grouping can enforce the status quo against liquidation, or perhaps at 60%.

5.40   Before the close of the deal the market price will usually edge upwards in the belief that an offer for the whole company is about to take place, rather than an offer merely for some level of control. This is a form of speculation and you would not automatically take the share prices during that period as representing the company's ordinary earnings or return on capital for any particular size of holding. The price has snapped to something between a 75% and 100% ownership value. Yet, that price will include one or more of those other value elements mentioned in 5.37, and we can therefore say that the premium may not be a pure control holding premium.

5.41   In summary, the quoted price (and accompanying PER) of a normal quoted minority interest share can be said to be good for any size holding up to at least 60% and possibly up to 75% or 90%. Any control premium would be measured by the premium differential between the 60–90% level and 100%. Therefore, the ordinary quoted share price (and its adjusted PER) may be close to a *control-holding* value, and consequently a private company shareholding of anything up to those levels would be entitled to a discount for lack of marketability.

5.42

(*a*)   The Share Valuation Division's view (see 5.43) of discounts from *pro rata* value to reflect the differences in voting power of control holdings is that there is no discount for a 90% holding, a 5% discount for a holding around 75%, and (by extrapolation) an 11% discount for a 60% holding.

(*b*)   The discount for lack of marketability is given from *pro rata* value (100% control holding). Therefore the adjusted PER must be applicable to a *pro rata* value before we apply the discount.

(*c*)   The adjusted PER for a private company applies for any shareholding up to at least 60% (and possibly 75% to 90%).

(*d*)   The adjusted PER is therefore to be increased by a premium to properly represent a 100% control holding as follows:

(i)   for private company shareholding of up to 60%, there is no premium to add (see (*c*) above);

(ii)   for a shareholding of between 60% and 100%:
    (A)   adopting the Inland Revenue discount rates below (between 11% and 5%), the premium to add would be between 5% and 12%;
    (B)   adopting the author's discount rates below (between 16% and 5%), the premium to add would be between 5% and 19%.

(*e*)   Having stabilised our adjusted PER to represent a quoted company 100% *pro rata* value, the PER can now be discounted to reflect the size and lack of marketability of the private company shares being valued. Included in the tables of discounts and premiums that follows are the Inland Revenue's Share Valuation Division discounts which they express only in respect of earnings and control holdings not in respect of dividends and minority interests.

5.43   The work done so far has been to bring the particular *industry sector* PE into the world of private companies within that sector (let us say the engineering sector) and also into a sort of 'social unit' within that sector (e.g. small private family engineering sector company, or large private multi-shareholder engineering sector company). The discount for lack of marketability recognises that in general amongst private companies the smaller the shareholding the less valuable it is because it becomes progressively less easily marketable. However, this marketability may vary between companies within the same social unit (e.g. two companies may appear exactly the same but one is very young and the other very established). It is therefore impossible to give hard and fast discounts for lack of marketability — the following discounts are averages that apply to a broad range of private company types within any particular social unit, and the aim now is to choose the discount that best reflects the level of marketability relating to the specific shareholding we are valuing, having regard to the desirability of the company and all the concomitant surrounding circumstances. So, the adjusted PER applicable to the subject company may be *further and finally discounted* as follows.

For a holding of	Discount suggested by SVD	Discount suggested by author
100% down to 90%	nil	nil
under 90% down to 75%	0%–5%*	0%–5%
under 75% but above 50%	5%–15%	10%–20%
50%	20%–30%	25%–45%
50% (casting vote with someone else)	30%	50%–55%

Although minority holdings are usually valued on the dividend basis there may be occasions where an earnings basis can apply. Where it is appropriate, the following discounts might be in line with those above:

50% (casting vote with someone else)	50%–55%
Under 50% but above 25%	60%–65%
25% down to 10%	70%–75%
under 10%	75%–80%

In a tax related valuation it would not be unreasonable for the Inland Revenue SVD to require supporting arguments for the adoption of a particular discount or premium.

Example

5.44   **Sunshine Property Investments Ltd** — *Valuation of minority shareholding at 16 July 1996*

Assume current revalued net asset value to be £3,000,000 principally comprising good quality long-term let industrial and office units (serviced by the company) valued at £5,000,000 and long-term borrowings of £1,500.000.

Accounts to 31 December	Pre-tax adjusted profit	RPI (rounded)	Present day value	Earnings growth	Weighting	
1991	105,000	136	115,800		×1	115,800
1992	120,000	140	128,600	(11%)	×2	257,200
1993	148,000	142	156,300	(12%)	×3	468,900
1994	159,000	146	163,300	(10%)	×4	653,200
1995	172,000	150	172,000	(10%)	×5	860,000
					15	2,355,100

The 5-year weighted average is: £2,355,100 ÷ 15 = £157,000

All things being equal, it is unlikely that future maintainable profits would be less than £157,000, having regard to the continuous growth in adjusted profits. Given the continuous growth (and assuming research has been undertaken into the assets on which the earnings are dependent and into the property market or the appropriate sector thereof) we may assume that future maintainable profits are not £157,000 but can reasonably be determined as £172,000 (the adjusted profit of the latest available accounts), or maybe £186,000 if we reflect the current year's expected growth pattern — say, 8%.

	£
Therefore, maintainable future earnings taken as	186,000
less: corporation tax at 24%	14,640
	141,360

Comparable quoted company PER — 16 July
Companies having market capitalisation under £50M

Company and market capitalisation	Share price (and discount from net assets)		Net assets per share (est.)	Published earnings per share	Historic PER	Estimated current earnings per share	Prospective PER
Bourne End (£26.2M)	43p	(51%)	87p	1.5p	28.6	2.0p	21.5
Ewart (£18M)	58p	(13%)	67p	3.1p	18.7	4.0p	14.5
Five Oaks (£26.1M)	25.5p	(27%)	35p	2.5p	10	1.8p	14.1
Hemingway (£44.6M)	27.25p	(17%)	33p	1.6p	17	1.6p	17
London Industrial (£41.7M)	269	(23%)	350p	20.2p	13.3	21.2p	12.6
McKay Securities (£30.2M)	126	(43%)	222p	6.7p	18.8	6.3p	20
Panther (£13.7M)	72	(30%)	102p	7.1p	10.1	4.1p	17.5
Average		(29%)				16.6	16.7

The average PER for companies with a market capitalisation of under £50M is 16.65. If SPI were a quoted company its PER would be at a discount from this average to reflect its smaller size, etc. The usual approach in the case of property investment companies is to look at the price as a factor of (and at a discount to) the net assets. Applying the above quoted company average discount from net assets of 29% to SPI's net asset value of £3,000,000, the company's value is £2,130,000. It would be normal practice to discount the PER, but where the net asset value is £3,000,000, this discount would be at the lower end of the range. In this case, to arrive at a value of £2,130,000 the PER discount for SPI as a non-quoted company might be only 10% or 15%. Looking now at SPI's post tax maintainable future earnings, and a discount of, say, around 10%:

(*a*)   discount the quoted average historic PER of 16.65 by around 10%, giving 15, and

(*b*)   multiply the post tax maintainable future earnings of £141,360 by 15, giving £2,120,400 as a control holding.

In this case, then, a reasonable value for a *minority interest* would be £2,130,000 less a discount for a non-quoted minority interest, as to which, see 5.43.

The required yield basis

5.45   By ignoring a specific quoted companies comparison and assuming that no other comparison data is available, the capitalisation of future maintainable profits must be by reference to a required yield. This is discussed, in relation to the dividend basis, at 4.46.

5.46   One alternative approach to the quoted companies comparison route is to take the average yield for the appropriate industry as shown in the Financial Times Actuaries Share Indices which is published in the *Financial Times*. Because the companies whose performances are taken into the FTASI are large and the yields heavily biased towards blue-chip companies, an adjustment should be made as described in 5.32–5.36 to reflect the differences of size, vulnerability, expertise, etc. between the private company and the FTASI companies. The use of FTASI data should be sparing. The Shares Valuation Division would not be too happy about its own valuation officers taking an appeal case to the Special Commissioners and relying only on FTASI data to support their valuation of private company shares.

5.47   The required yield will not be less than the yield available from gilts. The impact of the Euro may have an uncertain effect for some valuations undertaken around the time of its introduction and for some time thereafter, with effects on currency exposure, interest rates on bank deposits and bonds, debt settlement and so on.

5.48   For small companies, say with value no more than £300,000, a yield of around 50% may be appropriate; a lower yield might be appropriate if dividends or fees or bonuses in lieu are being paid. Above that value the yield will fall and an average of around 30–35% may be expected. Much depends on the facts of the case: the condition of the company, its management and the economic climate.

5.49 It may be argued that the potential investor in private company shares chooses that form of investment in preference to the alternatives because he is some special sort of investor. However, he will be taking the decision in the full knowledge of the alternatives available to him and he would be most unwise to invest in a private company without expecting to make his money work for him no less effectively than if it was placed elsewhere. If the immediate income to be derived from the holding is paltry then he might expect to make up the difference either by personal involvement in the business of the company or through the longer term prospects for growth and capital gains. For valuation purposes, the former is usually ignored: it is a personal reason that would be absent from the rest of the market and is not commercially valuable, unless, in the circumstances of the case, that particular purchaser is recognised as a 'special purchaser', but not one influenced by personal reasons (see 2.77). Having said that, there are many businesses whose values are determined by reference to the earnings capacity of the worker/owner, and where this is appropriate, it will come into the equation. The role of a special purchaser in the context of share acquisitions is considered in the interesting case of *Hawkings-Byass v Sassen*. This case also analyses the detailed reasoning behind the choice of valuation base on the facts of the case.

5.50 The required rate of return might therefore be weighted by the growth factor that can be discerned from the company's results and all the surrounding circumstances. The formula for this exercise is given, in relation to dividend basis valuation, at 4.16 and 4.21.

Capitalising the earnings

5.51 Given the PER (or the required yield) the next step is to apply it to the company's earnings. The earnings for the last or the current year are not satisfactory in isolation because the exercise is to capitalise the future maintainable earnings and the current year's profits are no more than one element pointing towards what that figure may be. Several years should be examined to discern the profit (or loss) trend, the impact of inflation, and the measure of growth. The purpose is to identify an inflation-free amount in today's value of tomorrow's promised profit, profit that one can be fairly certain will be maintained *all things being equal*. There may be a good chance that those promised profits will be exceeded in the future, but equally there will be some risk that they will not be reached. A rational view must be taken of the level of maintainable profits that the company can sustain without any significant change in the *status quo*. One method of measuring such earnings is the weighted average model, which looks at the results of the past five or so years as adjusted for inflation to give today's values, taking the average of those values (using the 'sum of the digits' basis) and adjusting the average for expected growth. What if all things will not be equal? If there are known facts that will affect the maintainable future profits they must, of course, be considered and reflected appropriately in the valuation, whether early on in the fundamental assessment of profit levels or in the final capitalisation exercise.

Cyclical trends

5.52   It is important to reflect properly the impact of cyclical profitability. For example, it is clearly not helpful if only a part of a cyclical trend is incorporated in any model of historic or prospective maintainable profits. A cyclical trend may have a marked effect on any growth factor to be introduced. In cases of fluctuating earnings apart from cyclical trends, it may help to smooth the model if the highest and lowest results (after adjusting for inflation) are removed from the calculation of the weighted average.

5.53   In the following examples figures are rounded for convenience.

Example:

Accounts to 30 September	Pre-tax adj profit (£ 000's)	RPI (rounded)	Profit adjusted to present-day (30 Sept 1996)	(1)	Weighted Profits (1)	(2)	Weighted Profits (2)
1987	120,000	103	178,000	1	178,000		
1988	100,000	110	139,000	2	278,000		
1989	(10,000)	119	(13,000)	3	(26,000)		
1990	40,000	130	47,000	4	188,000		
1991	180,000	136	202,000	5	1,010,000		
1992	140,000	140	153,000	6	918,000		
1993	30,000	142	32,000	7	224,000	1	32,000
1994	90,000	146	94,000	8	752,000	2	188,000
1995	200,000	150	204,000	9	1,836,000	3	612,000
1996	140,000	153	140,000	10	1,400,000	4	560,000
				55	6,758,000	10	1,392,000

Weighted average (1) $\dfrac{6,758,000}{55}$ = (say) £123,000

It will be seen that a four-year cyclical trend is in operation, and 1997 promises to be significantly down on 1996, with an upturn expected in 1998 (all things being equal). Perhaps a more accurate result would be obtained by taking the weighted average of the latest cycle.

Weighted average (2) $\dfrac{1,392,000}{10}$ = (say) £139,000

A question arises as to what, if any, growth factor should be introduced. The weighted average (2) of £139,000 seems to be a reasonable expression of what could be regarded as future maintainable profits at 1996 prices, but if each successive cycle shows growth over the previous cycle it may be appropriate to increase the maintainable future profits accordingly — remembering that it will theoretically take a year or two to reach the maximum cyclical profit level.

In adjusting for inflation using the RPI, it is not unusual to find that a smooth profit trend based on the company's accounts figures turns into a fluctuating series, or, more seriously, a declining profit trend where the company's performance has not kept up with real costs.

5.54   If a cyclical trend is present, this must be reflected in the future maintainable profits if it is not reflected in the PER. It is important to ensure that the effect of a cyclical trend is not missed, but neither should its effect be incorporated more than once.

5.55   If the cycle is short — say three to five years — it could give rise to inaccuracies unless the earnings model ranges well beyond one cycle. Even so, it is important to identify when, within that cycle, the valuation date falls. This will assist in deciding which end of a range of possible earnings should be chosen as the maintainable profits. Great care must be taken where cyclical business is involved: a change of product, management, location or fashion may destroy cyclical business and appropriate caution — and enquiry — is necessary. Long-term cyclical business is even more difficult to deal with because a longer period for comparison of profits, growth and wider economic trends etc. is needed. It could be argued that rather than fine tune maintainable profits by reference to cycles greater than, say, ten years, the PER or yield should be adjusted. Quoted company PERs may indeed reflect cyclical business in appropriate cases.

Linear trend analysis

5.56   A statistical model that can be of assistance to the valuer is the linear trend analysis model where the object is to take a series and smooth it into a steady pattern; this does not always provide a helpful answer. The future year's profit is given by solving the simultaneous equation:

$$\varepsilon(y) = na + \varepsilon(x)b$$

$$\varepsilon(xy) = \varepsilon(x)a + \varepsilon(x^2)b$$

Hopefully the following example can, with a little patience, be followed through.

Annual growth	Year to 30 April	Profits	RPI at 30 April	Profits at 1991 value	(x)	(xy)	(x^2)	(a) solved below	(b) solved below
	(1) 1984	78,000	88.6	116,000	× 1 =	116,000	1	54,038 + 1 (41,047) =	95,085
13%	(2) 1985	94,500	94.8	31,000	× 2 =	262,000	4	54,038 + 2 (41,047) =	136,132
33%	(3) 1986	129,000	97.7	174,000	× 3 =	522,000	9	54,038 + 3 (41,047) =	177,179
20%	(4) 1987	162,000	101.8	210,000	× 4 =	840,000	16	54,038 + 4 (41,047) =	218,226
18%	(5) 1988	200,000	105.8	249,000	× 5 = 1,245,000		25	54,038 + 5 (41,047) =	259,273
15%	(6) 1989	249,000	114.3	287,000	× 6 = 1,722,000		36	54,038 + 6 (41,047) =	300,320
16%	(7) 1990	315,000	125.1	332,000	× 7 = 2,324,000		49	54,038 + 7 (41,047) =	341,367
23%	(8) 1991	411,000	131.9	411,000	× 8 = 3,288,000		64	54,038 + 8 (41,047) =	382,414
				1,910,000	36	10,319,000	204		
	∴ n = 8			= Σ(y)	= (x)	= Σ(xy)	= (x^2)		

(i)   1,910,000 = 8a + 36b, and

(ii)   10,319,000 = 36a + 204b

multiply (i) by 9 and (2) by 2 =

(iii)   17,190,000 = 72a + 324b, and

(iv)   20,638,000 = 72a + 408b

Subtracting (iii) from (iv) gives a value of 41,047 for b. Substituting b's value in (iii) gives a value of 54,038 for (a) and, extrapolating the final column's figures for 1992 gives 382,414 + 41,047 = £423,461.

(1)   This is a small increase only over the actual 1991 profits, and with the recent RPI adjusted profit growth rates proven by performance (1989 — 15%, 1990 — 16%, 1991 — 23%). It is unlikely that anyone would really expect, merely on the profit trend, that the increase in 1992 would be just 3% — more likely somewhere in the region of 411,000 + 15% = 472,000, or 411,000 + 20% = 493,000.

(2)   Linear trend analysis of the years 1989, 1990 and 1991 alone gives an extrapolated 1992 profit of 467,000. This would appear to be the minimum maintenable level of future profits and represents a growth rate of 14%. It may take pretty hard evidence to prove that a 20–23% growth rate could be achieved, but if the evidence is available it could quite easily take precedence over the figures thrown up by the statistical models. This particular example of linear trend analysis shows that with strong, persistent growth the model does not truly reflect reality. However, if those profits were uneven and a simple forward extrapolation not possible, the linear trend model would provide a straight line of best fit and a future trend in keeping (within the overall growth rate) with past performance. That is when this approach comes into its own.

(3)   Looking retrospectively at a valuation based on a linear trend analysis, it is important to remember that the extrapolation is at the date of valuation and the *actual* performance of the company in later years, cannot be known at that date.

Chapter 6

The Assets Basis

Asset backing

6.1   The value of the company's assets per se will figure in a valuation only if the company is about to be liquidated or their net realisable value is greater than the capitalised value of dividends and earnings. Goodwill as an asset is a special matter (see Chapter 12). Assets which are separate from those which generate the company's earnings would certainly influence the share price. See 7.14. Consider two companies, Ayco and Beeco. Each pays the same dividends and enjoys the same level of earnings (and their shares would be valued at the same price if adopting a normal dividend or earning's basis). Ayco's net realisable asset value is negligible whereas Beeco's net realisable value upon a liquidation happens to equal its share value on a going concern basis. An investment in Beeco's shares appears to have an advantage if a liquidation or a surplus asset sale is contemplated. Perhaps the value of those assets means the shares would be easier to sell — should this value then influence (increase) Beeco's share price? If Ayco has no fixed assets to speak of, there would clearly be a major distinction between the activities of the two companies. Ayco would be generating its earnings from goodwill, whereas Beeco's earnings are derived from fixed and current assets. Earnings-generating assets occasionally need replacing, updating, moving, all of which promise to be a financial burden. Probably, the complete picture of Beeco, including its assets, would already be fully represented in its share value. If, on the other hand, Ayco has the same quality earnings-generating assets as Beeco, the disparity between the companies respective net asset values suggests that Beeco's shares are more attractive. The consequence would be that Ayco's share value is downgraded rather than Beeco's value is increased. However, if the difference can be identified as additional asset value that stands to one side of Beeco's business activities then Beeco's shares would be increased in value.

6.2   There are situations where the assets themselves will be the basis for valuation instead of either the dividend or earnings basis, or where they will be important added-value elements to a parallel valuation on one of the other bases. They will tend to constitute the principal basis of valuation where greatest current value can be derived from selling them (whether as individual fixed assets, or discrete business activities) rather than continuing to use them in a business context.

6.3   In *Attorney-General of Ceylon v Mackie*, Lord Reid said 'If it is proved in a particular case that at the relevant date the business could not have been sold for more than the value of its tangible assets, then that must be taken to be its value as a *going concern*'. That is not to say that the business is *deemed* to be a going concern, but a going concern business cannot necessarily be regarded as worth more than the value of its assets. If the business is *not* a going concern, presumably a break-up asset valuation will be appropriate, but see below.

Alternative bases

6.4   There are several different asset bases.

Straight net asset basis

6.5   This is the full current market value (not the book value on the balance sheet) of business or non-business assets within the company, and this basis is adopted when it is not expected or necessary to realise the assets. Some assets, e.g. freehold property, might be expected to increase in value while they will remain within the company. However, many types of asset, e.g. fixed plant and machinery, may depreciate over a period of time. It is necessary to separate out those assets which contribute to the company's earnings because their value should automatically have been reflected in the value of capitalised earnings. However, it is possible that the realisable value of business assets, including, for example, premises is greater than the capitalised value of going-concern earnings. Whilst this is unusual, it can arise.

Break-up basis

6.6   This is the value that would be realised upon the liquidation of the company and the sale of individual assets and stock, collection of debts and so on. The full market value for each asset (not necessarily the balance sheet value) is ascertained and this value must then be discounted by an element for loss on or cost of realisation. For example, upon a liquidation of a trading company, to get in all the debts within a reasonable period of time — say 30 days or even 60 days — it may be realistic to accept that at least 5% or 10% of these debtors may not pay — and that it would not be economical after a certain period to pursue them. Alternatively, the entire debtor list may be sold to a debt factoring agency, or debt collectors used. Stock and work-in-progress more often than not consists of perishables and 'wasted' work that cannot be realised upon a liquidation. A much higher discount may be necessary in these cases — often 50%, but depending upon the nature of the items. Additionally, the valuer must take into account possible redundancy pay and compensation; a provision of at least 10% of the annual staff costs would be a prudent move — but a precise cost can often be determined. The early repayment of loans may carry a penalty, as may the cancellation of a lease. Short-term leaseholds may have a balance-sheet value but may in fact be impossible to assign, not to mention possible dilapidation liabilities and deferred tax charges (basically the claw-back of capital allowances on a discontinuance of trade or disposal of cars, plant, machinery or industrial buildings).

6.7   The primary objective is to value the shares, not the individual assets, but the question is what would someone pay for the shares with the object of taking over all these assets so that they can be sold and the company then liquidated or the residue reinvested by the company? On the break-up basis we have to take into account the asset-stripper's profit. In *Re Courthorpe*, the Court accepted that a shareholder who did not have control but who *might* have been able to compel a winding-up would want a 50% profit — i.e. a one-third discount from the realisable value of the assets. The profit mark-up is unlikely to change significantly where the majority of the shares are for sale, unless it can be shown that the assets are readily saleable, in which case one might argue down to 30% profit or a 23% discount, perhaps less in some cases. The possibility of a special purchaser should not be forgotten. The exercise is to realise as much as possible from the sales — so one would look at all the possible permutations of asset disposal, whether piecemeal or as a block and not forgetting the possibility of auctions.

Forced-sale basis

6.8   This is something like the break-up basis but is a rather more serious version. It may be evident that at the date of valuation the only way to realise any value from the assets of the company would be to dispose of them within a limited time. This basis more usually applies where to delay the liquidation of the company or the disposal will actually cost more than to sell at an unusually large discount and the obvious example is where funding costs are exceptionally high, the interest rate is high and there are no or insufficient earnings from which to meet the interest charge. Suppose a loan of £200,000 at a real rate of interest of 16% has been made to a company and the loan is secured on a factory valued at £350,000. There are no earnings as the business has just collapsed. The property's full value may only be realised after it has been on the market for six to twelve months, yet the interest cost over twelve months will be £32,000. On top of this the lender may be able to take possession of the property, sell it at any price above £200,000 and return the net proceeds after costs of disposal, legal fees, interest unpaid, etc. All in all it may be better to dispose of the factory with least possible delay, and this may require an immediate and heavy discount from the current market value.

6.9   Additionally, in this case, whatever is in or around the factory that constitutes separate stock or assets would have to be disposed of before the new tenant takes up occupation: a further forced sale at 'knock-down' prices. In the case of leased property, it may be a condition of giving up the lease that the premises are completely vacated — and this may mean that rather than any realisation of assets on the premises, there are costs of removal, dumping or storage.

Taxation

6.10   Having determined a valuation for the assets the next matter to consider is the effect of taxation. So far as the realisation of stock and work-in-progress is concerned this would only give rise to a corporation tax charge if sold at a price above the balance sheet provision. Plant and machinery disposed of below its tax written-down value would create a further tax allowance (which may or may not be utilisable against current or past profits, depending upon a variety of factors). If sold at above that value, the sale would create a balancing charge and if, as is unlikely, it is sold above its original cost, it may in some circumstances give rise to a chargeable gain.

6.11   On the basis of a break-up or forced sale the resultant tax charge must be brought into account for it is the value net of tax that the liquidating shareholder would be able to realise outside the company (but no account would be taken of post-liquidation taxation outside the company).

6.12   In the case of the straight net asset basis the underlying capital gains tax liability would not be taken into the net value calculation if disposal is not being contemplated. It may not be unreasonable, however, to allow a discount from the full value to recognise the latent liability should a disposal be contemplated within, say, three to five years. This discount very largely depends upon the full facts of the case (including the likelihood of any 'roll-over' or 'hold-over' tax relief for business assets), and particularly the economic benefit that would accrue to a purchaser of the shares if he had power to dispose of the asset.

6.13   Tax problems may be encountered, in relation to real property under *ICTA 1988, s 776*, and generally, under *ICTA 1988, s 703*. Where groups of companies are concerned *TCGA 1992, s 139* may be relevant. Indeed, the tax consequences of any disposal arrangement should be considered, and to the extent that they could have an immediate impact within the company in a real sale, it may be appropriate to reflect that impact in a deduction from net asset value. In any major disposal of shares, tax warranties will be a feature of the negotiations — see 2.37.

Precedence of asset basis

6.14   In summary, the principal situations where the assets basis takes precedence over other bases are as follows.

(1)   Where a company is in liquidation or about to go into liquidation. In *Re Courthorpe* it was shown that a heavy discount on the value of the company's shares would be in order (one-third in this case) where the motive behind the acquisition of the shares is to liquidate the company and take a profit on the sale of the company's assets. It will be realised that in calculating the present value of the shares (i.e. before this discount) the costs of disposing of the assets and the discounted value

of the assets on a break-up basis will already have been taken into account.

(2) Where the asset backing is substantially under-utilised and there is no prospect of improving the profitability of the company's current activities. In *M'Connel's Trustees v IRC*, the company made a loss in each of the three years after its formation and there was never any prospect of the company earning profits or being in a position to pay a dividend. Lord Fleming held that the holder of the company's shares would be in a position to put the company into voluntary liquidation and to realise the whole assets and divide the value thereof amongst the shareholders.

(3) Where the assets stand to one side of the business and have a value in their own right.

(4) In the special case of investment etc. holding companies (see 6.16).

Minority shareholders

6.15 In the event of impending liquidation the minority shareholder will be entitled to a *pro rata* share of the net asset value. This would not be the case in other asset based valuations where the value would therefore have to be discounted because the minority shareholder's entitlement would only be on paper. The amount of the discount depends upon the size of the minority holding, the 'quality' of the asset backing and the likelihood of the value being realised. Shareholdings of less than 10% might be discounted by 50% or more (before any discount for lack of marketability). This matter is more fully discussed in the example in 7.14 *et seq.*

Investment etc. holding companies

6.16 In the case of a company that has assets in a form readily convertible into cash, and which have their own investment value irrespective of any current business use, a majority shareholding in such a company may be valued solely on a net assets basis, or on a 'hybrid' basis (Chapter 7), and thereby reflect the respective importance of the assets on the one hand and the earnings from those assets on the other. If the investment assets can be separated from the business assets it will be necessary to add the value of the investment assets (or their income derivative) plus the capitalised earnings as two separate factors in one total value. By business assets is meant those assets which are the source of or used for the purpose of earning investment income or trading income, which income can be capitalised.

6.17 Alternatively, the value of the business assets may be very great yet produce a low yield in income terms, such as in the case of property investment companies. Here, the real value of the underlying assets would often be reflected in a very high capitalisation factor for the earnings.

6.18   Typically, these approaches will apply to property or investment companies and possibly also to companies owning intellectual property (patents, copyrights, licences etc.) or possibly a ship-owning company; but it will be realised that the asset value will be taken only if demonstrably greater than the other possible bases. It may well be that the reason the earnings basis is low is a general decline in the particular industry or the economy generally, and that a corresponding problem could be found in disposing of the company's assets. For example, during a temporary decline in the shipping industry it might be found that perfectly good ships simply cannot be sold, and the discount that it would be necessary to apply to the current value to find a disposal value would be surprisingly, albeit factually, large. So, the earnings basis may still be appropriate after all when these factors are considered. Other relevant factors will be the quality of the underlying assets, and the geographical and economic spread of the assets.

Minority shareholders

6.19   A minority shareholding would usually be valued not on an assets basis but on a dividend basis, that value possibly being influenced by the strength of the company's asset backing by way of adjusting the discount for lack of marketability to reflect that strength and therefore the attraction of the shareholding. However, if the company is in liquidation or about to go into liquidation a minority shareholding will be valued on an asset basis. The asset basis may also be appropriate for a minority shareholding where there is a clear asset-strip opportunity.

6.20   In *M'Connel's Trustees,* in considering purchasers buying shares as an *ordinary investment* Lord Fleming said:

'A purchaser of a small lot of shares would naturally have assumed that purchasers of the remaining shares would wish to make the most they could out of their shares and would concur with him in taking the necessary steps to have the assets of the company realised to the best advantage.'

6.21   Where investment assets are owned in addition to assets used for business purposes, they would be valued independently of the business assets. See also 'the combination basis' at 7.14 *et seq.*

Balance sheet values

6.22   In every case of share valuation, the net asset value of the company must be investigated to determine how it is relevant to the valuation. The company's balance sheet will show the historic cost or revaluation of such assets and such values should be used as a starting point to identify the true market value at the required date. Even if the net asset value is not expected to be used in the calculation of the share value, it may nevertheless be a useful cross-check for the valuation basis that has been adopted and, as mentioned above, the net asset value may well influence the discount for non-marketability (see 5.37). If an asset value is grossly at variance with the proposed valuation obviously it would be necessary to investigate the reasons for this. For example, if the net asset value is vastly in excess of the capitalised earnings, the valuer may have discovered something about the company that the directors or owners did not know or refused to accept. Alternatively, it may simply show that the valuer has under-capitalised the earnings.

6.23 Generally speaking, it is the *net* asset value that provides the true asset backing figure. We may ignore net current liabilities if they will simply wash out through normal trading activities and do not contribute an extraordinary drain on reserves, but other liabilities must be taken into account, for if the company's assets are to be liquidated, creditors must be paid off. Such matters are dealt with below. The market value of each asset and liability must be considered independently but any inter-dependence or relationship should be brought into account as appropriate. If, for example, a loan is secured on a specific asset, the value of the asset in excess of the outstanding loan debt will be a surplus belonging to the company, unless the reality is that, on a break-up, after costs of sale etc., it would be cheaper to give the asset to the creditor in full and final settlement. As another example of asset inter-dependence a set of antique boardroom furniture will be of greater value than the sum of the individual knock-down prices of each item. In valuing the assets of a company which is a *going concern* it would not be correct to look at the break-up basis unless there is a clear indication that the asset should be disposed of and not replaced.

Valuing assets

6.24 The normal requirement is that open market value is to be taken. The principles of such open market price are discussed in Chapter 2. The rest of this chapter considers special points to keep in mind in respect of specific assets, although in just about every case of valuation of land and buildings and intellectual property specialist valuers will be required to determine the open market value. Therefore, the points made in respect of land and buildings, plant and works, rental property and so on are to assist the share valuer to understand the elements involved in the specific valuation exercises undertaken by the specialist valuer. Goodwill is usually valued by reference to earnings derived otherwise than directly from the asset (as in the case of rent, interest etc.). The matter is considered in Chapter 12; intellectual property, is dealt with in Chapter 13.

Land and buildings

6.25 Normally, existing or current use value would be taken (i.e. the value of the land on the basis of the use to which the land is put at the date for valuation), but additionally a value should be given for any actual development permission, although great caution should be exercised over putting 'hope' value on the land. In the case of *Raja Vyricherla Narayana Gajapatiraju v RDO, Vizagapatam*, which was an Indian compulsory purchase case heard by the Privy Council, Lord Romer said that it has been established by numerous authorities that land is not valued merely by reference to the use to which it is being put at the time at which its value has to be determined, but also by reference to the uses to which it is reasonably capable of being put in the future. Alternative use value of the land certainly should be considered if it is realistically possible for the use to be changed, whether as a practical or legal matter, but that value would only displace the existing use value if the land is not required for the company's business, or if the alternative use value is demonstrably greater than the value of the company's business — which is not entirely unusual.

6.26   If valuing the land on an alternative use basis the cost of approvals and regulatory matters, site clearance, levelling, infilling etc., should be taken into account, and regard should be had to any plant and/or machinery or structure on the land for, in such a case, they could not be valued on a current use basis unless the valuation of both land and buildings together on a current use basis is greater than the alternative use basis. It may be necessary to adopt a break-up basis for the plant etc., in which case the costs of dismantling, removing and restoring would have to be taken into account.

6.27   Existing tenancies and sub-tenancies, licences to occupy and covenants must also be brought into account. These may be of particular relevance in the case of farmland which requires particular valuation specialism. The case of *Walton (Executor of Walton deceased) v IRC* is important for its consideration of several valuation principles concerned with the open market value of a deceased partner's share in a farming partnership, having as a partnership interest an agricultural tenancy the landlords of which included the deceased.

Plant and machinery and structures

6.28   The valuation of land and buildings will usually be determined by a chartered surveyor who may also be skilled in valuing plant and machinery, especially where it forms part of a building or structure. Examples include transformer sub-stations, generating plant, escalators and lifting gear rails, boilers, air conditioning plant, sprinkler systems and other items forming an integral part of the structure of the building or other edifice.

This would not normally include plant or machinery which is installed wholly or primarily in connection with industrial or commercial processes and other 'loose' plant and machinery. For example, although the rails and gantry for an overhead crane may be included in the valuation of the building of which the rails or gantry form part, the crane itself would be valued as a separate and distinct asset.

Structures which have been installed or erected in or on buildings or land for the provision of the services attaching thereto and *not forming part of any particular industrial or commercial process* would normally be included in the value of the building or land. Examples are boiler houses, chimneys, stagings, permanent partitioning and internal buildings, railways and bridges, fences, roads and hardstandings.

6.29 For civil engineering works, plant and industrial structures, and major installations and complexes, where there is no ready market and no clear open market value can be determined, the valuation may be resolved by taking the current depreciated replacement cost discounted to reflect the remaining efficient and productive life of the asset. This exercise would take into account any degree of technological and economic obsolescence of the asset, continuing maintenance costs, and technical and production specifications of the existing versus new replacement assets.

6.30 If the company is to be liquidated or the trade is to cease the assets would be valued on a break-up basis, special care being taken to separate those assets having continuing value and those with only scrap value, and to establish the costs of dismantling and transportation. There may be a special market for the assets. For example, in the case of heavy industrial plant, a developing country may be prepared to acquire the whole or usable parts of it. Also, if there is any obligation under a lease or local or national law to leave the site in any particular state, i.e. completely levelled or landscaped etc., the cost of doing this should be taken into account. Environmental laws may today have a considerable impact on the value of land where, for example, reinstatement of a 'safe' condition of the land is necessary.

RICS open market price

6.31 In the Royal Institution of Chartered Surveyors' (RICS) *Statement of Asset Valuation Practice No 2* (revised June 1992), the definition of open market value is the best price at which the sale of an interest in property might reasonably be expected to have been completed unconditionally for cash consideration on the date of valuation, assuming:

(*a*) a willing seller;

(*b*) that, prior to the date of valuation, there had been a reasonable period (having regard to the nature of the property and the state of the market) for the proper marketing of the interest, for the agreement of price and terms and for the completion of the sale;

(*c*) that the state of the market, level of values and other circumstances were, on any earlier assumed date of exchange of contracts, the same as on the date of valuation; and

(*d*) that no account is taken of any additional bid by a purchaser with a special interest.

6.32 Of course, these guidelines will provide a value, but not necessarily the appropriate value for tax purposes. For example, the special purchaser cannot be dismissed for the purposes of a valuation for tax purposes, and the RICS value must be adjusted, if appropriate, to reflect the presence of such a purchaser; see 2.77.

6.33   RICS also defines the forced sale concept — this is the open market value as above except that the vendor has imposed a time limit for completion which cannot be regarded as a 'reasonable period' as required in (*b*) above.

Partial construction or development

6.34   In some cases property may be in the course of construction or may be held as trading stock. Specialised properties will be valued according to the existing stage of construction on a depreciated replacement cost basis, particularly having regard to whether the proposed current use would be the same after the share transfer. For example, it may be necessary to discount the proposed current use and substitute an alternative use basis, e.g. because the particular business for which the building is being constructed is to cease: in such a case the cost of removing or adapting the partially completed building must be brought into account. A non-specialist property is valued at the open market value of the land for the proposed use plus the cost of the development to the date of valuation. Alternatively the estimated current use value of the finished building, less the costs of completion, may be used.

Land as trading stock

6.35   Properties held as trading stock, if purchased and resold in the same unaltered condition, could be valued at the lower of cost or current market value, or where this cannot be ascertained, at original cost plus the cost of any development. See below for partially completed investment property. On liquidation market value would be the proper measure of value if ascertainable.

Rental properties

6.36   In the case of let properties it is necessary to look first at the current lease and secondly, if appropriate, at the rent potential after the expiry of the lease. First, the rent for the remaining period of the unexpired lease payable under the terms and conditions of the lease is capitalised, having regard to the basis and dates of rent reviews. Secondly, the anticipated future open market value rental income based on normal lease terms would be capitalised and then discounted to a present day value.

6.37   Outgoings such as rates and water rates, agent and management fees and rents payable to a superior landlord must also be taken into the equation. So too should any liability that can be identified and quantified with a reasonable degree of certainty. A repair and refurbishment clause, or a covenant to improve, putting the responsibility on the shoulders of the lessor, for example, would be an important future liability that should be provided for out of rents. There may already be a fund in existence out of which the future liability will be met, and if this is the case no further provision would need to be made unless the fund is calculated to meet the future liability by taking a contribution from future rents. Usually, of course, the lease will be a full repairing and insuring lease making the lessee responsible for the rates, repairs, maintenance, management and insurance (either directly or by way of service charge).

6.38   Other factors that can affect the value of property, whether or not rented, are:

- option to purchase, or for a new lease;

- planning applications or decisions (consents or refusals);

- zoning or compulsory purchase possibilities;

- mortgages and charges;

- easements.

Properties for letting which are in the course of being constructed will be valued according to the capitalised value of the expected rents when completed, less the estimated cost of completing the construction or development. If completion of construction or development is some way off it may not be appropriate to value in this way but rather to take the current land value plus the costs of the construction or development to date. Large developments of houses or flats for resale will probably be treated as trading stock (see above).

Negative value

6.39   Properties which constitute a net liability to a company will have a negative value. These normally are leasehold properties occupied by the company as tenant where the rent exceeds market value or where the lessee is bound by onerous covenants. As mentioned above, if there is responsibility to reinstate land to its former character at the end of some special use permitted by a local authority or under, for example, environmental laws, the costs of so doing may be greater than the expected market value of the land at that time. It is even possible that the costs would be indeterminate. This has always been the case. However, today's environmental laws which cross national boundaries and can pass through companies to land squarely on shareholder corporations mean that valuers need to take care about environmental liabilities, which will be particularly relevant to certain industries.

Premises and goodwill

6.40   For certain specialist commercial premises the building will itself form part of or include some or all of the goodwill of the business in which it is used. Examples are hotels, restaurants, cinemas, and 'theme' parks. In such cases the value of the 'whole', i.e. the business, will presumably, in the case of a going concern, be greater than the alternative use value of the 'part', i.e. the premises in which the business is carried on. The premises themselves would only be valued independently of the goodwill on a break-up basis, when presumably there would be no 'goodwill' to value, and in this case the premises would be valued on an alternative use basis or simply land value, possibly with costs of demolition brought into account — but take note of the effect of a 'special purchaser' in the market — see 2.77 and see also Chapter 12 *et seq* for the valuation and accounting treatment of goodwill that is not inextricably linked to the premises from which a business is conducted.

Wasting assets (other than leaseholds)

6.41   Fixed assets which, when consumed, cannot be renewed in the existing location will be valued according to the net current replacement cost basis. This includes mineral-bearing land, waste tips etc. The factors that will be relevant to this valuation are:

- volume of remaining reserves and royalty value;

- quality of remaining reserves;

- cost (revenue and capital) of recovering the remaining reserves;

- supply, demand and transportation factors;

- tenure, costs of concessions, royalty payments;

- alternative use value after exhaustion;

- alternative use value of land not yet required for working;

- costs of exploration, testing etc., incurred or yet to be incurred.

Non-mineral-bearing land such as rubbish tips will be valued similarly but by reference to filling-up rather than emptying. It may also be necessary to consider the value of a hole for such a purpose (planning permissions allowing) after minerals have been extracted by quarrying etc. Again, environmental issues may be relevant, especially to waste tips.

Investments and subsidiary companies

6.42   If valuation is not being carried out on the basis of consolidated accounts, shares held in a subsidiary unquoted company will need to be valued according to the appropriate share valuation basis — not necessarily using the same valuation basis as that adopted for the valuation of the parent company shares; as with all share valuations, the valuation basis depends upon the full circumstances and the size of the holding. Minority shareholdings in unquoted companies must also be treated on their own merits. If a valuation is being carried out on the basis of consolidated accounts, it is no less necessary to review the underlying entities and, indeed, the structural, management, and business inter-relationship and assets.

6.43   Shares held in quoted companies would be valued by reference to their quoted price on the day. Shares quoted on the AIM, however, are not treated as quoted shares for tax purposes. See 2.98 and Appendix 2, paragraph 19.

6.44   For the purposes of the taxation of capital gains, corporation tax on chargeable gains and inheritance tax, the value of quoted shares and securities is determined as follows:

'The market value of shares or securities listed in The Stock Exchange Daily Official List shall, except where in consequence of special circumstances prices quoted in that List are by themselves not a proper measure of market value, be as follows:

(*a*)   the lower of the two prices shown in the quotations for the shares or securities in The Stock Exchange Daily Official List on the relevant date plus one-quarter of the difference between those two figures, or

(*b*)   halfway between the highest and lowest prices at which bargains, other than bargains done at special prices, were recorded in the shares or securities for the relevant date,

choosing the amount under paragraph (*a*) if less than that under paragraph (*b*), or if no such bargains were recorded for the relevant date, and choosing the amount under paragraph (*b*) if less than that under paragraph (*a*):

Provided that—

(i)   this subsection shall not apply to shares or securities for which The Stock Exchange provides a more active market elsewhere than on the London trading floor, and

(ii)   if the London trading floor is closed on the relevant date the market value shall be ascertained by reference to the latest previous date or earliest subsequent date on which it is open, whichever affords the lower market value.'

6.45   The foregoing 'quarter-up' or 'halfway' rules are specified in *TCGA 1992, s 272* and are adopted for inheritance tax purposes. The Stock Exchange Daily Official List records all the day's bargains up to 2.15pm. Bargains after that time are recorded in the next day's list and are flagged.

6.46   The quoted price will include allowance for accrued dividends or interest, which will belong to the owner as at a specified date after the date the dividend is declared. A sale before that date will take the expected dividend with the shares; a sale after that date will exclude the recent dividend. Once that date has passed therefore the List shows the share price as being 'xd' (i.e. ex-dividend or without any right to the latest declared dividend).

6.47   If no quotation is available for the day of valuation (for example, because the Stock Exchange is closed) the last quoted price or the next following may be taken. For foreign shares, the UK quoted price, if there is one, will normally be accepted by the Inland Revenue's Shares Valuation Division.

6.48   If there is no UK quotation and the foreign stock market quotes both a 'bid' and an 'offer' price for any particular day, it is the lower of the two, the bid price, which will be accepted by the Revenue.

6.49   Where, exceptionally, the quoted price is not a proper measure of the market value, it cannot be taken for tax valuation purposes. For example, there may have been no bargains done for some considerable time or the shares are suspended for some reason. In such a case it would obviously be necessary to consider all the circumstances and information available concerning the shares.

Cash

6.50   A substantial amount of cash shown on the balance sheet indicates one of three things: first, a temporary reservoir of unallocated cash is held; secondly, a necessary cash reserve is maintained because the business requires ready cash; or thirdly, a surplus of reserves is held in cash form. It may be possible to confirm which of these is the case by comparing balance sheets of earlier years and satisfying oneself that there has been no inherent change in the conduct of the business or in its activities.

6.51   In the case of the third possibility, it may be argued that the cash represents undistributed reserves which are having no impact on the business itself or on the income and growth generating factors, in which case the cash and interest thereon should be regarded as an asset to one side of the business assets and therefore to be brought separately into account in the valuation. Alternatively or additionally, such a reserve may have a marked effect on a dividend basis unless the cash could be shown to be retained necessarily for a future business development purpose. This point raises an interesting debate concerning the rights and oppression of minority interests; see 2.108.

Chapter 7

The Hybrid Basis and the Combination Basis

The alternative bases

7.1   There are occasions when a single valuation basis will not be appropriate, for example because there are quite different expectations with regard to different assets in the company or simply because the assets themselves lend themselves to different valuation bases.

7.2   In such a case it may be appropriate to apply each of the valuation bases (assets, earnings and dividends and yields) separately to the different assets, or to weight them according to their respective importance. Some authorities bring into account a weighting for prior sales, but this is questionable. A prior sale may certainly be used as a means of checking a current value but should not be used to distort values calculated under the standard valuation bases.

7.3   This chapter is concerned with two variants on the standard valuation basis; the hybrid basis and the combination basis.

7.4   The *hybrid basis* is the use of two or more valuation bases in tandem, a full valuation under each base being undertaken but only a percentage of each value being used according to the relative importance of each to the total value. Suppose Aco's A's shares would be valued as follows: on an asset basis £3 per share; on an earnings basis £4 per share; on a dividends basis £1 per share. It is required to value a shareholding comprising 30% of the issued share capital. It is considered that the relative importance of each of the bases of value to the shareholding in question is: assets 60%; earnings 30%; dividends 10%. In this example the value of each share comprised in the shareholding would become (60% × £3) + (30% × £4) + (10% × £1) = £3.10 per share (before any discount for lack of marketability).

7.5   A hybrid basis cannot apply if there are no earnings and no future earnings in prospect. In that case there can be no future dividend stream in prospect either and value can be found on an assets basis only.

7.6   If there are no assets or, more likely, only nominal assets and no prospects for future dividends, only an earnings basis can identify value in the shares; with the result that minority shareholders will probably have nil value shares.

7.7   It is unlikely that the hybrid method of valuation can be relevant to a going concern trading company for shareholdings outside the range of 20% to 74%. Below that range the dividend basis cannot be ousted; above it the earnings basis must surely be supreme.

7.8   For investment companies however the range may be from 0% to 74% because the value of solid asset backing may percolate through to the smallest of shareholdings. Above the range, the asset basis will probably be appropriate unless capitalised earnings exceed the asset value, in which case the earnings basis will apply.

7.9   Within these ranges of shareholding the hybrid basis may be used and the problem is to identify when to use it and to choose the appropriate percentage of each valuation basis.

When to choose the hybrid basis

7.10   The hybrid basis can be appropriate in many cases and the valuer should consider using it when he feels, having looked at all the underlying facts relating to the shareholding, the company, its business, assets and future, that there is more (or less) to the value of the shares in the context of the size and influence of the shareholding and the circumstances of the valuation than a straight application of one basis would give.

For example, a small minority shareholding would normally be valued on a dividends basis. However, if the earnings of the company are extremely high and the dividends have been kept very low or are non-existent because earnings are retained for business purposes, and if the reserves are accumulating and the business is progressing well, clearly there is an argument that the benefit of holding the shares may be found in the accumulating earnings which will enure for the future benefit of the shareholder, and therefore some weighting might be given to the earnings basis (from which value is clearly evident), and to the asset basis in respect of accumulated cash reserves, as well as to the dividend basis.

7.11   Where the company has under-utilised assets, or the alternative value of the assets is greater (or there is a distinct impression that they might be greater) than the capitalised value of the earnings they are producing, some weighting should be attached to an asset valuation. Clearly, where assets are minimal and value stems from the utilisation of labour the weighting should be in favour of earnings rather than assets, and so on. As has already been mentioned, particular attention should be paid to investment companies whose asset value may well exceed capitalised earnings and dividends.

Weighting

7.12   Attempting to approach this in some scientific fashion it is necessary to categorise the possible different shareholding environments within the hybrid valuation range:

1.   the shareholding has control (above 50% to under 75%);

2.   the shareholding has effective control because it is the largest single shareholding and exceeds 25% (above 25% to 50%);

3.   no shares have effective control (above 25% to 50%);

4.   no shares have effective control (up to 25%);

5.   other shareholding(s) has control (under 50%).

7.13   The following are merely broad suggestions for weightings, which will be influenced by the facts of each case:

Shareholding Environment	*Asset*	*Earnings*	*Dividend*	*Total*

Shareholding Environment	

Weighting %
(investment company in parentheses)

Shareholding Environment	*Asset*	*Earnings*	*Dividend*	*Total*
1. Control (above 50% to under 75%)	20 (50)	75 (50)	5 (—)	100 (100)
2. Effective control (above 25% to 50%)	20 (40)	65 (20)	15 (40)	100 (100)
3. No controlling interest (above 25% to 50%)	10 (30)	40 (20)	50 (50)	100 (100)
4. No controlling interest (up to 25%)	10 (20)	25 (10)	65 (70)	100 (100)
5. Control elsewhere (up to 49%)	5 (20)	20 (5)	75 (75)	100 (100)

The combination basis

7.14   The combination basis applies simply where, notwithstanding that an ordinary share in a company does not entitle the shareholder to ownership of individual assets, certain separable assets need to be valued independently of the other business assets of the company in order to get a full valuation picture. In this case the total share valuation is the combined value as independently determined.

7.15   *Separable assets* stand alone from other assets of the company or can be separated from other assets of the company without causing damage (individual or combined loss of value) to the financial integrity of those assets when operating together. For the shareholder, the realisable value of those assets (or the capitalised value of the income derived from them) would be aggregated with the capitalised earnings or the capitalised dividends of the company, or with any other value basis adopted for valuing the other assets of the company. Alternatively, the additional value may be incorporated by way of a reduction in the discount for lack of marketability; or a percentage of the minority shareholding value might be attributed to the value of the company on an assets basis, under the hybrid basis, explained above; or the income (if any) could be capitalised with the earnings from the company's business, either by adding the income and the earnings together and applying a single PER, or by applying a separate PER to each and adding the totals.

Example

Suppose the asset market values of a company were:

Non-business assets   £100,000 (non-income producing)

Business assets   £75,000 (yielding post-tax earnings of 20%)

A dividend policy has been established and 30% of profits are regularly paid out. A minority shareholding of 5% is to be valued. The required yield is 12% (i.e. capitalise gross dividends at 100/12). Assume ACT and tax credit to be 20% at the date of valuation.

Dividend basis valuation

1.	Earnings — £75,000 at 20% yield	= £15,000
2.	Dividends — £15,000 at 30% paid	= £ 4,500
3.	Gross dividends — £4,500 at 5/4 (ACT)	= £ 5,625
4.	Capitalised value £5,625 at 12% grossed	= £46,875
5.	Discount for lack of marketability, say 40% (= £46,875 at 60%)	= £28,125
6.	5% shareholding — £28,125 at 5/100	= £ 1,406

Separable assets

There are also additional assets of £100,000. 5% of that value would be £5,000, but there is no likelihood of the 5% shareholder actually receiving that value until the company realises the cash and either distributes it as a dividend or upon liquidation. The chances of that happening must be quantified if at all possible because it is a material factor to the current value.

It is assumed that there is a less than 10% chance of that money being realised within the next five years, but a good chance of it being realised thereafter. It can also be assumed that there will be someone in the hypothetical open market who is prepared to wait some considerable time before taking the fruits of his investment. He may not be prepared to wait forever. On the other hand, he might expect to find another such purchaser at some future time who is likewise prepared to wait to recover his investment.

Long-term investors will want a sound and secure investment and an adequate return for their patience to compensate them for the loss of income and opportunity that would have been available if the investment had been placed elsewhere. The risk involved must be quantified. It might rule out making the investment or it might mean that a higher return is required.

We may assume that a yield on a secure asset that is likely to be realised for cash in between five and ten years time — say, seven years as an acceptable working figure — is 11%.

There is some uncertainty whether the asset will be realised for cash for the benefit of shareholders; there is also uncertainty that the asset will maintain a growth in value that will equal or exceed inflation, the asset itself may carry intrinsic depreciatory factors or be subject to possible fluctuations in value; it might be found in time that the asset cannot or will not be realised within the expected time scale.

Because of the uncertainty a return higher than the 11% associated with a secure and certain investment will be required. Assuming that the asset is sound enough, nevertheless the risks are there. It will also be recalled (see 3.1) that no shareholder has a right to any specific portion of the company's property. He cannot expect to force the company to sell the asset and distribute the proceeds unless he has voting control or perhaps in a case of oppression of minority interests.

A discount of 50% from the present day value of the asset is a sensible, commercial discount from which to start. This may of course vary according to the precise description and circumstances of the asset, but where such a long-term delay before possible realisation is concerned 50% is a reasonable, one might say modest, rate. Because the proceeds from the realisation of the asset would still be locked into the company and are a constituent part of the value of the company's shares, the potential future realised value would also be reduced by the discount for lack of marketability — taken in this case as 40%. The present day value of £1 at the end of seven years, discounted at 11% is approximately 48p. A valuation of the asset may then proceed.

Asset based valuation of non-business asset

1. Present day value — £100,000 @ 48p per £   = £48,000

2. Discounted for uncertainty — £48,000 @ 50%   = £24,000

3. Discount for lack of marketability deducted
    (40%) — £24,000 @ 60%   = £14,400

4. 5% shareholding — £14,400 × 5/100   = £   720

There are still some problems to consider.

(a) The possibility that the asset is realised by the company and distributed to the shareholders as income. If there is a latent capital gains tax liability this should be reflected in the realisable value of the asset. If the asset was income producing and there was no evidence to suppose that the asset would be sold then, perhaps, capital gains tax liability would not be a realistic reduction and the capitalised value of the income would be taken, but in other circumstances where a valuation is being based on the premise of a future realisation of value there is no reason to ignore the tax liability.

(b) Alternatively, the company might be liquidated and the asset paid up by way of liquidation distribution.

(c) A third possibility is that the company would sell the asset (or borrow against its value) and then use the funds in the company and not distribute them to shareholders (it should be said, however, that the share valuer's job is not to speculate on imponderables). This alternative might have the effect of increasing the earnings, and thereby the notional dividend basis would increase accordingly.

7.16 Another special case concerns business assets with value exceeding capitalised earnings value. Although there may not be assets that are additional to income-producing assets in a company there may well be income-producing assets that have more value for their capital appreciation potential than for their current income earning capacity.

Example

An investment company owned real estate investments valued at, say, £5M, and increasing in capital value at 5% per annum, returning 5% post tax in rents on an historic value basis, 60% of which is paid out in dividends.

A 20% interest in this company on a dividend basis is likely to give an erroneous value because there is an undeniable underlying value.

On a dividend basis, taking a required yield of 5.5% for average property investment company investments, and a discount for lack of marketability of 35%, the value might be as follows.

Dividend basis valuation

1.	Earnings — £5M @ 5% yield	= £ 250,000
2.	Dividends — £250,000 @ 60%	= £ 150,000
3.	Gross dividends — £150,000 @ 5/4 (ACT)	= £ 187,500
4.	Capitalised value — £187,500 @ 100/5.5	= £3,409,091
5.	After discount for lack of marketability at say 35%	= £2,215,909
6.	20% shareholding (20/100)	= £ 443,182

The value of the 20% shareholding, on a break-up basis, would be £1,000,000, less corporation tax on the gain made by the company less costs of sale and liquidation. A 20% shareholder is quite unable to influence such a realisation, but if the evidence is that the growth in the value of the asset backing is out-pacing the normal growth in property values plus inflation perhaps some additional value should be brought into account in the share value.

Assume then that the annual growth in value of the assets is outpacing normal 'industry' growth by 3% per annum. So, the present day value of one year's growth would be £5M @ 3% = £150,000. It is assumed that this growth is not actually contributing to any increase in earnings (but in the case of property investment companies, the value of rent revisions may be material to the valuation). We cannot bring in a revised dividend basis because there is no evidence (in this example) that the growth in capital value will be turned into additional earnings. Neither can we bring in any taxation provision because the assets are business assets producing income and the business is a going concern. One is therefore restricted to an assets valuation of the growth differential.

Asset based valuation of growth in capital value

1. Present day value of growth × 3 years*   = £450,000
2. Discounted for uncertainty @ 50%   = £225,000
3. Discount for lack of marketability say (35%) leaving 65%   = £146,250
4. 20% shareholding — £146,250 @ 20/100   = £ 29,250

Thus, the combined values of the shareholding would be £443,182 + £29,250 = £472,432.

* The three-year projection is obviously arbitrary in this example. Between one and three years should be fairly easy to rationalise, but beyond that some serious research into real estate (or other relevant asset) economics should be necessary.

Note in the foregoing examples, the discount for lack of marketability has been taken at maximum rates. In the case of good property asset backing, the discount could be as low as 10% and will, of course, depend upon the facts of each case. In any investment company share valuation the make-up of the investment portfolio (including geographical spread etc.) is of paramount importance as also is the management ability. Specialist advice regarding individual valuation of investment must be sought because only intimate knowledge of the appropriate investment market will provide an accurate valuation.

The circumstances in the latter example particularly lend themselves to the hybrid valuation basis, which would attribute some of the valuation to the earnings basis and some to the assets basis. The example is considerably simplified, and it is likely that in reality the growth would be reflected in additional future earnings because it would increase borrowing power; this growth potential would therefore be reflected in the PER and certainly in a public quoted company comparison the quoted PER would reflect future growth expectations. The example is useful to illustrate how to deal with other appreciating assets and with companies that cannot sensibly be compared with quoted companies.

Chapter 8

Other Valuation Methods

Introduction

8.1   One of the expert witnesses called by the Inland Revenue in the leading estate duty share valuation case of *Re Holt* was Mr Henry Samuel Loebl, the senior partner in a firm of stockbrokers. When reviewing Mr Loebl's evidence, Danckwerts J said that as far as he could see Mr Loebl had reached his value by some process of intuition and noted that dividend yield was a matter of indifference to Mr Loebl. Despite such a technically dismissive approach Mr Loebl's estimate was closer than any of those of the Revenue's other expert witnesses to the share value determined by the judge.

8.2   The objective of any share valuation is to estimate either a specific value or a range of values. The way of getting to that value is not written in stone. Even intuition may have a place in a share valuation exercise if it is the internalised technical knowledge and professional experience of an expert and is used in conjunction with facts and figures.

8.3   The valuation methods described in Chapters 4 to 7 are sound and are the bedrock on which, using the additional facilities of experience and common sense, a value can be built. There are, nonetheless, other valuation methods worthy of mention which may be more appropriate in some valuation situations, although they suffer (at least equally with the more traditional methods) from the need to bring in value judgments at critical points along the valuation path.

Discounted cash flow

8.4   The discounted cash flow (DCF) approach is to find the *present day value* of the future cash flows arising to investors. In fact, for private unquoted companies, it is easier to look at the DCF method in terms of valuing not the shareholding itself but the underlying businesses.

8.5   The methodology lends itself to computer modelling. Certainly in the realm of the valuation of unquoted companies this technique is not well-developed in the UK. However, it is a leading valuation methodology in the United States.

8.6   An investor is looking for a satisfactory return through a combination of dividends, growth in earnings per share and growth in value per share. The relative importance of each of these financial facets to any shareholder is largely a personal matter and may change according to personal circumstances, but the overall value of the shares will be found in an appropriate mix of these facets. In DCF terms each facet will manifest itself over time as a cash return and the present day value of this expectation is today's value of the whole bundle. The DCF approach cannot avoid looking at all the economic intricacies of the company's segregable interests and will bring into account the opportunity cost of capital as well as risk and growth assumptions. Its major drawbacks are its complexity and the fact that it has to depend upon certainly as many assumptions as the price to earnings method, and is more dependent upon determinations of future events.

8.7   DCF offers a methodology that theoretically can be applied consistently to all types of companies in many situations. Supporters of DCF are critical of the fact that the earnings basis relies heavily on historic earnings, occasionally taking into account one year's comparable quoted company prospective earnings. Detractors from DCF criticise its dependence on future cash flows that may be estimated five or ten years or more into the future. If the earnings basis offers a benchmark from which a valuer can determine probable future earnings within acceptable commercial limits, DCF offers a system to estimate future cash flows where there is no history or experience of earnings. Any projection into the future has risk attaching, and the risk can be reduced only by meticulous methods of analysis and estimation. That having been said, DCF may be particularly applicable in valuing new technology companies, start-ups and unique operations or projects, and preferably those of a size that relate more easily to large scale economics, rather than tiny sectors where the economic variables are just too many.

8.8   There are often several ways to get to the same answer, and there is no reason why different methods should not be employed in conjunction with each other, whether on the basis of each specifically contributing to a part of a valuation, or as a cross-checking device.

8.9   The basic formula for determining present day value is:

$$\frac{C_1}{1 + K} + \frac{C_2}{(1 + K)^2} \cdots \frac{C_n}{(1 + K)^n} + \frac{R}{(1 + K)^n}$$

Where:

C   =   the cash flow forecast for each of the years 1 to n.

K   =   the discount rate (otherwise known as the cost of capital, or interest rate for the year, or required rate of return) expressed as a decimal.

R   =   the residual value of the business at the end of year n, less any remaining debt.

8.10   In order to compute C the following facts must be known:

(*a*)   the estimated cash profits for each year from year 1 through year n; this will necessitate ignoring charges such as depreciation, but taking into account the timing and amount of taxation, and particularly having regard to growth expectations;

(*b*)   the estimated investment each year in working capital, such as stock-in-trade and debtors, and particularly having in mind the demands that will be made by the growth assumptions made in respect of the future cash profits;

(*c*)   the estimated capital expenditure each year;

(*d*)   debt repayment schedules.

8.11   For R, we need to know what will be the residual value of the business. This is a major problem and is at the heart of one of the principal criticisms of the DCF approach. The ideal is to let n be infinite, or so long as not to require a terminal value. In that case the model will drive itself through cyclical trends, periods of unbelievable growth and dark ages of miserable depression, with the net result that an 'average' growth will have been achieved, and, if it is not possible to determine a residual value of the business that averaging will be necessary — with an appropriate alteration to the formula.

8.12   If C and R present problems, what do we do about K? It has been mentioned above that we need to look at averaging in some cases, and this must be the case with the discount rate. We are basing our figures on present day assumptions and should therefore start from that position. The factors that go to determining our required rate of return (see 4.12 and 4.46 *et seq*) come into play here, and we have to keep in mind the n years over which this required rate of return is at risk.

Dividend growth model

8.13   Where the value of a shareholding depends upon dividends, most notably a minority interest in a company that has a very wide shareholding and a cast-iron dividend policy, it may be appropriate to consider a more sophisticated version of the dividend basis which takes into account dividend growth.

8.14   The basic formula for a *constant growth* is:

$$\text{Share value} = \frac{\text{Projected dividend}}{\text{Required rate} - \text{Dividend growth rate of return}} \times 100$$

The formula is discussed in some detail at 4.12.

8.15   This formula is also applicable where, over a long-term period (say twelve years or so), the year on year growth fluctuates but averages out over the period to the same compound result.

8.16   The formula has its shortcomings. For example, dividends are unlikely to represent 100% of earnings. Whilst we may not concern ourselves too much over earnings retentions that are strictly in line with normal liquidity requirements of a growing business, if the retention is greater or less than that there are a number of alternative problems.

8.17   If the earnings retentions are greater, then regard should be had to the additional earnings arising from the utilisation of that additional cash in the business:

(*a*)   it may be equal to its current return, in which case it can be assumed that there is a constant increase in reserves that are not being distributed but may be one day;

(*b*)   it may be greater, in which case the increase in reserves will be greater;

(*c*)   it may be less, in which case reserves will effectively be eroded — this will affect the future dividend payout as the average return will be reduced.

8.18   If retentions are less than required then reserves will be eroded because of the adverse impact on business performance.

8.19   The point should be made again that all businesses will experience ups and downs on a year by year basis and, therefore, short-term variances might not impact seriously on the long-term effect of the formula; but if long-term variances are foreseen, some adjustment may be necessary. This needs to be taken in stages.

Assume: dividends of £5M

required rate of return 20%

annual dividend growth 4%

The basic formula is $\dfrac{£5M}{20\% - 4\%} \times 100 = £31.25M$

Now assume: dividends are reduced to £2.5M, and

retained earnings are 50%, and

average return on capital employed in the company is 16%

The formula becomes $\dfrac{£2.5M}{20\% - 4\% - (0.5 \times 16\%)} \times 100 = £31.25M$

8.20   The 0.5 × 16% represents the underlying additional return on the retained earnings.

8.21   If the company's return on capital employed is less than 16% the value of the shares begins to reduce, and questions are then raised concerning whether that 16%, as an average return on capital employed, is less than it might have been by virtue of retained earnings exceeding their optimum level within the company; or indeed, whether the £5M dividend is a true reflection of what the company can afford to pay and, in turn, whether the propositioned 4% annual growth factor is justified.

8.22   Note that these calculations are basically concerned with the valuation of the whole company. In valuing minority interests on a dividend basis, retained earnings can hardly be said to be money in the bank (of the shareholder). Depending upon the circumstances, some regard may have to be had to a discount for uncertainty in respect of receiving the additional earnings. In most cases of minority interests it will be impossible for the intending purchaser to obtain sufficient information to determine a value using the dividend growth model.

Chapter 9

Taxation

Introduction

9.1   The event giving rise to a share valuation is likely to have some tax consequence. In particular, inheritance tax (and its predecessor taxes) and capital gains tax or stamp duty are possible contenders. However, income tax (under Schedule E) is relevant in the event of a transfer or issue of shares to an employee and capital duty may be payable where the event is connected to an increase in corporate share capital, e.g. upon an acquisition of a company by another. This chapter considers in outline those parts of the tax legislation which deal specifically with share valuation, and particularly the ascertainment of market value for determining the taxable amount. It looks at capital gains tax, inheritance tax, income tax and stamp duty and also at some topical issues. Depending upon the date and circumstances of the transaction giving rise to the valuation, various other rules or taxes may, of course, be relevant.

9.2   Valuations for tax purposes have to be agreed with the Inland Revenue, and this often means with the Shares Valuation Division, not just the Inspector of Taxes dealing with the client in question. Valuations may be agreed without trouble or may be subject to discussion, examination and even negotiation, and sometimes may be agreed by the Inland Revenue on a 'without prejudice' basis: this usually meaning without prejudice to the Inland Revenue's position regarding other related or similar transactions. Chapter 11 deals more fully with the Shares Valuation Division.

9.3   Under Self-Assessment, Form CG34 may be used by individuals (and trustees) to submit capital gains tax share valuations (and other capital gains tax valuations) prior to the filing date for submission of the self-assessment tax return with the intent to agree the value before that date. The Inland Revenue have said that they expect it to take a minimum of 56 days to agree a valuation or provide an alternative and in 'a few very complex cases we may not be able to provide you with any alternative valuation before the filing date for your return'. This matter is considered at 11.2.

Capital gains tax

Bargains made otherwise than at arm's length

9.4   When there is a disposal or acquisition of shares otherwise than by way of a bargain made at arm's length, the market value (see 9.22) of those shares is generally taken as the consideration for the shares. This is particularly relevant to gifts, transfers into settlement or distributions from a company in respect of shares in the company.

Market value will also be taken where the consideration (or some of it) cannot be valued. For example, a restrictive covenant or an option to acquire something in the future subject to the happening of some event outside anyone's control, or if the acquisition or disposal is in connection with an office or employment (*TCGA 1992, s 17*).

In the case of *Fielder (Inspector of Taxes) v Vedlynn Ltd*, it was held that in valuing consideration paid on a sale of shares a guarantee that certain supplemental sums would be paid did not increase the monetary value of the actual cash consideration because (in this case) the guarantee was part of the terms of the sale agreement in respect of which the cash consideration was paid. This convoluted argument won the day and it may be that the wrong argument was raised by the Inland Revenue because the vendor received £19,529 cash consideration which was taxed and £1,429,915 in supplemental sums which was not! The supplemental sums were calculated by reference to losses 'if such ever were agreed', and the secondary holding was that if the guarantees were to be taken into account as part of the consideration that part of the consideration could not be valued!

9.5   If a disposal and acquisition of shares is between 'connected persons', the transaction will be treated as being made 'otherwise than by way of bargain made at arm's length', and the market value of those shares taken as the sole consideration for capital gains tax purposes (*TCGA 1992, s 18*).

The meaning of connected persons is set out in *TCGA 1992, s 286*. Broadly, this includes spouses, brothers, sisters, ancestors and lineal descendants; partners and their relatives; settlors, trustees and companies whose shares are held by trustees; companies under common control; and, in relation to a company, any two or more persons acting together to secure or exercise control.

9.6   As a result of indexation and re-basing to 31 March 1982, it is nowadays not unusual for a capital tax loss to arise on a disposal. It should be borne in mind that losses on a disposal to a connected person can be offset only against gains arising on another transaction with the same connected person, whilst still connected, in that same or a future fiscal year. Such losses cannot be applied against gains arising from any other disposals. In respect of disposals after 29 November 1993, indexation relief cannot be used to create or augment a loss on disposal.

9.7   The market value rule in *section 17* (above) does not apply if there is *no corresponding disposal* of the asset and there is no consideration in money or money's worth, or the consideration is less than market value. This is an anti-avoidance rule to prevent an uplift in base value in certain situations.

9.8   Normally, the value of consideration given in kind will be its open market value, but in *Stanton v Drayton Commercial Investment Co Ltd*, where shares were offered in exchange for an asset and a sale contract specified the price of those shares, the shares were not required to be valued on a market value basis as was contended by the Inland Revenue. The agreed value of the shares had been honestly reached between the parties and the transaction was by way of bargain at arm's length.

9.9   *Section 18(6)* requires that if the person making the disposal (or a connected person) has power to enforce a right or restriction in respect of the asset transferred, the market value of the asset is determined initially free of any such encumbrance and is then reduced by 'the market value of the right or restriction or the amount by which its extinction would enhance the value of the asset to its owner (whichever is the less)'. However, such rights will be ignored for these purposes if, upon enforcement, the asset's value would be substantially impaired and no advantage would be brought to the disposer (but consider *TCGA 1992, s 29* as to value shifting). In the case of incorporeal assets, rights of extinguishment are also ignored for this purpose.

9.10   In certain circumstances, capital gains tax, which would otherwise be due on a disposal of an asset, can be held over until the transferee makes a subsequent disposal of the asset. These circumstances include, *inter alia*, the disposal for no consideration of a qualifying business, which embraces a gift of shares in an unquoted trading company (*TCGA 1992, s 165*). Hold-over relief is also available for gifts which are not potentially exempt but chargeable transfers for inheritance tax, such as gifts into and out of discretionary trusts (*TCGA 1992, s 260*). When hold-over relief is claimed, it is not necessary to agree with the Revenue the market value of the asset transferred, although the value may be agreed and the held-over gain calculated if the taxpayer wishes (Revenue Statement of Practice SP 8/92).

Settlements

9.11   When a person becomes absolutely entitled to settled property as against the trustee, the assets forming part of that property are deemed to be disposed of by the trustee and immediately re-acquired by him as trustee for a consideration equal to the market value (*TCGA 1992, s 71*). A gain or loss may therefore accrue to the trustees although, in the circumstances outlined above, an election may be made to hold over the gain to the person taking the assets.

9.12   A similar market value rule applies on the termination (upon death) of a life interest in possession in settled property, except that no chargeable gain accrues (because no capital gains tax is payable on death) except to the extent that assets were originally acquired by the trustees under a hold-over election.

Value shifting

9.13   If control over a company is exercised in such a way that value passes out of shares in the company and passes into other shares, the transaction may be treated as one otherwise than by way of bargain made at arm's length and thereby market value would be taken (*TCGA 1992, ss 29–34*).

31 March 1982 market value

9.14   For determining the chargeable gain (or loss) on a disposal of an asset acquired *before* 31 March 1982, the base cost of the asset is calculated by reference to its market value on 31 March 1982 (*FA 1985, TCGA 1992, s 35*). There are exceptions to this rule: disposals which would give rise to a loss under the pre-1988 rules but a gain under the present rules (or vice versa), and no-gain/no-loss transfers specified in *TCGA 1992, s 35(3)(d)*. It may therefore be necessary to arrive at a value on the former base date of 6 April 1965 in order to determine liability. Such complications can be avoided by an election for the computation of all relevant disposals to be based on market value at 31 March 1982 (*TCGA 1992, s 35(5)*).

9.15   Indexation allowance for a chargeable gain arising from the disposal of a pre-31 March 1982 acquisition is also calculated by reference to the 31 March 1982 value (*TCGA 1992, s 55*).

9.16   If part only of a taxpayer's shareholding is transferred, the base value is nevertheless determined by reference to that taxpayer's total shareholding at 31 March 1982 but, according to the Inland Revenue, reduced by any disposals that were made between 6 April 1982 and 5 April 1985 (1 April to 31 March for companies). This can be significant where a minority shareholding is transferred out of a majority holding, and runs counter to the general capital gains tax rule that it is the shares transferred, in isolation, that have to be valued (Revenue Statement of Practice SP 5/89 and Extra-Statutory Concession D34). The case of *R v IRC, ex p Kaye* considered the Inland Revenue's rights (and duty of fairness) in applying their Statement of Practice SP 5/89 — or rather in *not* applying it retrospectively — and found in favour of the Inland Revenue.

9.17   Extra-Statutory Concession D34 has been extended to enable the transferee who has acquired shares in a no gain/no loss transfer to elect to have their base value determined as a proportionate part of the whole of the transferor's holding at 31 March 1982. No gain/no loss transactions are principally between spouses and group companies under *TCGA 1992, s 58* or *TCGA 1992, s 171(1)*.

Negligible value

9.18   If shares have become of negligible value, the owner may claim for them to be treated as having been sold and immediately re-acquired for the value claimed. The Inspector of Taxes must be satisfied that the value has become negligible (*TCGA 1992, s 24(2)*).

Company ceasing to be a member of a group

9.19   If a company leaves a group of companies it may be regarded as having sold and immediately acquired at market value an asset previously acquired from one of the group members (*TCGA 1992, ss 178, 179*). This is an anti-avoidance provision and would apply for instance if the company has received shares in another company that was previously owned by another group company and transferred under the hold-over provisions in *TCGA 1992, s 171*.

Liquidations

9.20   Liquidation distributions are part disposals for capital gains tax purposes. However, where the liquidation of an unquoted company is completed within two years of the first such distribution, the Inland Revenue will accept any reasonable valuation rather than demand a formal valuation of the residual value on each occasion as an interim measure (Revenue Statement of Practice D3).

Series of transactions

9.21   Where there is a series of transfers of shares in a company to connected persons (as explained above) there is a requirement in *TCGA 1992, s 19* to aggregate the transfers made within the previous six years and take the market value of the aggregate number of shares and recalculate the value of the smaller transfers accordingly. This is an anti-avoidance provision to defeat the transfer of a large shareholding by occasional transfers of small holdings.

Market value

9.22   For capital gains tax purposes 'market value' is defined in almost exactly the same terms as for inheritance tax as 'the price which those assets might *reasonably be expected to fetch* on a sale in the open market'. There is to be no reduction in the estimated market value to reflect any market forces that would reduce the value because of flooding the market (*TCGA 1992, s 272*); but there are important 'information' requirements — see 2.20.

9.23   Specifically in relation to unquoted shares or securities, in determining the market value it is to be assumed that, in the postulated open market there is available to any prospective purchaser all the information which a prudent prospective purchaser of the asset might reasonably require if he were proposing to purchase it from a willing vendor by private treaty and at arm's length. For a wider discussion, see 2.24.

9.24 Securities dealt in on the AIM are treated as unquoted securities for tax purposes.

9.25 Under the *Capital Gains Tax Regulations 1967* (*SI 1967 No 149*), if there is a capital gains tax liability in point in respect of a transaction and provided that there has been no tax appeal, any of the parties to the transaction can apply to the Commissioners of Inland Revenue, via an Inspector of Taxes, to determine the market value.

9.26 The determination of a market value on an appeal is final as between the Board, the Inspector, parties to the appeal and third parties who were entitled to be joined in the appeal. Market value can also be finally determined if it was a material factor in an appeal notwithstanding that it was not in dispute. However, this does not apply where the question may be varied by a higher court or there has been fraud or wilful default.

9.27 A taxpayer and the Inland Revenue cannot reach binding agreement on the value for capital gains tax purposes if a third party could be joined in the appeal unless he joins in an agreement in writing or is given due notice and does not apply to be joined in the appeal.

9.28 Questions in dispute on an appeal against an assessment (including an amendment to a self-assessment) for capital gains tax or corporation tax on chargeable gains in respect of the value of unquoted shares or securities in a UK company are determined by the Special Commissioners (*TMA 1970, s 46B*): in the case of the value of land or of a lease of land the question is determined by the Lands Tribunal (*TMA 1970, s 46D, s 47(B)* in respect of the value of land under the Business Expansion Scheme).

9.29 For valuations prior to 6 March 1992 the transitional rules in *TCGA 1992, Sch 11, Pt 1* may be applicable. The Schedule considers gifts and transactions between connected persons before 20 March 1985; valuation of assets before 6 July 1973 (allowing the application of the *Lynall* decision rules in *TCGA 1992, s 273*; valuation of assets on 6 April 1965; references to the London Stock Exchange and Exchange Control restrictions; depreciated valuations referable to deaths before 31 March 1973; and estate duty.

Deductible costs of valuation

9.30 For capital gains purposes on a disposal, 'costs reasonably incurred in making any valuation or apportionment required for the purposes of the computation of the gain, including, in particular, expenses reasonably incurred in ascertaining market value', can be deducted (*TCGA 1992, s 38(2)*). The Inland Revenue does not agree that this provision includes the professional and related costs in agreeing such values with the Shares Valuation Division. That would probably be a reasonable stance if the position of the Revenue were simply to accept the values produced by independent experts, but while they continue to question, refute, negotiate and otherwise 'intermeddle' with valuations from experts, it hardly seems that a market value can have been 'ascertained' until all parties have accepted the jointly determined valuation, for the entire procedure of 'negotiating' the valuation can be described perfectly correctly as 'making' a valuation required for the purposes of the tax computation.

In *Couch v Administrators of the Estate of Caton (deceased)* it was held that those expenses were not an allowable deduction — and that the natural interpretation of the class of allowable costs referred to in *section 32(2)(b)* did not include the costs which were incurred in carrying out negotiations with the Revenue. Rimer J appeared to believe that negotiations following the submission of a valuation to the Inland Revenue were 'an exercise of negotiation . . . as to the amount of any actual or proposed assessment'. This perhaps suggests that the cost of the valuation report itself up to the time of its submission to the Inland Revenue should be allowable. See also 2.50 with regard to notional expenses on a disposal.

Inheritance tax valuations

9.31   The market value of an asset for inheritance tax purposes *on a death* is to be taken as the market value for capital gains tax purposes — this is for establishing the base cost to the recipient of the asset as there is no capital gains tax on death.

9.32   Inheritance tax reliefs — such as business assets relief — are usually ignored for capital gains purposes, but it is understood that the inheritance tax reliefs that recalculate the value of assets at death, such as in cases of dispositions within three years of death, will be taken into account for capital gains tax valuation purposes (*TCGA 1992, ss 62, 274*).

9.33   If the value has not been 'ascertained' for inheritance tax purposes, for example because the beneficiary was exempt or 100% business property relief was due, it may be that at the time of a subsequent disposal by that beneficiary it will then be necessary to agree a value at the date of death of the person from whom he or she inherited the shares.

Inheritance tax

Market value

9.34   The definitions follow almost exactly the market value definitions for capital gains tax.

9.35   Market value is 'the price which the property might reasonably be expected to fetch if sold in the open market . . . but the price shall not be assumed to be reduced on the grounds that the whole property is to be placed on the market at one and the same time' (*Inheritance Tax Act 1984, s 160*).

9.36   For unquoted shares 'it shall be assumed that in that market there is available to any prospective purchaser of the shares . . . all the information which a prudent prospective purchaser might reasonably require if he were proposing to purchase them from a willing vendor by private treaty and at arm's length' (*Inheritance Tax Act 1984, s 168*). For a wider discussion, see 2.20.

9.37   Capital transfer tax (the forerunner of inheritance tax) succeeded the old estate duty and many or most of the legal principles governing estate duty continue to govern inheritance tax. In the case of *Crabtree v Hinchcliffe* Russell LJ intimated that the principles of estate duty were the same as those applicable to capital gains tax; this can be extended to inheritance tax.

Potentially exempt transfers

9.38   Except in the circumstances outlined below, a gift by an individual during his or her lifetime is not a chargeable transfer for inheritance tax purposes unless the transferor dies within seven years of making the gift.

Chargeable lifetime transfers

9.39   The principal chargeable lifetime transfers are transfers into and out of discretionary trusts (but not accumulation and maintenance trusts). In such cases and where a transfer becomes chargeable because of the death of the transferor within seven years, *Inheritance Tax 1984, s 3(1)* has special relevance in the case of unquoted shares. That section provides that: '. . . a transfer of value is a disposition made by a person (the transferor) as a result of which the value of his estate immediately after the disposition is less than it would be but for the disposition; and the amount by which it is less is the value transferred by the transfer'.

9.40   Where a disposal of shares out of a majority shareholding results in the transferor retaining a minority shareholding only, the disparity in the valuations creates a larger IHT liability than would be the case if the transferred shares were capable of being valued in isolation. Note also that for IHT purposes the transfer of a minority interest out of a majority interest which is still a majority interest after the transfer will be valued effectively on the same basis as the majority interest because what is valued for IHT is the difference between the original holding and the reduced holding, both of which will be valued as a majority holding. Because of this there can be quite a disparity between the values for IHT and for CGT purposes even though exactly the same transfer is being valued.

9.41   The failure to exercise the right to take up a rights issue might result in a shareholding becoming of less value as against the remaining shares in the company, and this would constitute a diminution in the value of the transferor's estate.

Related property and the 'estate' concept

9.42   Where the value of shares in isolation is less than the value they would have if they and 'related property' were valued together and that value was apportioned between them, the larger value is taken (*Inheritance Tax Act 1984, s 161*). Related property will include shares held by a spouse (but not by sons or daughters). Shares held in a trust in which the transferor has a life interest also have to be taken into account since for IHT purposes they form part of the transferor's 'estate' (*Inheritance Tax Act 1984, ss 5 and 49(1)*).

Associated operations

9.43   Where any two or more operations affect the same property, whether directly or indirectly, or are effected by reference to each other, they are deemed to have occurred at the same time — *the time of the latest such operation*. However, if an earlier operation gives rise to a transfer of value at that time the transfer of value deemed to take place when all the transactions are taken together is reduced by the earlier value. This is in the same vein as the capital gains tax provisions dealing with a series of transactions, but goes much wider (*Inheritance Tax Act 1984, s 268*).

Deferred shares

9.44   The Inland Revenue, since September 1991, has taken an increasingly aggressive line in respect of the inheritance tax consequences resulting from the 'enfranchisement' of (time) deferred shares. In respect of such deferred shares issued after 5 August 1991 claims for inheritance tax will be raised under *IHTA 1984, s 98* where they subsequently come to rank equally, or become merged, with shares of another class. This is because the Inland Revenue now take the view that when that happens there has been 'an alteration in ... rights attaching to [unquoted shares ...] [which] shall be treated as having been made by a disposition ...' (*IHTA 1984, s 98(1)(b)*).

9.45   In most cases of deferred shares their value would take a very gradually steepening trajectory to meet the 'merged value' at the earliest possible time that they can rank *pari passu* or merge. In case of time span of over, say, three years, but depending upon the actual length of time and the strength and proven longevity of the company, the curve would be relatively flat until the potential market for the shares could 'see' the effect that the convergence would have on the deferred shares — the increase in value would then be geometric. The curve of the value of the ordinary shares with which the deferrals would rank or merge would mirror that of the deferrals. Thus, immediately before the ranking/merger values would be very similar, so that any alterations in value upon the actual trigger point should be minimal.

9.46   The foregoing applies to majority and minority shareholdings as well as for holdings that would 'switch' because of dilution from a majority to a minority. This is because the effect of even a large value shift caused by deferred shares 'switching on' would be smoothed over the final period of years — that period depending upon several market related and company factors.

Close companies

9.47   Transfers of value made by a company are related back to the shareholders and are treated as net transfers, i.e. for IHT the 'gift' is grossed-up. Any alteration in the share capital of an unquoted company or in the rights attaching thereto, is treated as a disposition made by the shareholders (*Inheritance Tax Act 1984, ss 94, 98*).

Payment of IHT by instalments

9.48   Any IHT arising out of a transfer of shares or securities of a company on death which gave the deceased control of the company immediately before his death may be paid (under election) by instalments over ten years. The instalment payment is also available if not less than 20% of the IHT is attributable to the value of shares, or if the shares have a value exceeding £20,000 and represent not less than 10% of the company's share capital (*Inheritance Tax Act 1984, ss 227, 228*). Similar conditions apply where a potentially exempt transfer becomes chargeable, provided the shares remain unquoted and are retained by the transferee between the date of transfer and the date of death of the transferor.

Business relief

9.49   Where the value transferred by a transfer of value is attributable to the value of any *relevant business property*, business relief may be available as follows (but subject to all the applicable rules and these reliefs have changed over the years):

100%

- unquoted shares or securities (including AIM or USM companies) and unquoted securities which with unquoted shares give the holder control;
- a business or interest in a business;

50%

- shares or securities which gave the transferor control of a quoted company;
- land, buildings, machinery or plant used by a company or a partnership.

The property must have been owned for (or replaced within) two years preceding the transfer (*Inheritance Tax Act 1984, ss 103–114*).

Agricultural relief

9.50   100% of agricultural value: Transfer of land with vacant possession (or with right to obtain vacant possession within twelve months) and land let on tenancy, after 31 August 1995 (*Inheritance Tax Act 1984, s 116*). 50% of agricultural value: Other cases For agricultural relief the value of the agricultural property (which includes the cultivation of short rotation coppice) and assets is restricted to the value as if the property were subject to a perpetual covenant prohibiting use otherwise than as agricultural. This eliminates any development or hope value for IHT relief purposes. 'Where the whole or part of the value transferred is attributable to the value of shares in . . . a company it shall be taken . . . to be attributable . . . to the agricultural value of agricultural property . . . if the agricultural property forms part of the company's assets . . . and the shares gave the transferor control . . .' (*Inheritance Tax Act 1984, ss 122–124*).

9.51   Agricultural property is defined in the *Inheritance Tax Act 1984, s 115(2)*. This case of *Starke and another (Executors of Brown deceased) v IRC* sought to interpret the meaning of 'agricultural land or pasture'. Morritt, LJ said: 'With the exception of the inclusion of "woodland" all that follows the words "agricultural land and pasture" is concerned with the buildings of one sort or another which are to be included. In such a context it would be surprising to find that buildings were already included in the phrase "agricultural land or pasture" ' .The consequence of this is that buildings or other structures not specifically included in the defining section were not to be regarded as forming part of agricultural land and pasture. See also 6.25 and 6.27.

In *Walton (Walton's Executor) v CIR*, a case concerning the valuation of a partnership interest in a non-assignable agricultural tenancy, it was held that it was for the Lands Tribunal to determine whether a special purchaser would be prepared to pay a premium and the amount of any such premium.

Control

9.52   For certain business relief and agricultural reliefs prior to April 1996 'voting control' was required. 'A person has control at any time if he then has the control of powers of voting on all questions affecting the company as a whole which if exercised would yield a majority of the votes capable of being exercised thereon' (*Inheritance Tax Act 1984, s 269*).

Death

9.53   Death is an occasion of charge for IHT, which is charged as if, immediately before death, the individual made a transfer of value and the value transferred thereby had been equal to the value of his estate *immediately before his death*. So shares held by the deceased are valued for IHT immediately before death as part of his estate and related property is taken into account (*Inheritance Tax Act 1984, s 4*).

9.54   If the death itself causes a diminution in value of the shares — such as where the shareholder is also the source of the earnings of the company — then that diminution is treated as taking place immediately before the death (*Inheritance Tax Act 1984, s 171*).

9.55   In *Gray (surviving executor of Lady Ex) v IRC* it was held that if any assets which are component parts taken together have a greater value than valued independently, they should be valued together for IHT if that was the course that a prudent hypothetical vendor would have adopted in order to obtain the most favourable price without undue expenditure of time and effort. Thus, in this case (a capital transfer tax case) the deceased's freehold reversion of land let to a farming partnership was aggregated with the deceased's 92.5% interest in that farming partnership.

Surviving spouse exemption

9.56   If shares were left by a deceased person (who died before 13 November 1974) in trust for a surviving spouse, the shares will not suffer inheritance tax on the death of the transferee. However, if that surviving spouse held other shares in the same company, in determining the value of those other shares the total holding would be valued and then that value apportioned between the chargeable shares and those subject to the exempt life interest (*Inheritance Tax Act 1984, 6 Sch 2*).

Settlements

9.57   Where shares are held in trust they will be regarded as forming part of the estate of a beneficiary who has an interest in possession (that is an entitlement to any of the income of the trust).

9.58   The termination of an interest in possession is treated as a transfer of value; which will be potentially exempt in the circumstances described above. Shares held by the settlement will be valued separately from any similar shares held by the person who had been entitled to the interest in possession (*Inheritance Tax Act 1984, ss 49, 50*).

9.59   Discretionary settlements are charged to IHT at 30% of the lifetime rates on each ten-yearly anniversary from the creation of the trust falling after 31 March 1983 (*Inheritance Tax Act 1984, ss 58–76*). There is also a proportionate charge on distributions from such settlements before the first ten-yearly anniversary and between ten-yearly anniversaries.

9.60   There is no IHT charge on transfers of assets out of an accumulation and maintenance settlement to the beneficiaries.

Income tax

Share incentives and options

9.61   Shares issued to an employee would normally be taxable under Schedule E on the market value (*ICTA 1988, s 131* and *Weight v Salmon*) to the extent that market value exceeds the amount paid for the shares. The legislation does not define market value for the purposes of *section 131*; therefore the general understanding of the words should probably prevail; and the special importation of terms and conditions for other tax purposes would not apply for *section 131* purposes — such as that requiring information to be assumed to be available to a prospective purchaser (*TCGA 1992, s 273*; *Inheritance Tax Act 1984, s 168*) and the assumption that there is no discount for a disposal of all the shares at one time (*TCGA 1992, s 272*; *Inheritance Tax Act 1984, s 160*). However, in practice it would probably be that the capital gains tax valuation rules would apply. See also *Ede v Wilson* (issue of shares at par); *Tyrer v Smart* (gift of shares to directors).

Share incentive scheme shares fall within the Schedule E rules by virtue of *Finance Act 1988, ss 77–89* where a person acquires shares in a company in pursuance of a right conferred on him or an opportunity afforded to him by reason of his employment, when the removal, creation or imposition of a restriction or right has the effect of increasing the value of the shares. For these purposes, *Finance Act 1988, s 87* provides that '"value", in relation to shares or a benefit, means the amount which the person holding the shares or receiving the benefit might reasonably expect to obtain from a sale in the open market'. The concept of the hypothetical vendor does not therefore apply in these circumstances and it must be assumed that knowledge personal to the actual vendor will affect the value. That knowledge could include, for example, details of a proposed flotation. See also *ICTA 1988, s 162* for shares acquired partly paid and bought on instalment terms. Capital gains tax market value rules apply. See *ICTA 1988, ss 186, 187* and *10 Sch* as to profit-sharing schemes. Capital gains tax market value rules apply.

Share options

9.62   Gains derived from the exercise, assignment or release of a share option fall within the Schedule E rules by virtue of *ICTA 1988, s 135*.

9.63   The gain realised on the exercise of an option is the difference between 'the amount that a person might reasonably expect to obtain from a sale in the open market at that time of the shares acquired and the amount or value of the consideration given whether for them or for the grant of the right' (*ICTA 1988 s 135(3)(a)*). The expression 'market value' is not used in this provision and it is therefore probable that the stamp duty valuation principles will apply. However, the capital gains tax market value rules are imported for certain other applications in *ICTA 1988, ss 135, 136*.

9.64   The value on which tax is charged under Schedule E is to be taken as the acquisition cost for subsequent capital gains tax purposes.

Revenue approved share option schemes

9.65   If options are granted under savings related share option schemes and executive share option schemes, which conform with the provisions of *ICTA 1988, 9 Sch*, capital gains tax is payable only on the eventual sale of the shares acquired as a result of exercising the option, on the difference between the sale price and the exercise price. In the case of unquoted shares, prior to the grant of the option the exercise price has to be agreed with the Shares Valuation Division specialist department: Inland Revenue Savings and Investment Division (Employee Share Schemes). Valuation again follows capital gains tax rules (*ICTA 1988, ss 185, 187* and *9 Sch*).

Trading receipts

9.66   A capital receipt of a trader consisting of shares in exchange for some business interest or property is valued at open market value according to the capital gains tax rules (*Wolf Electric Tools Ltd v Wilson*).

9.67   If the shares are received as trading income as a result of a sale or exchange, the money value, or market value of the shares would have to be ascertained and taken as at the end of the trader's accounting period. A discount may be appropriate for shares not capable of being realised until a future time (but not to wipe out the value of shares on that basis alone) (*Gold Coast Selection Trust Ltd v Humphrey*). This market value would be determined for income tax or corporation tax purposes only. There would not be a capital gains tax charge if a charge to income tax arises. See 9.77 *et seq* for a discussion of money value.

Transactions in land

9.68   In relation to the Schedule D Case VI charge on gains arising from transactions in land — under *ICTA 1988, s 776* — including gains underlying a shareholding, 'all such valuations shall be made as are appropriate to give effect to [*section 776*]' (*ICTA 1988, s 777(6)(b)*).

Stamp duty

9.69   Stamp duty on transfers otherwise than for consideration require to be valued under the *Finance (1909–10) Act 1910, s 74*.

9.70   Assets may be transferred between associated companies without giving rise to a stamp duty charge — see *Finance Act 1930, s 42*.

9.71 The sale of shares or a transaction involving the exchange of shares is liable to stamp duty as a conveyance or transfer on sale and therefore attracts *ad valorem* stamp duty. Under the *Stamp Act 1891, s 55*, where the consideration, or any part of the consideration, for a conveyance on sale consists of any stock or marketable security, the conveyance is to be charged with *ad valorem* duty in respect of the value of the stock or security. Where assets of different character are agreed to be sold for one consideration for the whole, a *bona fide* apportionment of the consideration among the various assets is required to be made (following *West London Syndicate Ltd v IRC*). The case of *John Foster & Sons v IRC* indicates that the value of the consideration is to be made by reference to the value of the property conveyed or transferred. See also *Carlyon Estate Ltd v IRC*.

9.72 In the case of *Stanyforth v IRC*, it was confirmed that the value of property conveyed is by reference to the value on sale in the open market.

9.73 It should be noted that for stamp duty valuation purposes the special prohibition against flooding the market (in *TCGA 1992, s 272(2)* and *IHTA 1984, s 160*) and the assumption that information is to be available as on a sale by private treaty (in *TCGA 1992, s 272(3)* and *IHTA 1984, s 168*), are not to apply as they do for capital gains tax purposes and inheritance tax purposes. This therefore allows a possible reduction in open market value in appropriate circumstances.

9.74 A sale at undervalue is stamped as a voluntary disposition (*Lap Shun Textiles Industrial Co Ltd v Collector of Stamp Revenue*).

9.75 Under the *Finance Act 1994* stamp duty on land and leasing transactions are based on a valuation of the property or lease or of the consideration for the transaction. Under *section 241*, where land is exchanged for property, stamp duty is chargeable on the market value of the property. Under *section 242(1)*, however, where the whole or part of the consideration is unascertainable stamp duty is charged on the market value of the interest in land transferred or leased. *Section 242(2)* provides that if the rent under a lease is unascertainable stamp duty is chargeable on the market rent.

9.76 The Stamp Office has indicated that the value of the consideration determined by the parties in arm's length transactions will be accepted as evidence of market value if accompanied by a professional valuation. The alternative is to refer the valuation to the district valuer, in which case stamp duty may be postponed without interest or penalty pending the district valuer's determination of value. The cash flow advantage may not be worth the uncertainty attaching to this course of action. There may be a practical problem arising in the circumstances of these valuations because the date of valuation under both *sections 241* and *242* is immediately before the execution of the instrument. This date may vary from the date of valuation of, for example, shares in an unquoted company, which may have been determined for negotiation purposes at an earlier time. The point should therefore be kept in mind when such shares are being offered in exchange for interests in land.

Section 209 distributions

9.77   For the purposes of *ICTA 1988, s 209* there is scant assistance in determining how the value of a distribution is to be arrived at. Under *section 234* a company which makes a qualifying distribution shall, if the recipient so requests in writing, furnish to him a statement in writing showing 'the amount or value of the distribution'. Under *section 209(4)* in respect of a transfer of assets by a company to its members, the amount or value of the benefit received by a member is determined according to its market value. There is no such importation of market value concept in *section 209(2)(b)*.

9.78   However, it is unlikely that it could be argued that the value of the distribution would be anything less than the value that the recipient could receive on realising it. Some assistance can be found in the case of *Gold Coast Selection Trust Ltd v Humphrey*, in which Viscount Simon said 'if the asset is difficult to value but is nonetheless of a money value, the best valuation possible must be made'. In that case he said that the fact that the asset could not be realised at once may reduce its present value although there was no reason for treating it for the purposes of income tax as though it had no value until it could be realised. He also made reference to the case where the assets take the form of fully paid shares, saying that the valuation would take into account the prospective yields, marketability, the general outlook for the type of business of the company which has allotted the shares and similar issues. However, the fact that a discount might be available because the shares could not necessarily be realised at once, and the absence of the prohibition against flooding the market and the absence of the requirement to assume information would be available to the potential purchaser, might remove the income tax market value concept considerably away from the CGT and IHT market value concept.

9.79   The question also arises whether a distribution is to be valued in terms of the benefit received, or in terms of the value of the asset that is distributed, i.e. before or after any fragmentation. In the case of *Short v Treasury Commissioners* it was held that to impute a controlling interest valuation to a minority interest is not correct. Although this case may not be on all fours with the distribution of shares in a subsidiary company or other investment to members of the distributing company, it is likely that the same principle would apply to the distribution of a controlling interest in a subsidiary to a number of shareholders of the parent.

9.80   An unquoted trading company buying back its own shares, or issuing redeemable shares, under *Companies Act 1985, ss 162–181* is exempt from *section 209* by virtue of *section 219*, provided the exercise is undertaken to benefit its trade (or the trade of 75% subsidiaries). This rule applies also to unquoted holding companies of a trading group. 'Unquoted' includes a company dealt with in the AIM and the Unlisted Securities Market.

Recent Share Purchase Incentive Arrangements

Venture capital trusts

9.81   Companies that qualify as Venture Capital Trusts (VCTs) within the provisions of *TA 1988, s 842AA etc* offer the individual taxpayer a range of tax reliefs. To qualify as a VCT a company must:

(1)   be quoted on a recognised stock exchange;
(2)   derive its income wholly or mainly from shares or securities;
(3)   have at least 70% by value of its investments in shares and securities in unquoted companies;
(4)   have at least 30% by value of its investments in unquoted companies in the form of ordinary shares;
(5)   have not more than 15% by value of its investments invested in one company.

9.82   Value for these purposes is taken as the value of the investment when acquired, which will normally be its cost.

9.83   It is further provided that any company in which the VCT invests must have gross assets not exceeding £10M prior to the investment and £11M thereafter. Assets for this purpose include goodwill and other tangible assets not shown in the company's accounts. Fixed assets will have to be re-valued. Any valuations produced by the VCT could be challenged by the Revenue and could delay the investment process.

9.84   Income tax relief granted to the initial subscriber in a VCT will be withdrawn if his shares are sold within five years of his subscription. It is thus likely that unless the value of the VCT increases to such an extent that loss of income tax relief is a minor consideration, there will be very little activity in the VCT's shares in the first five years of its existence. It may be therefore that on the death of a shareholder within five years of his subscription the quoted price of the VCT will not be a proper measure of its market value. There may well be scope to negotiate a reduced value for inheritance tax purposes. Shares in VCTs do not attract inheritance tax business property relief.

Enterprise investment scheme

9.85   The Enterprise Investment Scheme (EIS) was introduced by *FA 1994, s 137* as the successor to the Business Expansion Scheme and applies to shares issued after 1 January 1994. Subscription for ordinary shares in a qualifying company reduces an individual's income tax liability by tax at the lower rate (20% in 1995/96) on the amount subscribed, or by an amount sufficient to reduce the individual's tax liability to nil. There is an upper limit of £100,000 on which an individual may obtain relief in one year.

9.86   Issuing companies must be unquoted and carry on qualifying trades which do not include such things as dealing in land, shares or commodities, banking, oil extraction and providing legal or accountancy services.

9.87   The tax relief may be restricted if the investor 'received value' from the company within five years of subscribing for the shares. Receiving value would include a re-purchase of the shares by the company and also a sale of shares to a person connected with the company. Relief would be restricted by the amount receivable, or, if greater, the market value of the shares. Negotiation of the value with the Revenue may be necessary in those circumstances.

Reinvestment relief

9.88   Where a chargeable gain accrues to an individual (and most trustees) the gain can be deferred by being reinvested in qualifying unquoted trading companies, without limit, or by subscribing for shares in a VCT up to a limit of £100,000 in one year (*TCGA 1992, s 164A(1)*). Qualifying companies must carry on a qualifying trade, which does not include such things as dealing in land or commodities, banking, insurance, providing legal and accountancy services and farming. The list of non-qualifying trades is similar, but not identical, to that for Enterprise Investment Relief.

9.89   If any part of the value of the investment is returned to the investor, the shares are treated as no longer being eligible for relief.

9.90   If the qualifying investment is acquired otherwise than by a transaction at arm's length the open market value of the investment will have to be agreed with the Revenue.

Chapter 10

The Share Valuation Report

Introduction

10.1   This chapter is principally concerned with what is generally referred to as a 'speaking' valuation. This is, a report style valuation that sets out all the background facts and progresses through the thought processes and computations and other determinants to a resultant value or range of values. The format of a 'non-speaking' valuation would be appropriately truncated, although the elements covered will figure in the processes that go into determining a non-speaking opinion of value.

10.2   Whether a speaking or non-speaking valuation is to be adopted will depend upon the particular case in point. If underlying the valuation requirement there is a disagreement between shareholders or private litigation, a speaking valuation may simply exacerbate the situation. The more elements there are to take dispute over, the less likely it is that a conclusion will be reached, and the share valuation exercise might end up having been a waste of time. If the Inland Revenue is involved, it is probable that the detail of the valution will need to be laid bare.

10.3   An accurate valuation report in respect of private company shares cannot be prepared without a full understanding of the purpose of the valuation, the background to the valuation, share valuation principles (Chapter 2) and the company.

10.4   Although this chapter attempts to cover a wide field of sources of information it is not believed (and this view is supported so far by *Grenier v KPMG Peat Marwick*) that the valuer has a responsibility to go into the detail that perhaps a 'due diligence' investigation requires — and is certainly not expected to seek to discover information that is not provided freely and timeously by parties to the valuation objectives. This view may be overridden by the terms of engagement.

10.5   It is imperative to know whose shares are being valued, and to identify the full shareholding in the subject company belonging to that person (or persons), including shares of different classes, debentures and so on. In ascertaining the true value of any particular shareholding it may be necessary also to have regard to other securities or rights that the person has in or over the subject company (Chapter 3). Clearly, the relationship of the shareholder with the subject company must also be established — the shareholder may be a parent company, a director or simply an individual shareholder.

10.6   Having arrived at the starting post, the valuer can commence the exercise by assembling the necessary facts and documentary evidence ready for his eventual valuation report. The valuer's special position may, depending upon the size of the shareholding that is being valued and other circumstances, give him access to far more information than an ordinary purchaser of shares would have. The degree of information that would be available to potential purchasers in the particular case should be decided upon (see 2.20), and the valuation report prepared accordingly, by reference to the following relevant matters.

Sources of information

10.7   Having established who the shareholder is, it is useful to schedule the initial sources of information. These will include the client, principal officers of the company and third party advisers such as estate agents or accountants or solicitors. The company accountant, and particularly the company secretary, are in a position to provide valuation information, as also may be long-term shareholders who are closely involved with the activities of the company.

Purpose of valuation

10.8   The valuation report should state clearly the purpose of valuation and should indicate which, if any, tax is in point and why. The identity and number of shares should be given, along with the date for which the valuation is required. At all times, in respect of all matters concerning the valuation, the date is of fundamental importance (see 2.44), and facts and figures which cannot be substantiated as at that date will always be suspect. In practical terms this can give rise to difficulties, for example, where the date of valuation falls, say, halfway through a company's accounting period.

10.9   The balance sheet at the end of that period cannot be taken automatically as a reflection of the state of affairs of the company as at the date the valuation is required. The same can be said of the company's trading profits for that year. It is necessary to see what has happened during the year and it would be usual to take the balance sheet at the end of the previous year and amend that accordingly to take account of events occurring between that date and the date of the valuation. It is not always a practical possibility or appropriate, however (for example, in minority interest cases), and sometimes it is necessary to estimate increases in value or profits that have been made during the period on a time basis or in some other way. Even so, if the valuation is for tax purposes the Shares Valuation Division may take issue with apportionments that are made arbitrarily. It will rather depend upon the facts in each case, and indeed the scale of the valuation.

The subject company

10.10   Obviously, it is necessary to identify the subject company, its business address and registered office, and its professional advisers, and the valuer needs to have a knowledge of the company's trading history. To some extent these may be taken from the directors' report on the annual accounts, but very often this is rather brief and a more detailed knowledge is required, especially if there has been any material change in the trading activities, particularly any notable cyclical trends.

10.11   Any parent and subsidiary companies must be identified and their relationship fully understood; the capital structure of each company must be noted and the shareholding identified. The valuer must understand whether or not he is valuing shares from trading results taken from consolidated accounts, and whenever subsidiary companies are involved, the valuation exercise may require an individual inspection of each subsidiary and cognisance of its impact on the parent and the parent's activity and value. A schedule of parent, subsidiary and associated companies and their capital structures should be prepared, and inter-company trading activities, guarantees, debts etc. noted.

10.12   A schedule of the capital structure of the subject company must be prepared and the shares which are the subject of the valuation identified in the context of this structure (see 3.1 and 3.25). Such a schedule could also be the base for identifying previous transactions (sales, acquisitions, bonus or rights issues and other transfers (see 2.115, etc.). Any known prices would be recorded here and the valuer must ensure that any transactions that would appear to be material to the valuation of the shares in the current circumstances are brought into account.

10.13   Within reason, a list of shareholders should be made and so far as possible previous shareholders identified and brought into the schedule. This may have relevance for capital gains tax and inheritance tax purposes, especially if there have been transactions between connected parties or members of the same family (see 9.4 and 9.34). For this purpose all shareholders' relationships with each other should be identified, not only family relations, but also any trusteeships, nominee holdings and company or director connections.

10.14   This will enable decisions to be taken as to whether there are any groupings of shares to be made for the purpose of valuation under the various tax rules which deal with related party transactions, and may be relevant in identifying whether somebody has *de facto* control (such as where a person holds shares on his own account, and also as trustee, and the holdings together constitute effective control (see 3.11)).

Basis of valuation

10.15   At some stage in bringing the information together, a decision has to be taken by the valuer as to which basis of valuation is appropriate — whether dividend basis, earnings basis, assets basis or hybrid basis. The probability is that by looking at the size of the shareholding in question, the trading activities of the company and the net asset backing, the valuer will have come to an early decision as to what basis would be appropriate (see 3.78).

10.16 In any valuation report (as distinct from an 'opinion' of value as discussed at 1.5 and 2.57) the basis must be stated and the reasons for choosing the basis explained. It is certainly not unknown for the valuer to change his mind as to the appropriate basis once he has immersed himself in the detail of the valuation. For example, in looking at the current (that is at the date of valuation) trading activities of the company, the valuer may consider that the directors are carrying on the business with insufficient funds with the result that an initial view that, say, a dividend basis applies, is put aside in favour of an asset value on a break-up basis. As long as a firm decision on the valuation basis is eventually made, there is no reason why the valuer should not leave open the question of which basis to adopt until quite late in his examination. Indeed, one of a valuer's greatest assets is an open mind. He should be wary of first impressions and should not be influenced by any preconceived idea that the client may have concerning the value of the shares or the viability or otherwise of the company.

Statutory rules

10.17 It is certainly most helpful to the valuer to identify those statutory rules that are pertinent to the valuation, and schedule and re-read them before commencing the valuation itself. If he is not well versed in taxation he would do well to seek confirmation of the rules that will or may apply. These can normally be set out in fairly short terms (Chapter 9).

10.18 The valuation report should specify the tax valuation legislation for the avoidance of doubt and it also helps to list those valuation concepts to which the valuer has had regard in putting together his valuation. Similarly, any company law requirements, such as the valuation rules under *Companies Act 1985, ss 103* and *104* in relation to the issue of shares for non-cash consideration, should be referred to where appropriate.

10.19 A suggested form for setting out such principles is given in the model valuation report in Appendix 1.

Memorandum and Articles of Association

10.20 Most companies use standard forms of Memorandum and Articles of Association and these usually draw on the standard clauses in Tables A, D or E as set out in the *Companies Act* (see 3.8). It can be useful to have a summary of the company's main objects clause but it is particularly important that the pre-emption articles are recorded. Any other restrictions on transfer of shares, along with any special articles concerning casting votes and the like, should also be recorded.

10.21 Any clause restricting share transfer is particularly important because of the discounts usually given from quoted company comparisons for the private company shareholding which is subject to such restrictions (see 2.101). Any change in rights must certainly be checked and, if currently relevant, stated in the valuation report.

10.22 Also to be recorded would be any shareholders' agreement in relation to profit distributions or share dilution as they may have a material effect on the rights of shareholders (see 3.18).

10.23 Special resolutions that have an effect on rights of members should also be noted.

Financial and management background

10.24 The real detail of the valuation commences with a review of the financial and management background of the subject company. At this point it is worth reiterating that the valuer is in a privileged position in terms of having access to company records and accounts and statutory books. It is most unlikely that in the case of a minority holding much information beyond that which is in the hands of the shareholder would be made available to any prospective purchaser (see 2.20).

10.25 A director is under no obligation to disclose confidential company information to anyone, including the company's shareholders, and therefore the information drawn upon for the purposes of the valuation report should be weighed in relation to the impact that that information would have on any price offered for the shares. If the information would be material in this respect, the valuer should determine whether it would or would not become available to that purchaser and determine the value accordingly.

10.26 By way of example, the existence of a possible take-over bid or offer by one company for another may have a material effect on the share value of the latter. If the valuer discovers that this information is known only to the directors and no one else, there would be no *prima facie* reason to reflect this potential bid in the value of a minority interest, unless it could be said that in the circumstances of the case a 'reasonable' director would divulge that information (without jeopardising the affairs of the company in any way).

In the unlikely event of a controlling shareholder not being aware of an impending takeover offer, the question arises whether a potential purchaser of that controlling interest (not being the actual takeover bidder) would discover the potential bid or offer upon normal investigation of the company and enquiry of the officers of the company. Could there be a real case where at the date of valuation disclosure to a controlling shareholder of the offer might prejudice the interests of the company (see 2.20)?

10.27 Again, it is worth pointing out that the financial and management information to be investigated is for the purpose of establishing a value as at the date for valuation. There is therefore little point in taking steps to find out about events happening after the date for valuation if there was no forewarning of such events before that date.

Balance sheet and annual accounts

10.28   The annual accounts, including the balance sheet, will contain the directors' reports and auditors' certificates, and between them these will set out some of the information required for the purposes of the valuation. If at all possible, accounts and balance sheets for the five years prior to the date for valuation should be collected and copies put on the valuation file. It can often be helpful to have copies of these accounts appended to the valuation report. Although this may not be strictly necessary, it indicates that the approach to the valuation is based on collecting and displaying all the appropriate evidence.

10.29   It helps to have all the background information on which the valuation report is being prepared kept in one file, together with correspondence between the valuer and all other parties, including the Shares Valuation Division, as this will help considerably if negotiation with the Inland Revenue is drawn out over a number of months or years.

10.30   The directors' report may be useful for getting a 'first feel' for the company's affairs but there is very little consistency between directors' reports of different companies and the valuer should obviously expect to look well beyond the directors' report on the accounts. The audit report also attached to the accounts should be read as this will identify whatever reservations exist in the mind of the auditor concerning the accounting and reporting quality of the company.

10.31   The accounts will also include a cash flow statement (Statement of Source and Application of Funds for accounting periods ending before 23 March 1992) which is useful for understanding the balance sheet changes that have occurred during the period for which the accounts have been prepared. In particular it may help identify material changes in, for example, stocks, debtors, creditors and bank balances during that period.

10.32   It is useful to prepare a summary of the trading and profit and loss accounts over the period under review, and this summary would show the turnover plus other income and gains, providing a total earnings figure per the profit and loss account. The summary would also give the net profit and loss and, at some stage, into this schedule can be inserted notes relating to extraordinary or exceptional items which, for the purpose of arriving at 'ordinary' net trading profits, will be added back or removed from the profit and loss account figure shown. It may be necessary to enquire of the directors what extraordinary items of expenditure may be present in the accounts ending after July 1993 since the SSAP3 definition of earnings per share changed after that date (see 5.7).

10.33   The schedule is also a useful place to record the Retail Price Index figures for the balance sheet date and also at the date for valuation. By adjusting all the results by reference to the RPI one will be able to see the company performance in the context of present day values (that is as at the date for valuation), which is vital for making any sort of estimate as to present day value of future maintainable profit (see the Model Valuation in Appendix 1).

10.34   A summary of balance sheets as such is probably of little value because a valuation exercise must look at market value of assets at the date for the valuation and not at net book values. However, it can be useful to see the relationship between the market value of business assets and the market value of non-business assets. By comparing the movement in the ratio of one against the other, an underlying movement may emerge that may help the valuer judge the company's state of health. For example, if the percentage of investment assets as against business assets is continuing to fall, this may indicate a long-term decline in the company's ability to cushion itself against adverse trading conditions. A trend the other way might well suggest that additional asset value should be brought into the valuation, whether or not the indications are that another basis is appropriate for the basic valuation. This schedule can be difficult to produce because it necessitates revaluing the balance sheet for each year under review. There is certainly no point in doing this unless one can identify assets on the balance sheet that could be regarded as not strictly required for business purposes.

10.35   In terms of exceptional and extraordinary items, some of the most common exceptional items are pension fund payments on or around the setting-up of a self-administered pension fund, and the sale or purchase of investments, but the valuer should watch for other unexpected items, such as heavy removal costs relating to a once-and-for-all move to new premises, or costs relating to the discontinuance of a trade.

Dividend policy

10.36   Any dividend policy (see Chapter 4) of the company must be ascertained and the criteria set down on paper so that the valuer understands fully what that policy is. The dates of previous dividend payments should be listed and the pre- and post-tax figures shown. This is of particular importance where minority interests are being valued. Whether or not a dividend policy is being followed it is necessary to determine the company's current and future cash requirements because, just as a history of no dividends can come to an end, so too can a history of dividend payments. It is difficult to foresee a future change in a policy that is already established, but any management projections which show either a deficit or surfeit of cash in the future will be an important indicator of an impending change.

Management projections and profit forecasts

10.37   The balance sheet and accounts will provide the historic facts. Current management projections and profit forecasts, provided they have been prepared on proper accounting principles, will be of great value in projecting those historic results forward. More often than not in the case of a going concern, the valuer will be trying to establish future maintainable profits, and therefore management accounts and forecasts based on sound accounting records can be very valuable in, if nothing else, establishing a reasonably acceptable view of the current position. Once again, it is important to stress that one is looking at the date for valuation. It is pointless to bring in as evidence any management forecasts, budgets and so on made after this date, unless it is reasonably certain that that information was available at the date for valuation. If there are budgets prepared regularly then a comparison of past budgets and management accounts with the actual financial audited accounts could be useful to see how accurate the projections and forecasts are.

Directors and personnel

10.38   It has been proved time and again that a company's trading position, its goodwill, its profit-earning capacity and its growth, are continuous hostages of management. A company, a business, a venture is as successful as the persons carrying it on. It is not uncommon to find that the private company is shareholder controlled and directed and its success depends upon its business goodwill in a locality or narrow specialism, often depending upon a personal relationship between the shareholder director and one or a few other parties. That is not to say that such a company has no value, but in the author's view, if the company's business is so personal to the shareholder director, there is much doubt that a dividends or earnings basis may be applied.

10.39   The valuer might prepare his own management review identifying the age and experience of each director and any specialist knowledge or qualification the person may have. He should consider that information against the business being carried on. For example, if, in a property development company, he discovered half a dozen directors all aged between 20 and 25, no one of those directors having any experience of property transactions and having no qualification in relation to property, then the valuer must seriously question the likelihood of success.

10.40   It is useful to point out that the valuer is not concerned with the potential of the business if it were subjected to major change; the valuer is projecting the *status quo* forward at the date for the valuation. The value of the company stems from that, at least initially. When looking at the market for the shares in the particular company it may be necessary to modify this view (see, e.g. 2.77 and 2.96).

10.41   A summary of management personnel would include current remuneration and brief details of any service contracts and their unexpired period. This may be of particular importance in the case of key executives; any 'keyman' insurance policies will help identify such individuals. Directors' remuneration would be listed along with pension contributions and benefit packages, which in many cases can be quite substantial. Not to be forgotten is any 'golden handshake' or redundancy liability on a future termination of employment.

10.42   It is imperative to record any agreement for the sale or transfer of shares, or subscription for new shares, to or by any directors or employees. Details of any share option/incentive scheme arrangement must be obtained and the impact of such schemes taken into account, obviously to identify what sort of dilution in existing share values there may be.

10.43   A brief summary of the company's employees might also be obtained along with a review of staff level changes made, especially if the business is labour intensive. If it is discovered that the company uses outside workers, it would be useful to check that control of such a workforce is properly conducted; a particular problem at this time is the company's responsibilities under PAYE regulations: 'homeworkers' and other 'casuals' may, in reality, be employees with the result that the company may have built up PAYE liabilities and penalties.

10.44   The company's pension scheme or schemes, especially small self-administered schemes, should be considered to identify what level of contributions have been made and will be made in the future and whether there is any other connection between the company and the pension scheme. For example, property occupied by the company may be owned by the fund and the valuer may wish to ensure that the fund has received all the necessary approvals from the Superannuation Funds Office.

Taxation

10.45   A review of tax provisions over recent years might disclose irregularities or special situations (e.g. ACT irrecoverable) that might have an impact on value.

Assets and real estate

10.46   The assets owned by the company and the uses to which the assets are put should be identified. The assets' current market value must be determined (6.22 *et seq*) and in the case of a going concern the valuer must see whether there is any extraordinary value attaching to business assets which might identify a particular strength in the asset-backing of the business. He must also identify any valuable assets standing to one side of the business assets.

10.47   The current value of plant and machinery in the case of a going concern probably will not enter into the valuation except in the unusual circumstance of a going concern business being valued on an asset basis rather than an earnings basis. In the event of likely liquidation, the valuer will be seeking to establish the break-up basis (see 6.6) and some advice may have to be taken either from the company directors themselves, or, more probably, from outside experts, as to the likely value of the plant and machinery on a break-up basis or in a forced sale.

10.48   If plant and machinery accounts for a substantial part of the value of the company, then it would certainly be advisable to obtain an outside opinion as to what the sale value might be. Otherwise, subject to the valuer's opinion, it might be perfectly acceptable to make his own estimate of what the assets might realise on such a sale, taking into account the costs of the sale and the use to which the purchaser would put the assets, and bearing in mind that the purchaser may be planning to sell on the assets and would require a profit himself. The more specialist the equipment the more necessary it will be to look for specialist assistance.

10.49   With the balance sheet items should be included any assets that are not actually shown on the balance sheet (for example goodwill — see 6.52 and Chapter 12), but only if there is such a separable asset that stands to one side of the actual business that the company is carrying on, i.e. the actual share valuation itself will reflect ultimately the goodwill in the undertaking being carried on by the company.

There may be other assets, including copyrights, with undisclosed value attaching. The valuer must therefore look for any patents, trade marks, registered designs, publications, technical designs, computer programs, recordings etc. that are not actually contributing to the earnings of the company. Any contracts and agreements should be inspected and the importance of the 'asset' to the business and the company must be ascertained. It is very likely that specialist expertise will have to be used in the process of ascertaining the value or confirming a value given by the company directors. If the valuer can see that the goodwill attaching to any such asset is already reflected in the earnings of the company, it will not be necessary to ascribe an independent value because that will be reflected in the capitalisation of the earnings of the company. See Chapter 13 regarding intellectual property.

10.50   In the case of leasehold property there may also be obligations which must be ascertained. In a property portfolio, it will certainly be necessary for a professional valuation to be undertaken by a firm of property valuers, who will also be able to value any leasehold obligations. It should not be overlooked that this will involve expense and the valuer would do well to ensure that provision has been made to meet his costs and the costs of third parties.

Liabilities

10.51   In addition to liabilities in respect of leasehold interests, mentioned above, there may be other liabilities, contingent or otherwise. In the case of an asset value in contemplation of the liquidation of the company, there may be redundancy payment obligations, pension payments to be made, and contract cancellation penalties.

10.52 Any current litigation should be looked into and the possible outcome considered in terms of the effect on the company. Expenditure commitments should also be considered; these may include research and development costs that are expected to continue into the future, or perhaps are expected to start at some future time (but only if as a consequence of current activities and commitments). Ongoing construction costs may be relevant and there may be stage payments required under existing contracts with outside parties.

10.53 Environmental issues may also impact upon a valuation, particularly for certain industries. Land restitution can be expensive. Litigation can be devastating.

Order book

10.54 If available, the valuer could look at the order book at the time for the valuation, and compare that with the past performance of the company, looking particularly for cancellations through lack of delivery, or any other fall, or indeed increase, of orders. An increase in unfulfilled orders may indicate not only that demand is growing, but that the company is unable to meet the orders in time. That failure may be due to under-capitalisation, labour disputes, out-moded machinery or bad management. Any material change in past trading activities should be identified and explanations obtained from management. Such changes could be in product or method of production, type of customer or type of outlet. Any change, especially in the recent past, may indicate that the historic trading performance may bear little relevance to future activities and future maintainable earnings.

Suppliers, joint ventures and third party commitments

10.55 It is always useful to know the number of suppliers to the company as this may indicate strength or weakness. For example, a supplier of widgets who has all his widgets turned by the only widget-turner in the world clearly is exposed in commercial terms and may be a hostage to the fortunes of the one and only widget-turner. A principal requirement for a healthy company is that suppliers of important commodities should be capable of being replaced easily and quickly. If this is not the case then there must be some risk factor.

10.56 Joint ventures, franchise arrangements and other third party commitments, especially of any size, should be examined to identify their relevance to the trading activities of the company and the importance to the profit-earning potential and growth of the company. In these cases there are likely to be contracts or agreements which should be read. Joint ventures may carry continuing liabilities. There may therefore be a negative value attaching to a joint venture if it has not been carried on for a sufficient time to show a return. The identity of the joint venture parties may be relevant and of course the full terms of the arrangement must be understood and noted in the valuation report if appropriate.

10.57   The impact of the EU and the Euro may introduce novel problems in the valuation exercise.

Bad debts

10.58   To get an idea of the risk attaching to the company's business it can be useful to look at the bad debts over a period of years. In the case of a company approaching liquidation it may also help to indicate what problems will exist in collecting money from debtors. A list, as at the date for valuation, of aged debtors and creditors should be prepared, and in the case of debtors it should identify which are bad and which are doubtful. Debts which are older than the average trade terms normally found in the particular type of business should be investigated to see whether they will turn bad, and the reasons for that should be ascertained.

Foreign trading and currency exposure

10.59   Any foreign subsidiaries or branch operations should be examined in the same way as the company's UK trade and business is investigated. Obviously it is more difficult to investigate activities overseas, where different emphasis is often found to be placed on the share valuation elements.

10.60   Currency exposure is a problem of growing relevance as international trade increases. Many businesses now conduct their entire trade in $US and convert into £ sterling for accounting purposes. Now, we also have the Euro to consider, and especially the special issues arising where the three currencies are being used in tandem; possibly hedged, possibly not! The risks particularly appear where trade is being carried on in more than one currency and debtors and creditors exist in differing currencies. The valuer may need to consider the protective measures that the company may or may not be taking in terms of currency exposure.

Financial rates and data

10.61   It is useful to identify various data relating both to the company and to general economic conditions at the date for valuation. Whether or not a quoted company comparison is to be used it is useful to take the FT Actuaries Share Index for the appropriate industry sector as at the date for valuation, and show the index figure for the date twelve months (or whatever may be appropriate to the case) previously. The FT Share Index for those dates can also be given. Clearing banks base rate is useful, as is the yield on undated gilts and often currency rates of exchange.

10.62 Aside from the profit margin percentages measuring gross profit, trading profit, and pre-tax profits against sales or operating income, other financial ratios which may assist in the assessment of the subject company are as follows.

(1)   *The credit ratio.* This is the ratio of trade creditors to trade purchases. A high credit ratio indicates that the company is, for good or ill, extracting the maximum patience from its suppliers.

(2)   *The debtor ratio.* This is the ratio of debtors to sales. A high debtor ratio shows that the company is having some difficulty in collecting debts from its customers.

(3)   *Creditor debtor comparison.* A high credit ratio and a low debtor ratio indicate *prima facie* that the company is maximising its trade related cash flow. A high debtor ratio and low credit ratio indicates the opposite and indeed could point to cash flow difficulties.

(4)   *Turnover of stock.* The rate of turnover of stock is a very valuable indicator of the success of the business and many trade associations publish average stock turnover rates. The rate is determined by dividing the cost of sales by the average of stock levels. The cost of sales is the annual purchases plus opening stock figure, less the closing stock figure, and will also include any manufacturing costs or added value.

(5)   *Return on capital.* The return on capital is considered to be an important piece of information, calculated by dividing the pre-tax net profits by the average net value of capital employed (including intangibles and investment grants) multiplied by 100. Many factors can create a distortion in this figure and it would be quite dangerous simply to take the return on capital at the date for valuation by reference to the net worth at that time and current estimated net profit. Reference must also be made to long-term and short-term cyclical trends as well as short-term distortions in trading activities.

(6)   *The ratio of assets to liabilities.* Ignoring fixed assets and shareholders reserves, this is a useful ratio for identifying whether, by reference to the movement in the ratio over a period of months or years, there is a sufficiency of working capital. Any suggestion that additional working capital is required is likely to have an adverse effect on the value of the shares.

(7)   *The liquid asset ratio (acid test ratio).* This is similar to the ratio of assets to liabilities but excludes stock and work in progress. If current liabilities exceed current assets it indicates that the company is unable to meet its current debts without realising the value of assets. This may well indicate a serious trading problem, or indeed insolvency.

(8)   *Dividend cover.* This is the ratio of the earnings to the dividend yield. The dividend cover shows the number of times that the net dividend can be paid out of current net earnings. A high cover indicates considerable security for future dividends; low cover leads to less certainty that the dividend can be maintained.

Future trading prospects and special factors

10.63   It is helpful to have from the company's management not only immediate profit forecasts but their views on the future trading prospects of the company in the context of the general economic climate. Any special factors relating to the company, the trade or the industry should be noted. For example, a company in the transport industry may in fact be a specialist business dealing with the transportation of heavy engineering items. The company may not be trading in any other area. It may also be that the directors know of a forthcoming decline in the transport industry generally, but have reason to believe the transportation of heavy engineering items is and will continue to be stable.

Supporting documentation

10.64   When a share valuation report is to be supported by comprehensive documentation the following should be included if possible:

● accounts and balance sheet for the past (five) years;

● independent valuations of real estate or other assets;

● copy of Memorandum and Articles of Association;

● pertinent minutes and resolutions;

● copies of material contracts which are referred to in the share valuation report;

● schedules of financial data;

● signed statements by any party certifying any particular facts or figures.

General economic outlook

10.65   The company's management may direct the valuer to a range of publications and a variety of information sources relating to the general economic outlook for the company and its trade. In addition to the information so provided, the valuer should seek independent views, and a particularly valuable source would be trade associations and trade journals. If the names of competitors and companies carrying on comparable businesses can be identified, further information can be gleaned from the Extel Card System (from Extel Financial Ltd). Information relating to quoted companies can be had from Datastream International Limited, and much information on a range of economic and trade matters can be obtained from the Department of Trade and Industry.

10.66   It is important to identify the place of the subject company in the context of its general economic surroundings, which are undoubtedly bound to have an effect on the value of the business as a going concern. This matter today needs to take into account the wider world as it shrinks through the effect of ever improving communications.

Valuation approach

10.67   By the time the valuer has gathered all the above details, he will have a good idea of how he intends to approach his valuation; where he thinks the emphasis should be placed in terms of the proper basis of valuation; whether he will need to adopt a hybrid basis approach; whether he must take into account any particular quirk in the asset base or earnings of the company; and which facts he expects to give special weight, and maybe which facts he intends to ignore.

10.68   He may, for example, decide to ignore the fact that a particular product that was developed by the subject company during the year proved a total failure in all respects and has cost a great deal of money. He may decide that this should not unduly influence the future prospects for the company, perhaps because the individual who devised the product is no longer with the company. This may be of sufficient moment to note in the valuation report, and equally it would be of sufficient moment to note that the results of the exercise are to be removed from the assessment of future maintainable earnings.

10.69   The valuation approach is very much a statement of the valuer's experience brought to bear on the subject company. It is likely to be regarded by the Shares Valuation Division as opinion and may be attacked as such. Nevertheless, it is valid as such, for more than one judge will admit that a valuation is often no more than an arbitration of opinions.

Comparisons

10.70   As mentioned in 10.65, if any comparisons, whether with quoted companies or other companies, can be made, they should be brought into the valuation report, and any distinctions noted. If one uses a comparable company, then the comparison needs to be justified. More often than not, if a private company is being compared with a public quoted company, one would be concerned to identify the inevitable divergences. This is a most important area and it is the area where the valuer can expect to have most difficulty with the Shares Valuation Division if opinions differ. The matter is considered in some detail in Chapters 4 and 5.

Calculation

10.71   Eventually, the valuer comes to the actual calculation. Just as the data has been presented in the valuation report, so the calculation should be unambiguous and capable of being followed through by someone who has not been a party to detailed examination of the affairs of the company. The figures used must be capable of easy reconciliation with the accounts, independent valuations and comparisons with other companies. A comprehensive share valuation report is a working document and should be quite explicit, starting with a basic statement of figures, showing calculations for values that are to be taken into a final calculation, giving reasons why particular figures or fractions or percentages are being used.

10.72   The eventual valuation on a per share basis may then have to be adjusted according to any tax rules that are pertinent, for example, IHT reliefs. It may well be that the actual calculation of the value chargeable to one or other of the taxes is then worked out by someone other than the valuer.

Review

10.73   When the valuer has determined his value and any tax liability or other consequence has been identified, it is wise to have the entire valuation report reviewed by another person. Having been involved in depth in a complicated share valuation, small points can easily be missed.

Finally

10.74   The major technical decisions the valuer will have to make relate to the required yield or the PER, the weighting to be given in a hybrid valuation, and the discounts, whether from the PER of the quoted company comparison, or to reflect the lack of marketability of a private company's shares.

10.75   It is not constructive to choose a deliberately high or low figure simply because one expects the 'opposition' to take the other extreme and negotiate towards a point midway between the two. Such positioning gives weight to confrontational bargaining at the expense of what should be essentially a highly professional and absolute determination. A fully considered opinion is more easily adhered to through lengthy negotiations with the Revenue, and is less likely to engender polarisation of views.

Chapter 11

Dealing with the Shares Valuation Division

The Shares Valuation Division (SVD) is a department of the Capital Taxes Office of the Inland Revenue. The address is Fitz Roy House, PO Box 46, Castle Meadow Road, Nottingham, NG2 1BD. The 'DX' address is DX 701203 Nottingham 4. For companies incorporated in Scotland, the address is Mulberry House, 16 Picardy Place, Edinburgh, EH1 3NB.

Introduction

11.1   The usual procedure for examination of tax related share valuations has been that the department responsible for making the tax assessment will request the taxpayer's valuation, and then pass it to the SVD for examination and negotiation of agreed value. There are specific procedures within the Inland Revenue to deal with a variety of different situations.

11.2   Under self-assessment, form CG34 is used to submit a capital gains valuation of private company shares (and other assets) for agreement in advance of the filing date for the self-assessment tax return. There is no guarantee that agreement will be reached before the filing date however, and a period of around two months should be allowed. It is perfectly possible for the period to exceed that limit and in complex cases to run beyond a year.

The form requires the value to be expressed as the value *per share,* rather than a value for the whole shareholding to be given. Also the form asks for the company share capital to be given, the capital gains tax computation and particulars of available reliefs, a copy of any valuation report plus three years accounts to the valuation date and any further information that would assist in the examination of the valuation. If not already included in the share valuation report, the business of the company should be described fully; restrictions on share transfers should be detailed (per the Articles of Association or other agreements), and the full rights attaching to all classes of shares (including on a liquidation) should be detailed.

In the absence of a form CG34, an estimated share value used in a capital gains self-assessment will be referred to the SVD and if there is to be a challenge to the value this will be by way of an enquiry under *TMA 1970, s 9A*, which may bring into question other related tax issues.

11.3   The SVD will refer land values to the appropriate District Valuer for an informal value (where a precise property value is not crucial to the share value itself), or for a formal valuation which may involve direct negotiations between the District Valuer and the taxpayer. A formal valuation will usually only be sought in respect of investment property or farmland, or if the return on net assets is so low that a break-up basis valuation is appropriate (see 6.4). Negotiating with the District Valuer often leads to additional delay in agreeing final figures, although it should not prevent the two sides agreeing other elements in the valuation, leaving the matter open to final adjustment when the land value has been agreed. However, this may not be the best course of action if the land value is significant in relation to the share valuation.

11.4   The Shares Valuation Division maintains a file (or several) for every company, and a prominent note is made of any 31 March 1982 value (for capital gains re-basing purposes — see 11.9 and 9.14). These files will not only have details of previous valuations of shares in the company, but also copies of accounts and copies of the Memorandum and Articles of Association and other matters, sometimes including press cuttings. The SVD valuation officers also have access to other Inland Revenue files also, including, for example, files maintained by Technical Division and the Stamp Office, not to mention the taxpayer's Inspector of Taxes.

Agreed values — without prejudice

11.5   If sufficient information is available the SVD procedure is to decide first whether the particular valuation under examination can be agreed without further negotiation and conditions because it falls within a range of acceptable values. In limited circumstances, the SVD may be prepared to accept, on a 'without prejudice' basis, a value which is outside its considered range of acceptable values — which generally means that if any other tax issue or valuation arises with respect to shares (presumably even the same shares) in the same company the without prejudice value will have no status with respect to that issue or valuation. This approach is most likely to be adopted in cases where the tax charge in the particular circumstances is of little moment and where protracted negotiation may be of little benefit to either party.

Such an agreement may be just as convenient to the taxpayer in question (or his advisor) as to the SVD valuation officer. However, it would be as well for the taxpayer's advisor to be cognisant of the possibility of other related tax matters and how a valuation agreed on a without prejudice agreement may come back to haunt the advisor later if the taxpayer (or an affected related party) does not appreciate the terms of the valuation agreement. For example, it may suit the SVD to agree informally a relatively high share value for inheritance tax purposes because the total value of the estate falls under the IHT exemption limits anyway; yet the 'acquisition value' for capital gains tax value on death will still need to be agreed by further negotiation.

11.6   In *IRC v Stenhouse's Trustees* it was decided that evidence *inter alia* of previous agreements with the SVD was admissible in determining open market value, but was not necessarily conclusive. It was emphasised that valuations were a matter of fact and expert opinion which could be made after employing more than one measure, each legitimate but none necessarily conclusive by itself.

11.7 The Inland Revenue is not empowered (and indeed is forbidden under the rules of taxpayer confidentiality) unilaterally to inform one taxpayer of agreements on share valuations made with other taxpayers even if the same company is involved and the same number of shares is involved.

Employee share schemes

11.8 Special arrangements are available to deal with employee share schemes of unquoted companies. In the case of an unapproved share option scheme where it is proposed to grant options which can be exercised after seven years, because such options give rise to a tax charge upon the grant, the SVD will consider the proposed option price before the date of the grant and will comment on whether the price is less than market value — so long as the Inland Revenue Employee Share Scheme Unit (ESSU) has been informed of the scheme. Notification to the ESSU should include: the name of the scheme; the name and registered office of the company whose shares will be used; the class and nominal value of the shares; the company's tax office and PAYE office and respective reference numbers; and, correspondence address.

Where options have been exercised (whether under an approved or unapproved share option scheme) and there is an income tax charge under *TA 1988, s 135* on the exercise, then the SVD is prepared to negotiate the value immediately and directly with the company provided that the employees authorise the company to act on their behalf. A draft letter of authority from employees is available from the ESSU. The SVD will require a minimum of information to consider the valuation:

- company's accounts for last three financial years ending before the date on which the value is required, plus subsequent interim financial statements or dividend declarations for the company's current financial year;
- scheme rules;
- estimate of value with explanation of how arrived at;
- ESSU scheme reference number 'U...'.

The ESSU address is: Inland Revenue, ESSU, 1st Floor SW Wing, Bush House, Strand, London, WC2B 4RD.

31 March 1982 values

11.9 Where a 31 March 1982 value is required for indexation and the rebasing of capital gains to 1982 and shareholders with similar shareholdings agree, the SVD will begin valuation negotiation with them (or with a practitioner acting on their behalf) before receiving a formal request from the tax office (which is the normal 'proper' practice). The conditions for this procedure are that the requested valuations relate to unquoted shares at 31 March 1982 for capital gains tax purposes; a number of shareholders require the valuations; those shareholders having similar holdings are prepared to be bound by the value agreed; the SVD has a full list of the company's shareholders and the size of their holdings at 31 March 1982 and the date of disposal plus (if available!) details of the tax offices involved. There will still be a need for the taxpayer to disclose the gains in their tax returns and note the referral to the SVD.

Appeals and agreements

11.10   An appeal from a valuation determination by the SVD is to the Special Commissioners and is brought in the same way as other tax appeals. The decision of the Commissioners on a matter of fact is final and conclusive but on a point of law their decision can be appealed against to the High Court. Special Commissioners decisions are published. Agreements with the SVD are not safe in appeal circumstances unless under *TMA 1970, s 54* (see *Cash & Carry v Inspector of Taxes*).

Chapter 12

Goodwill and Unincorporated Businesses

Introduction

12.1   This chapter considers the valuation elements relating to goodwill, which is the 'earnings' capacity of a business whether incorporated or unincorporated.

12.2   In valuing an unincorporated business the essential elements are net assets and goodwill. A standard valuation approach in certain sectors — for example in the financial services industry — is simply to value the whole business as a multiple of turnover rather than to seek out the precise earnings of the business. This is because the earnings machinery and gross and net profit contributions are understood well. This approach will not operate in all unincorporated businesses, and even where it is operated, due diligence procedures will confirm that the foundations are stable — so that the expected profit contribution is confirmed.

12.3   In 'premises-bound' businesses the goodwill and the premises will be intimately bound so that the price of the property will incorporate the goodwill value of the business being conducted there.

12.4   The following text in its application to unincorporated businesses will need supplementing by Chapter 6, which deals with asset valuations, and may also require reference to Chapter 13.

Goodwill

12.5   In simplistic terms goodwill is an intangible appendage to a business or to a business asset; it cannot exist in isolation. Goodwill, in the valuation of a business in its entirety, will be that part of the total value that exceeds the value of the net tangible assets. In order for there to be such an excess, the expected annual maintainable profits of the business must be greater than a reasonable financial return from the investment in those net tangible assets.

12.6   When valuing a business on a break-up basis, where the business is to cease altogether, goodwill will not exist in respect of the business as a whole because it is implicit in goodwill that a profit-earning potential exists, yet there may be goodwill attaching to individual assets or groups of assets. A case in point might be a hotel group. Some hotels in the group may be profitable, some not so. On a break-up basis, each hotel will be segregated and looked at in isolation or, possibly, in viable groups depending on size.

12.7   Goodwill is:

'the benefit and advantage of the good name, reputation, and connection of a business. It is the attractive force which brings in custom. It is the one thing which distinguishes an old established from a new business at its first start. The goodwill of a business must emanate from a particular centre or source. However widely extended or diffused its influence may be, goodwill is worth nothing unless it has power of attraction sufficient to bring customers to the source from which it emanates. Goodwill is composed of a variety of elements. It differs in its composition in different trades and in different businesses in the same trade . . . The goodwill of a business is one whole . . .

. . . If there is one attribute common to all cases of goodwill, it is the attribute of locality. For goodwill has no independent existence. It cannot subsist by itself. It must be attached to a business. Destroy the business and the goodwill perishes with it, though the elements remain which may perhaps be gathered up and revived again.'

12.8   Having said all this, Lord MacNaghten, in the stamp duty case *IRC v Muller & Co's Margarine Ltd*, admitted that in his terms it may be difficult to localise goodwill where the reputation of a business is very widely spread, or where it is the article produced rather than the producer of the article that has won popular favour.

12.9   In the same case Lord Brampton distinguished two forms of goodwill. The first is goodwill together with the premises in which the trade is then carried on, whereby the value of the premises is enhanced. In this case the trade and the premises are inseparable so long as the trade is carried on there; it is, according to Lord Brampton, immaterial whether the business has been built up by reason of the personal good qualities of the out-goer, the goodness of his wares or merchandise, the good situation of the premises, or the absence of competition; the business and custom in fact have been attracted to the premises, and when the incomer takes possession he takes all the chances offered and conveyed to him by the purchase, of standing, so far as the business is concerned, in the shoes of the out-goer, and he must rely upon his own good qualities and aptitude of his undertaking to continue the prosperity of the business and thereby profit by his bargain.

12.10   The second is goodwill utterly unconnected with the premises in which it is carried on, and which is merely the advantage of the recommendation of the vendor to his connections and customers and his covenant to allow the purchaser to use his trade name and to abstain from competition with him.

12.11   If there are assets belonging to the business that can realise cash and are replaceable without changing the nature or the intrinsic value of the business, then those can be regarded as separate from the goodwill. However, if an asset is part of the very nature of the business and income can be said to emanate from it, it would be wrong to try to separate it from the goodwill of the business as a whole, unless it has value well beyond the earnings generated by the business in exploiting it, i.e. it is obviously under-utilised. Even so, if there is no clear indication that the asset can or will be separated from the business it may not be possible to place additional value on it, unless the company has been continuously unprofitable and is being valued on a break-up basis.

12.12   Certain trades, such as newsagents, milk delivery and bookmakers, may have their goodwill valued according to the custom of the particular trade, which may place greater emphasis on turnover than on profitability.

12.13   In the case of intellectual property, such as patents, copyrights, trademarks, licences, know-how, design registration (all intangible assets because they are 'rights' and as such have no physical presence in themselves) it would be wrong to regard such property as separate from the business including its goodwill element because they are the very source of the earnings of the business, but whether they constitute goodwill in themselves in whole or part is a moot point. See Chapter 13.

12.14   A trade mark is a classic goodwill item. It cannot be exploited in isolation. A trade mark or brand name is only of value when directly associated with some product or service. Therefore, the right to use a trade mark or brand name will have a goodwill value measured by its selling power *above and beyond the ability of the product to sell itself without that brand name*. Other valuation considerations include the additional marketing opportunities associated with the product/brand name. Any additional value attributable to the further — but unproven — exploitation of the trade mark would, however calculated, be speculative in the sense that such value would be based on the successful combination of a variety of factors all of which would suffer the uncertainties that attach to forecasting.

12.15   A patent right is not easily classifiable as goodwill. The patent rights in themselves may provide the patent owner with a unique market, but goodwill materialises from the profitable exploitation of that market — if the product is lousy or the marketing ineffective no goodwill would be created. The value of a patent right that is being exploited will be determined by reference to the revenue earned from that exploitation. However, it is quite possible that the market for the patented product can be exploited by other, differently designed, products — the point is that a patented right can only have value if it can be commercially exploited. As to additional exploitation potential, the same factors apply as apply to trade marks.

12.16   Assets that need replacing regularly, even if over a period of years, are unlikely to form part of the nature of the business because they are replaceable and replaced. An ice-cream van may be regarded as the actual source of income — the fixed premises — and the income earning potential of the business would last as long as the asset. Without the van, all the income would 'melt' away because the value of the vehicle and of the income earning potential are one. However, this is not the case (apart from the fact that ice-cream vans seem to survive for generations). For, like all businesses, ice-cream retailing is a composite of elements of which the van is a replaceable part. There is, for example, value in 'know-how': how to produce a proper ice-cream cornet, the most profitable route for the van to take, and the most profitable time of day to visit key sales areas. So, the ice-cream van when sold might carry with it the 'goodwill' of the business, but where is the real value? The cost of the van is one thing, the 'value' of the know-how is another. This value is probably close to the earnings that would theoretically be lost while discovering the information about routes, sales areas, etc. — if that is a practical alternative, of course.

12.17 In some businesses, particularly service industries, the goodwill is very personal to an individual and the business would cease if that individual died or retired. However, there are clearly many cases where the goodwill will continue beyond an individual's death or retirement, even where the goodwill originally derived from the individual.

Valuation of goodwill

12.18 Broadly speaking, the value of goodwill is the difference between the capitalised value of the earnings and the value of net tangible assets.

12.19 In the case of *Findlay's Trustees v IRC*, a case concerning the value of a newspaper business, it was common ground that for the purposes of ascertaining a business's net profits, those profits should be before tax and interest on debentures, and that the agreed profit figure — that which the purchaser could reasonably expect to earn from the business — should be multiplied by eight to give the total value of the business and from that figure the value of net tangible assets is removed to give the goodwill value. However, the parties disagreed on how to arrive at the appropriate profit figure. One party took the average of the last three years and the other party took the final year's profits.

12.20 Lord Fleming said:

' . . . when one is seeking to ascertain the profits which will probably be earned by a business in the future, it is quite usual to do so by taking an average of the profits actually earned for the three preceding years. This probably operates quite equitably when one is dealing with a well-established business, which has normal ups and downs, but has no violent fluctuations in either direction. But if there is a definite trend upwards or downwards, it may be different.'

12.21   In this particular case it was found that the last year in question showed a heavily reduced profit and Fleming said in respect of it:

'... it is impossible to avoid coming to the conclusion that the outlook in 1930 could not be regarded as favourable for the newspaper industry ... A prudent buyer would, I think, proceed upon the view that the business would not recover from the serious setback which it had sustained in 1930 for some years.'

12.22   Lord Fleming eventually settled for a profit figure (£135,000) that was almost exactly halfway between the three-year average (£147,510) and the final year (£124,721). He was seeking to achieve a profit that could reasonably be expected to be maintained by the business without the interference of any special outside influence or person — thus any 'personal' goodwill element would be excluded unless the right to exploit that personal goodwill was somehow retained in the business. At the same time it would be necessary to consider whether the business might be 'disturbed' by the actions of the vendor after the disposal, and to adjust the profits for any expected competition that might follow the sale. Normally, a shopkeeper (as many other types of entrepreneur) would be prevented from exercising a similar trade or business within a radius of, say, five or thirty miles of the location of the business being sold, or perhaps some other restrictive covenant would apply (provided it is not an oppressive or unenforceable restriction) and this may be brought into the formula.

12.23   As has been shown above, once a maintainable profit is determined, the profit must be capitalised by multiplying it by a factor appropriate to the type of business and economic activity. Deciding what that factor should be is difficult indeed, and better considered on the basis of the factors in Chapter 5.

12.24   Once the capitalised value for the whole business has been determined, the value of net assets is removed (but not of any assets which are necessarily bound into the goodwill, such as the sweet shop or hotel previously discussed). What is left is the value of the goodwill of the business. This is the total capitalisation method.

12.25   An alternative method is to calculate the annual yield that arises — or should arise — from the tangible assets used in the business, deduct that from the annual maintainable profits and then multiply the difference by a capitalisation factor. This method is known as the super profits method.

12.26   These two methods are common in valuing substantial businesses. Theoretically they should both give the same result and the value determined under one of the methods should be capable of being put into the formula for the other to give an acceptable yield under that formula. If that is not the case, then, in theory at least, the yields and/or capitalisation factors used in one or other, or both, of the methods must be suspect.

12.27   Goodwill and Unincorporated Businesses

12.27   Under the *total capitalisation* method, the maintainable profits are multiplied by a capitalisation factor which is determined by the yield expected from the investment in the business as a whole.

12.28   Under the *super profits* method, two yields are required: the first, a lower yield, from the investment in the net tangible assets; and the second, a higher yield, from the investment in the pure goodwill. The yields, one for tangible assets and one for goodwill, at best may be debatable and arbitrary. An example will help to show the two different methods.

Example

Suppose a business has proven maintainable profits of £100,000 and tangible assets valued at £400,000. What value should be placed on the goodwill of the business?

(1)   Looking first at the *super profits* method, the yield required from the investment in the tangible assets must be estimated, remembering the alternative investments available, such as gilts or bank deposits or the money market. It would normally be the case that the yield expected from tangible assets would be less than that expected from pure goodwill.

(2)   For the purposes of this example, let us suppose a yield of 12% is required:

Yield required from fixed assets – say 12%	£48,000	400,000
Super-profit £100,000 – £48,000 =	£52,000	
Three-year purchase of goodwill @ £52,000		156,000
Total value		£556,000

(3)   The other variable factor is the three year purchase of goodwill which gives a yield of 33⅓ rd.

(4)   The total capitalisation method will agree with the super profits method *if the capitalisation factor for the business as a whole* will give £556,000 when applied to maintainable profits. One way to determine the value of goodwill is to calculate the values under both methods and compare values falling within a common value range. It is helpful in the calculations only to use whole number capitalisation factors and to allow a margin for error of +/– 1. This gives the 'range'. If the two methods give comparable values within this range it might be reasonable to take the simple average of those two values.

(5)   Suppose, for example, that we consider the capitalisation factor for this sort of business as a whole in the current economic climate to be five (equivalent to an annual yield of 20%).

	VALUE RANGE		
	A	B	C
Total capitalisation method	(5–1)	5	(5+1)
Total value of business	400,000	500,000	600,000
(× £100,000)			
Less: tangible assets	400,000	400,000	400,000
Value of goodwill	NIL	100,000	200,000
Super profits method	(3–1)	3	(3+1)
Purchase of goodwill (× £52,000)	104,000	156,000	208,000
Add: Tangible assets	400,000	400,000	400,000
Total value of the business	504,000	556,000	608,000

(6)   The value range for the total value of the business under the total capitalisation method is £400,000 to £600,000.

(7)   The value range for the super-profits method is £504,000 to £608,000.

(8)   The total capitalisation estimated value of the business under (B) is £500,000. It will be seen that this is outside the value range for the super profits methods — it is lower than £504,000. Therefore, £504,000 should be taken as the minimum value.

(9)   The super profits estimated value of the business is £556,000. This is within the value range for the total capitalisation method (£400,000 to £600,000) and we may therefore regard £556,000 as the maximum value (had it been outside that value range, at say £606,000 the maximum value would have been limited to £600,000).

(10)   The average of these values (£504,000 and £556,000) is £530,000. As the assets are valued at £400,000, the value of the goodwill is £530,000 – £400,000 = £130,000.

(11)   Relating this to the first assumptions:

- On the basis of maintainable profits of £100,000 and a 12% yield from fixed assets, the resultant yield of £52,000 out of the goodwill value of £130,000 represents a 2.5 years purchase, or a yield of 40%. If this is considered to be too high, is the yield from the fixed assets too low?

- On the basis of maintainable profits of £100,000 the value of the business at £530,000 gives a capitalisation factor of 5.3, equivalent to an annual yield of 18.9%.

(12)   This example is merely a way of averaging out guesses within an arbitrary compass. Yet it may help to contain the inexactitude so often encountered in goodwill valuation.

Negative goodwill

12.29   A low level of profitability may give rise to a negative goodwill or to 'super losses'. This occurs when more value may be realised from disposing of the assets on a break-up basis. The cessation of trading may itself create further losses through crystallising a liability, for example, to make redundancy payments.

The one-man business

12.30   In the smaller, unincorporated 'one-man' type of business, less importance will be placed on establishing a yield from the tangible assets employed and it is even likely that no deduction will be made from net profits for remuneration to the owner. This resultant over-blown profit will be multiplied by a factor representing a number of years' purchase, or alternatively, goodwill may be derived from turnover.

12.31   In these cases the approach will be to value the business by reference to actual sales of similar businesses, and a good guide would be to obtain particulars of sales of businesses from the specialist press such as *Dalton's Weekly* or *Exchange and Mart*. More often than not, such businesses include premises and, as mentioned earlier, the value of the premises will effectively incorporate the value of the goodwill.

12.32   A number of cases (*Nielsen v London Borough of Camden; Perezic v Bristol Corporation*, and *Zarraga v Newcastle upon Tyne Corporation*) has shown that usually no remuneration should be deducted in determining profits for the purpose of valuing goodwill in the case of one-man or husband and wife businesses. In *R C Handley Ltd v London Borough of Greenwich*, however, a nominal deduction for management remuneration and 10% interest on capital were allowed from profits of £14,000 a year. This principle was extended to directors' remuneration in *Lewis's Executors and Palladium Cinema (Brighton) Ltd v Brighton Corporation* where the company's profits were generated by one man; but all these cases were compensation claims against local authorities for loss of goodwill, and although goodwill may form part of a company's assets, it is difficult to conceive of shares having a value which is based on no cost of earning the company's profits — i.e. the cost of labour and management.

12.33   As mentioned earlier, in many businesses — and this includes many small 'one-man' or family companies — the goodwill is attached to an individual and dies with him. The principle can also apply to companies with a single shareholder/employee, and also quasi-partnership companies where the abandonment of the office by one or more of the principals would eliminate the business activity of the company.

'Trade or industry values'

12.34   Over the years many types of business have been valued by reference to value 'generators' that their owners can understand as the real indicator of earnings. From that point they know (or believe they know) what financial end result there will be because after those measurable elements the respective underlying management issues are identical. There are many examples, ancient and modern:

- agencies — gross commissions;
- accountants — gross fees;
- bookmakers — turnover;
- brewers — barrel price throughput;
- care homes — occupied beds;
- fund managers — money under management;
- mining enterprises — mineral reserves.

These value generators are multiplied by the current value (e.g. £s per bed of a nursing home) or multiple (e.g. × 1.5 of gross audit fees), which may change over time because they are driven by the open market. Experienced entrepreneurs in the industries will have knowledge of the value multiplier and will have a weather eye open for changes. The approach can be accurate in some instances but it is dangerous to apply such 'norms' without absolute certainty that the formula being used currently in all other transactions on pure open market and *status quo* terms. In short, you have to know your onions! It is a little like Spanish holiday homes or Greek oil tankers; each of these industries has been through periods of serious depression but in most cases the owners would not sell their house or their ship at less than the 'industry' norm price. The result is usually that in times of depression nothing is sold, except in the 'fire sales' of unfortunate people. The prices secured by these people would be more like the real market value of the time.

Industry norms can also become established for new unique businesses. This is because they have no history of profits or performance or management success. However, someone has to take a stab, probably the corporate finance experts of the financial institutions investing in the business who will want to describe (probably backwards through the discounted cash flow valuation basis) a proof for escalating value despite initial heavy costs of development. The message is that there are trade customs and industry norms which the valuer should consider but discard if their expertise suggests that the figures do not add up (or down) to a proper 'open-market' value on the basis of what is being sold.

Chapter 13

Intellectual Property

Introduction

13.1   The valuation of intellectual property is a specialist matter. In this chapter we can only touch upon some of the essential issues. Because of the nature of intellectual property, the way in which it comes into being, how it is held and exploited and its importance in the commercial world today, some specific mention should be made of it in the valuation sense. Its existence is not always apparent, not even by documentation, yet it may lie dormant or quietly bubbling away in the financial or asset undergrowth and be generating income or profits or be capable of so doing.

In companies that incur expenditure on research and development, in particular, there may be intellectual property rights in existence. This is not limited to technological or scientific research establishments, however. The possibility lies with any company, in any business. More and more, management is beginning to recognise that intellectual property is a long-term asset, and is becoming concerned about identifying whether such property exists or is capable of existing within their company, and in what ways intellectual property might be utilised by the company (including internally within groups).

Intangible assets

13.2   Intellectual property is a sub-classification of intangible assets, which are assets that are not physical. Land and buildings, plant and machinery, stock, cash, are all tangible or physical assets. Goodwill, choses-in-action, rights of way, know-how, trade marks, copyrights — these are intangible assets. What tends to distinguish intellectual property from other intangibles is that intellectual property is derived from creative processes. Many types of intangible assets are capable of being legally protected, and by virtue of that legal protection can be commercially exploited, and it is largely this protection that bestows upon the intellectual property in question the possibility of having value.

Actual value is, of course, derived from the earnings or perceived earnings and from the market (knowing who or where the market is is one of the tricks to knowing what that value might be). There have certainly been many recent instances of companies which are almost wholly dependent upon their recently developed intellectual property, notably including untried and untested products, commanding 'heroic' (readers may substitute their own word) prices, especially bio-tech, IT and Netware software companies. These trends then set a pattern for related transactions and create short-term distortions in and around the particular markets.

Intellectual property

13.3   There are several types of intellectual property: copyright, patents, trade marks, designs, know-how, and some hybrids or composites. Within each of these descriptions there are various sub-categories of asset, so a rough summary of each description may be helpful (some sub-categories may appear in more than one description):

(a)   *Copyrights* — computer programmes, literary works (publishing rights and titles, and 'mastheads'), dramatic, artistic and musical works, films (cinematographic rights), broadcasting and music publishing, logos, trade marks, livery (e.g. British Airways' entire get-up), endorsements;

(b)   *Patents* — novel inventions or processes, drugs and chemical compounds, genetic designs;

(c)   *Trade marks* — including *Service marks* — unique motifs or characteristics, logos, brands, names and styles, endorsements;

(d)   *Designs* — physical appearance, packaging;

(e)   *Know-how* — unique knowledge, trade secrets (show-how — empirical experience).

13.4   *Hybrids and composites* — may include goodwill, distribution rights, trade agreements (which in some cases may be illegal) and assembled rights and licences and licensing packages, and not forgetting franchise rights.

Balance sheet values

13.5   There has been very considerable debate over the years concerning the possibility and advisability of valuing and showing intangible assets, particularly brands, as separable items on the owning company's balance sheet. Here is not the place to continue that debate, but it should be remembered that the matter arose in relation to mega-takeovers involving 'mega-bucks' and mega-gearing requirements. A vociferous school of thought believes it makes sense to 'orient' the market for a quoted company's shares by highlighting the intrinsic value of intangible assets that the company owns. It is rather like a company revaluing its real estate for the balance sheet to show the inherent value of the assets that are used in the creation of the company's earnings.

Looked at like that, it does seem to be a reasonable proposition; but a problem is that whereas the value of the company's fixed (tangible) assets (whether or not accurately recorded on the balance sheet) may change significantly without affecting in any way the quality of earnings of the company, a significant real change in the value of brands and intangibles (whether or not accurately recorded on the balance sheet) would indicate a real change in the quality of earnings. Therefore, do these assets sit comfortably side-by-side on the balance sheet? There are different 'types' of brand, some simple in character, others having multiple characteristics and in either case the brand market and marketing factors can further complicate an already complex picture.

13.6   The kernel of the brand accounting question has actually three legs. First, the acquisition of a company having valuable brands may be the acquisition of goodwill for accounting purposes, the treatment of which, whether it is being written-off over 20 years against profits or being written-off against reserves, is not satisfactory to those who believe that the acquired brands are rather more durable than this. Secondly, the 'quoted' share market often does not recognise the supervalue that may lie dormant in a company, and some believe that this weakness in the market for the company's shares needs correcting by highlighting (and maintaining) the brand values in the balance sheet. Thirdly, highly-geared borrowing for corporate acquisition (or protection) purposes needs justification which can sometimes be found in the realisation of 'hidden' asset value. It has been shown that a lack of understanding of the value factors by the senior management of companies which own intellectual property can lead to serious erosion of negotiating power in a takeover or merger, to impotence in resisting unwelcome bids and perhaps at best indicates market or business naiveté. On the other hand, the exploitation of ideas, even of protected rights, can be very expensive indeed. Without a cast-iron certainty that costly investment will be rewarded, who takes that jump into the unknown with an untried idea? 'Ideas are ten-a-penny' and 'Results are the end-game', are connecting epithets that sum up the essential world-view of the intellectual property valuer — and of enlightened management. The issue continues to be debated and the latest development is the publication of Financial Reporting Exposure Draft 12 which addresses the question of accounting for goodwill and intangible assets but does not yet reach a conclusion.

Valuation bases

13.7   Important as it may be, on this occasion we shall not attempt to answer the specific question about where the value of a brand or other intellectual property should be posted except to say that from the valuer's perspective the more accurate and available the information the better it must be. We need also to remind ourselves that we must avoid double counting, and where there is a possibility that a balance sheet carries assets with value that includes some of the capitalised earnings of the company such assets may need to be isolated, depending upon the share valuation basis that is being utilised. As valuers, we are here concerned about the actual value, whether or not it may actually be shown somewhere, and we shall now look at some of the valuation mechanics involved in an exercise to value intellectual property rights. It is rather important to remember that the different valuation bases that may be employed are not mutually exclusive.

The first step will be to identify precisely what is the intellectual property and to classify it and to discover whether it is protected in law or capable of being protected. The second step is to determine its relationship to the company's business activities and whether it is properly separable from the other business assets, whether it is transferable (or divisible) or subject to restrictions in terms of its use. The third step is to determine whether there is earning potential in the exploitation of the asset, the competition in the market, the asset's economic life, and obsolescence factors. The fourth step is to compare the resultant valuation with one determined using a different basis; to cross-check those valuations with any other empirical evidence of value that may exist; and to view the proposed value from the respective positions of proposed seller and actual, or most probable, purchaser.

13.8   Where a company has many different assets, fixed and intangible, which contribute to it's earning capacity it may be helpful, if not necessary, to ensure that earnings are properly allocated or apportioned to the appropriate asset. Obviously a proper understanding of the business and of the company and its management *modus operandi* is necessary.

Development cost basis

13.9   If it is reasonably possible to determine the cost of development of the asset, this might establish a minimum value on the basis that anyone starting from scratch would have to go through the various stages of developing, researching, testing, designing etc., and of legally protecting the asset. There are other aspects too. The possibility of error in development is avoided by acquiring the completed item — thus is saved cost of correction, re-engineering etc. Earnings or profits from exploiting the asset will be achieved sooner and more certainly than if the asset were developed from scratch. Often, intellectual property is derived from the application of other know-how, secret processes and so on.

It will be seen from the foregoing that the base cost may be substantial and very relevant to a current valuation exercise. However, there may have been over-expenditure (there may even have been copyright infringement by the developer); there may be a continuing cost of maintaining or enhancing the legal protection or the asset itself which will be found especially in the case of software or intellectual property rights that are sensitive to legislation or rapid developments in the field, such as in the ethical pharmaceutical industry.

13.10   To say, as was said in the previous paragraph, that there may have been over-expenditure is over-simplistic. Failure of one approach in the development of a product is more the norm than a direct line, without waste or delay, from nothing to something. To say that another party may have achieved the same results at less cost is probably impossible to prove one way or another because of the very nature of research and development; but then, there will be a line drawn at some point because, of course, between the cost and the earnings that are likely to be derived from the product there is a minimum required rate of return on the investment, and therefore some sanity must prevail in the assessment of economic costs of development. Against this, certain costs may have been incurred specifically to earn income that has been derived from the exploitation of the asset and it would not be correct to conclude such 'revenue' expenditure is the base cost of the asset. The costs may have been incurred over a short period or over many years, and some of that cost may have been entitled to tax relief or allowances. It would be equally relevant to consider what the current tax position would be for similar current development costs. The period of development raises the issue of present-day value of past costs, and the required rate of return from those costs to reflect the development/ investment risk. Both of these factors need to be incorporated in the cost basis approach. The further back in time that the development commenced the more difficult it may be to discover and differentiate different types of relevant expenditure.

It may also be that other intellectual property, for example know-how, management expertise or other propriety elements, have been brought into the development processes but do not appear as cost items; other companies in a group may also have contributed, successfully or not, in the process. There is always the possibility that failed technology can make a successful reappearance when applied in a different way or when a further technological or creative advance is made, and therefore a second or third string, or more, may emerge when researching the development history of any intellectual property.

It can therefore be seen that this approach is essentially a cash flow or, more accurately, a cash outflow model, projected for a finite period. It can be most complex and uncertain. Nevertheless, it may be essential to review this area as a valuation cross-check, if not as the prime valuation basis.

Example: development cost basis (all figures £'000s)

	Year-4	Year-3	Year-2	Year-1	Year-0	Total
Gross costs	400	900	1,300	1,900	1,100	5,600
Tax relief (1)	(100)	(270)	(429)	(495)	(363)	(1,657)
Net costs (1)	300	630	871	1,405	737	3,943
Inflation rate (2)	10.8%	7.0%	5.6%	3.2%		
Indexed costs (2)	332.4	674.1	919.8	1,450	737	4,113.3
Required return (3)	12%	15%	10%	8%	8%	
∴ return factor (3)	1.66	1.48	1.28	1.17	1.08	
Adjusted costs (4)	551.8	997.7	1,177.3	1,696.5	796	5,219.3

Notes:

(1)   The real cost of development of property that is to be commercially exploited will usually be the cost net of tax relief, such that is available of course. Some expenditure may be eligible for immediate tax relief, some not at all, and some relief may be restricted or deferred. It is a

moot point whether account should be taken of the actual relief obtained or future relief that would be available to, or other tax consequences for, an intending purchaser who would alternatively develop the product independently. In international situations, this matter may be more acute.

(2)   The costs borne over the years of development must be reflected at current prices at the time of valuation, hence the present-day value is determined by reference to the retail price index.

(3)   The required rate of return (see 4.46) is necessary to provide the developer a minimum risk return that would have been available to him had he placed the development funds in some alternative, safer, investment medium, or used the money in other ways in the business of the company. In the latter case, the rate of return may be the net return on assets that the company was currently earning at the time the expenditure was incurred, assuming that the business then had the capacity to absorb productively the available investment funds. Whichever approach is appropriate to the case, this rate of return may vary year by year.

(4)   In determining a realistic hypothetical cost of development to an intending purchaser, it may also be appropriate to reflect to some extent the loss of the earnings that would have been derived from the product if it was purchased at the beginning of, and actively exploited during, the purchaser's hypothetical development period. The sum of the costs and loss of earnings is the real alternative cost to an outright acquisition of the developed product.

Product intrinsic value

13.11   The result of the above valuation exercise gives the cost of development; it may have little to do with earnings potential and may be best described as a cash outflow model. Of course, at some time during the development period or at the end of it there is a product that has some value and possibly some on-going maintenance liability.

The earliest time that the product will have value will be the moment someone else is prepared to pay to acquire it, whatever its state of completion may be and notwithstanding that continuing development costs may or will be incurred. It might be helpful in a valuation exercise to know when this intrinsic value first arose — if it was at an early stage this might suggest that the likely purchasers were willing to take on the apparent risk of development, whereas if it arose only after development was completed, this may indicate that the development risk was great. In turn, this may help identify the required rate of return for the risk capital. It may not determine actual current value because interest in the product under development may simply have been the result of an industry-wide knowledge of its development, and other products may have been equally the subject of interest; on the other hand a knowledge of the history of interest shown in such a product by potential purchasers may help greatly in assessing the current market value.

Open market value basis

13.12   The prime basis of valuation will be the open market value. Obviously, a knowledge of the market is needed. This is likely to be rather specialist knowledge and is intrinsically connected with the detail of the intellectual property, and with experience of comparative values, prices etc. The standard basis of valuation of an income or earnings stream is the capitalisation of maintainable future earnings calculated partly from historic earnings and projected forward.

13.13   The alternative basis is the discounted cash flow basis (see 8.4). Whichever method is adopted, some authorities suggest that the value calculation does not necessarily end with the capitalised value of the earnings, because some possible purchasers might be prepared to pay a premium representing something less than the cost the purchaser would have to incur to develop a successful brand competitor. If the proper capitalisation factor has been used in the determination of the capitalised earnings, adding a premium for development costs is really double counting, and this additional element must be looked at with some caution; but the valuer is not there to prevent the open market operating and if such a premium is a real possibility, it should not be ignored.

There are two principal scenarios. The first is a straight (or even a complex) direct sale of intellectual property by a company to a purchaser of that property; the second is a sale or an exchange of shares in a company owning intellectual property. The market places may be different. In the first case, it is largely a matter of identifying comparative arm's length prices for similar property, by reference to a detailed knowledge of the specific end product or use. These prices tend not to be very public, and some 'inside' knowledge and experience of arm's length prices will usually be necessary to estimate the price at which some specific property might change hands.

The second scenario, a company acquisition or merger, is quite different in a technical sense. The various valuation techniques explained elsewhere in this book deal with the fundamental approach and will, in most cases, provide a correct answer. However, whenever intellectual property is included in a company's assets, care should be taken to identify the proper earnings or earnings potential (that is evidential potential rather than imagined potential) derived from that property, the treatment of development and maintenance costs and, as might be the case with other assets on the balance sheet, whether the intellectual property has an alternative use value or whether it stands to one side of the actual earnings from the business and thereby constitutes a separable asset.

13.14   Where the company is actually driven by its intellectual property, such as a major brand company, it should be valued in a wider sense than looking at the *status quo* (the *status quo* being the known earnings and those expected to be generated from the current business practices and proven success without regard to external matters such as the motives or management expertise of the most likely purchaser). The valuation should have regard also to matters such as whether the acquisition would carry with it a significant impact on market share, management expertise, or critical sales volume or production capacity, or other aspects of competitive advantage that an acquisition would bestow upon the purchaser. There are many public transactions of substantial size which will assist in this analysis.

Earnings basis

13.15   The third basis of valuation — where there are no comparatives available — will be an earnings basis valuation by reference to assumed economic and financial data, or factual historic financial data. Here, we are looking at an earnings basis (see Chapter 5) which may be a discounted cash flow basis (see 8.4) if the character of the earnings is such that it is not possible to identify a reliable industry or sector related PER with which to capitalise the expected future maintainable earnings. If the earnings from the intellectual property are most likely to be absorbed into a similar earning stream of a company whose earnings can be judged by reference to a published PER, then it may be appropriate to apply that PER to the intellectual property. Care must be taken to compare like with like.

13.16   An important factor to have in mind with intellectual property is its life. There may be a legal lifetime on the one hand (perhaps renewable) and a useful lifetime on the other, whether shorter or longer than the legal lifetime, and which may or may not be accurately ascertainable at the time of the valuation. It may have a 'shelf life' based on unfolding technology, and it may be in need of regular upgrading or servicing, advertising and management. There may also be a 'fad' or fashion life as may be particularly the case for newly developed 'simple' brands (and this may be part of an 'umbrella' brand strategy, where, for example, a major 'household name' producer brings into the market a newly branded product aimed to exploit a market created by, say, a recently successful film about dinosaurs). A related issue here is one of geography. Because the market for intellectual property is global, the question of durability and life takes on a global perspective, as does the vexed question of effective legal protection in foreign markets.

13.17   The same considerations apply here as apply in respect of the open market value basis (see above) in so far as it may be appropriate to consider the 'external' issue of competitive advantage to the acquirer and the impact that could have on the value derived by mathematical formulae based on *status quo* earnings.

Royalty basis

13.18   A fourth basis of valuation is a deemed royalty basis. For this, the factors required are a royalty by reference to annual unit sales or turnover, a licensing period, a net present value discount rate and a residual value. There are several uncertainties contained in this formula, also it really is necessary to use comparable arm's length royalties and to understand the nature of the intellectual property. It may be possible to construct such a model by reference to past actual royalties and circumstances and to capitalise the net royalties by a factor such as years' purchase; alternatively, a discounted cash flow model would be used, but it has to be said that without real comparatives this value would lack empirical evidence to support it.

13.19   In terms of valuing a pure income stream over a period of years, the cash flow model is probably the best method available. It seems to work relatively efficiently for simple income streams, whereas for valuing a complex business it becomes cumbersome and subjective. However, if the cash flow period used in the model is not co-terminous with the actual cash flow and a residual value has to be determined to take account of subsequent years' cash flow, the cash flow model begins to creak! Where there is no termination of the cash flow in prospect, the cash flow model may be taken to infinity, or rather to an approximation of infinity over a number of years which will depend upon the actual amount of cash flowing.

For most purposes, a period of 25 to 30 years will reduce present day values to a very small percentage of the future earnings (obviously depending upon the discount rate), but if this small percentage still represents a significant amount of cash in today's terms, the cash flow period will be extended further. The discounted cash flow methodology is described at 8.4. The model requires the following elements:

(*a*)   a financial source for the royalties over a given period (see below) into the future: whether a third party's gross turnover or a royalty price per unit sold, or a royalty rate per unit sold at an estimated price per unit;

(*b*)   the gross royalties receivable in each of the years in the given period;

(*c*)   expenditure wholly necessary for the maintenance of the intellectual property throughout the given period;

(*d*)   the net royalties arising;

(*e*)   tax chargeable on the net royalties;

(*f*)   royalties net of tax;

(*g*)   net present value discount factor to give a present day value to the future annual earnings over the given period, by reference to assumed inflation year by year over that period;

(*h*)   if it cannot be avoided, a residual value (see below) for the royalty flow at the end of the given period, discounted to the net present value.

The given period for the annual royalty flow should be the actual licence period or at least five years, but more importantly, should be accurate (which may not be easy to achieve). As mentioned above, a cash flow period into an approximation of infinity is better than having a compromise residual value.

The residual value is basically the estimated future value of the continuing right at the end of the given period to receive the perceived royalties. It is a multiple of the final year's royalty in the given period. An assumption has to be made that that level of royalties will continue for a further period of years. This period may be a further ten or whatever years, depending upon the rights, the property, knowledge of the market, the financing possibilities, etc. This residual value will be discounted at the same discount factor as the final year in the given period.

The net present value of the royalty flow is the sum of the discounted annual royalty earnings plus the discounted residual value.

Brand valuation (brand contribution basis)

13.20   The essence of brand valuation is to identify the supervalue that has been generated by the successful management and exploitation of the particular brand. This supervalue is the value that exists over and above the value of a notional unbranded product that enjoys all the attributes of the branded product other than the brand name. Different products may require different factors to be brought into the equation, for example point-of-sale control is becoming a vital issue for consumer goods with the powerful retailing companies extending their own brand retail names into a widening range of goods sold on their premises and manufacturer's own brand names are battling against these new competitors. Some of the warning signs in brand valuation are: if the branded products prices are more than 30% above the retailer's own-label products, or there are products of equal quality available at a lower price, or the price of the product has risen faster than inflation over recent years, or more than 70% of the branded products are sold through supermarket and similar outlets, and if the cost of essential advertising of the branded product is less than 10% of the sales. There may be perfectly satisfactory answers to these questions. The basic bases of valuation have been explained above.

The supervalue sought will be net of operating costs and tax. The accuracy of the methodology in practice is wholly dependent upon the quality of the available information and of the analytical power applied to the information. The exercise will be more subjective than is found in a straightforward valuation of a single piece of tangible equipment or even of shares, because it will generally be found that costs and especially management input can be divided up amongst several earning streams, some of which may be inter-dependent. The brand contribution basis may:

(a)   compare the branded product price with the price for sales of an unbranded but otherwise similar product, thereby identifying the premium price available in respect of the particular brand;

(b)   look at the usual prices charged for comparable but unbranded products, to determine a base to which the additional brand costs and profit margin can be added; or (*c*)   compare rates of return or profits derived from similar businesses that do not exploit brands.

In all cases the valuer must be awake to the contribution to the equation of any special distribution rights and facilities or constraints. Through these methodologies it should be possible to model gross earnings, which will be subject to specific costs, such as brand maintenance costs, advertising and special distribution agreement costs, marketing and research costs, and related executive and legal costs. Some of the factors to be considered in the valuation of a brand are:

- past performance;
- market share;
- market movement;
- current and prospective competition;
- vulnerability to fashion and trend;
- external regulation and restrictions;
- support and distribution requirements;
- outlet dependency;
- advertising and marketing dependency;
- research and development dependency;
- alternative use and annexe and competition value;
- know-how and development costs;
- trade mark, patent and copyright protection;
- current income and gross and net margins;
- manufacturing requirements;
- production and supply dependency;
- likely purchasers.

Internal licensing

13.21   By virtue of advance pricing arrangements with certain national tax authorities under their transfer pricing regulations, prices (such as royalty rates, charges for know-how or software support and development) for internal licensing purposes within a multinational group of companies may already have been determined by reference to arm's length comparable prices and values. The US, Japan and Australia are examples of countries having such arrangements (which are not voluntary!). These prices may be of some assistance in the process of valuing the underlying intellectual property, but probably equally important is the functionality test that should have been undertaken as part of the process of determining the arm's length price, for that test would identify where and what the various elements are which generate the ultimate earnings from the exploitation of the property in question.

Internal licensing is both an important commercial tool in directing the proper management objectives of a multinational group, and a facility to identify the proper taxing jurisdiction, the location of risk and reward and, ultimately, the amount of taxation arising from the individual parts of a multinational's disparate activities. Needless to say, these matters may have some bearing on the valuer's process, though they should not be allowed to dictate the outcome. Depending upon the circumstances, the internal licensing practices may be another source of confirmation or reference for the purposes of determining the value of any intellectual property.

The foregoing matters are part of the larger question of transfer pricing, a fuller treatment of which can be found in Chapter 14.

UK Transfer Pricing Rules

Introduction – the arm's length test

14.1   The UK transfer pricing rules enable the Inland Revenue to adjust for tax purposes an inter-company price which is charged between related business parties (one of which will usually be resident in another country) in situations where the inter-company price does not closely approximate the price that would be charged between parties dealing at arm's length.

In other countries the national tax authorities have their own, not necessarily similar, transfer pricing rules and regulations and practices and the interaction of these sets of rules and practices has become of major if not fundamental importance to any business operating across borders through the medium of controlled related entities.

The subject is naturally of particular importance to multinational groups of companies but it is also of relevance to any business that trades or invests in another country through a controlled party, whether a subsidiary or associated company or joint-venture vehicle, a branch office or other permanent establishment or dependent agent, or a partnership. Transfer pricing rules and practices of the UK and of the other country may apply even (or, perhaps particularly) where there is no actual or real economic activity carried out by one of the transacting parties. The UK Inland Revenue is now more positively addressing the difficult matter of transfer pricing practices and administration, particularly clearances to taxpayers, examination of transfer pricing issues and settlement of negotiations.

14.2   The OECD (see 14.24) has been most active in trying to bring order and consistency into the matter by studying the practices and approaches of different revenue authorities, identifying essential elements in the transfer pricing field and recommending standard approaches to resolving the problems that arise for taxpayers on the one hand and tax authorities on the other. These matters are all 'on-going'. Meanwhile, businesses of all shapes and sizes have no alternative but to gird themselves to battle with the inevitable complexities and intrusions into time and business practices that the respective country's approaches create. On the other hand, this is not an 'emerging' matter; many countries have sophisticated transfer pricing rules and plenty of experience in handling simple and complex cases. In particular, the United States has a complete and substantial code dealing with law and practice, and non-compliance can lead to very serious and costly difficulties — not just for US companies.

Advance pricing arrangements

14.3   The fundamental question for any group company potentially exposed to transfer pricing rules internationally is whether to seek to conclude an advance pricing agreement (APA) with the tax authorities, and indeed whether this should be a bilateral or trilateral agreement with other countries involved with the same transactions of the company. To reach agreement on this basis means that the company can carry on its inter-company pricing policy secure in the knowledge that there will not be subsequent enquiries and changes to its prices and that its tax position will be 'relatively' secure. APA procedures are not simple and there is certainly no guarantee that they will recognise current practices of the company as being satisfactory, indeed it is probably guaranteed that changes in such practices would have to be made for the tax authorities to agree an APA; nevertheless the transfer pricing compliance requirements in some countries, and particularly in the US, will drive companies into seeking them. There is currently no APA procedure in the UK.

The statutory rules

14.4   The UK transfer pricing rules are contained in *TA 1988, Sch 28AA* for accounting periods and years of assessment ending after 1 July 1999 (the commencement day for the company self-assessment rules). Prior to this the applicable rules are contained in *Part XVII of ICTA 1988*, principally *sections 770, 772* and *773*. All these provisions may be overridden by applicable articles of double tax treaties (see 14.12).

There are some definite technical differences between the old and the new transfer pricing charging provisions. The new rules include a requirement that the offensive practice confers a potential tax advantage whereas the old rules do not rely on any motive test. Also, the old *section 770* rules were not automatic but required a direction from the Board before the section could be invoked. The European Union Arbitration Convention requires the Board formally to inform the taxpayer of its intention to make a transfer pricing adjustment. If one party to a transaction is an oil and petroleum company or carries on a petroleum related ring-fence trade old *section 771* or *Schedule 28AA, paras 9–11* will be applicable.

The basic provisions

Schedule 28AA

14.5   For the new rules to apply in ordinary circumstances, *para 1* requires that:

(*a*)   provision which is different from what would have been made between independent enterprises has been made *or imposed* by means of a transaction or series of transactions;

(*b*)   as between any two persons, one of whom was at that time directly or indirectly participating in the management, control or capital of each;

(*c*)   and, a potential UK tax advantage is thereby conferred on one or both of them.

The consequence is that the profits and losses of those persons is computed for tax purposes as if the arm's length provision rather than the actual provision had been made.

Where the matter is subject to tax treaty override and the tax treaty in question incorporates OECD Model Tax Convention, Article 9 (associated enterprises) provisions (those as at 9 February 1988), the new, *Schedule 28AA* rules are to be construed in accordance with the OECD transfer pricing guidelines.

'Transaction' includes arrangements, understandings and mutual practices (legally enforceable or not). A 'series of transactions', appears to mean almost anything. 'Participation in the management, control or capital of a person' is very wide, catching direct control participation in a company or partnership, participation through a joint 40%+ interest in the company or partnership, and participation by the assumption of attributable future rights and powers, and rights and powers of nominees or connected persons.

The rules do not apply to foreign exchange gains and losses and financial instruments which are covered by separate legislation. Petroleum companies and petroleum industry ring-fenced traders have their own rules.

Where a party suffers a transfer pricing adjustment and the other party is a UK taxpayer that party may claim a corresponding adjustment — within two years of the filing of a tax return which includes the adjustment or the date of the notice of adjustment given to the first party.

Sections 770 and 773

14.6   *Sections 770* and *773* apply in the following circumstances:

(*a*)   where there are sales, lettings and hiring of property, grants and transfers of rights, interests or licences, or the giving of business facilities of whatever kind; and

(*b*)   the buyer controls the seller, or vice versa, or they are both under common control, and the actual price paid for the property is either:

- less than the arm's length price (i.e. the price it might have been expected to fetch if the parties to the transaction had been independent persons dealing at arm's length); or

- is greater than the arm's length price.

The giving of business facilities of any kind is regarded by the Inland Revenue as having a very wide application and encompasses the giving of credit or guarantees, loan interest, management fees and many other types of 'business facility' (Inland Revenue Press Release, 26 January 1981).

If *section 770* is applied, an arm's length price is substituted for the actual price in computing income, profits or losses for income tax or corporation tax purposes of the seller if he sold for less than arm's length price, and of the buyer if the price he paid was greater. The sale is deemed to take place at the earlier of the time of completion of the sale or transaction or when possession is given.

A pricing adjustment will not take place if a UK resident trader buys at an undervalue and brings that cost into his trading accounts; or if a UK resident trader sells at an overvalue and brings that receipt into his trading accounts. This provision removes from the section most controlled price transactions taking place within the UK unless one of the parties to the transaction is a petroleum company (see below).

For *section 770* there must be control by the seller over the buyer, or vice versa, or they must both be under common control. For this purpose control is defined in *section 840* as a person's power to secure through a shareholding or voting power that the affairs of a body corporate are conducted in accordance with the wishes of that person. Connected parties, under *section 839*, will be taken into account. For a partnership control is the right to more than one-half of the partnership assets or income.

Transactions with a petroleum company

14.7   Special provisions apply under both the old and new legislation to deal with transfer pricing practices between companies engaged in the oil business and related parties. Such companies include oil traders, importers and exporters, refiners and processors of crude oil, and petroleum extractors, and oil shippers and oil pipeline companies if under common control.

Enquiry powers

14.8   Under *Schedule 28AA*, the information disclosure rules of company self-assessment will apply and Inland Revenue enquiry powers will follow under those provisions. The onus is therefore placed squarely on the shoulders of the taxpayer to have transfer pricing values correctly shown in the self-assessment tax return.

Transfer pricing adjustments under *section 770* are made consequent upon a direction from the Board and for this purpose the Board have power under *section 772* to require details of a broad range of relevant transactions.

Controlled foreign companies are subject to the enquiry powers of *ICTA 1988, s 755* which gives the Board power to require company and accounting information concerning a foreign subsidiary.

OECD — A Code of Good Practice

14.9 An OECD code governs exchange of information relating to multinational enterprises between competent authorities under the double taxation treaties between France, Germany, the United States and the UK. The information exchanges are (1) upon request in relation to formal tax enquiries being carried out by one country, and (2) spontaneous exchanges where one country considers information would be useful to the tax authorities in another country.

EU — Mutual Assistance Directive

14.10 Provision is made by the EU Mutual Assistance Convention (EU Directive 77/799) for exchange of information between competent authorities of Member States to combat tax evasion and tax avoidance, including VAT. The Directive empowers unilateral disclosure of information, 'in particular where there appears to be an artificial transfer of profits between enterprises in different Member States or where such transactions are carried out between enterprises in two Member States through a third country in order to obtain tax advantages, or where tax has been or may be evaded or avoided'. The Directive also lays down criteria which, if met, require *spontaneous* disclosure of information to be made by one tax authority to another.

Under *FA 1978, s 77*, no information may be disclosed by the UK tax authorities except for tax purposes and unless they are satisfied that the competent authorities of the other State are bound by rules of confidentiality which are not less strict than UK rules.

The UK Inland Revenue practice on the operation of the mutual agreement procedure and the manner in which claims under the relevant article in the UK's tax treaties are handled, with particular reference to transfer pricing and multinational enterprises, is set out at page 346 of issue 25 of the Inland Revenue's *Tax Bulletin, issue 25, October 1996*. These guidelines include consideration of secondary corresponding adjustments, and advance pricing agreements.

EU Arbitration Convention

14.11 This Convention (EU Directive 90/436) establishes the approach that will be followed to resolve transfer pricing double taxation arising within the EU. The Convention applies if the same profits (or losses) are included or are likely to be included in the profits (or losses) of associated enterprises (including permanent establishments) in more than one contracting state by virtue of incompatible pricing adjustments made by different taxing authorities. The Convention came into force for proceedings commenced after 31 December 1994 and will remain in force until the year 2000. The Convention requires notification to be given by a taxing authority of an intention to adjust prices in such a way that the other parties and tax authorities can be advised in good time and that the mutual agreement and arbitration procedures may be implemented (within three years of first notification), and it sets out the appeal procedures.

Double taxation treaties

Introduction

14.12 Double taxation treaties deal with several matters that relate specifically to transfer pricing. The relevant articles in the OECD Model Double Taxation Convention are:

- (Article 7) profit-allocation methods in the business profits article;

- (Article 9) associated enterprises article;

- (Articles 11 and 12) 'special relationship' clauses in the interest and the royalties articles);

- (see also *ICTA 1988, s 808A* for the application of 'special relationship' rules in relation to payments of interest);

- (Article 25) mutual agreement procedure;

- (Article 26) exchange of information and administrative assistance article;

- special industry related articles.

Not all bilateral double tax treaties use the same article numbers in addressing the foregoing particular subject matters.

Business profits — Article 7

14.13 Under paragraph 2 of this Article each State must attribute to the taxable permanent establishment 'the profits which it might be expected to make if it were a distinct and separate enterprise engaged in the same or similar activities under the same or similar conditions and dealing wholly independently with the enterprise of which it is a permanent establishment'. The OECD commentary emphasises that this paragraph is not justification for tax administrations to construct hypothetical profit figures *in vacuua*. The general rule put forward is that the profits attributed to a permanent establishment should be based on the establishment's accounts if they represent the real facts of the situation otherwise adjustments to the profit figures may be necessary to recognise the arm's length principle. In relation to intellectual property the OECD suggests that the costs of creation of the rights might be attributed without mark-ups to all parts of the enterprise including permanent establishments who are users of them.

Associated enterprises — Article 9

14.14   This Article allows the competent authorities to adjust the profits of the enterprise that is resident in their State:

(*a*)   where an enterprise of one State participates directly or indirectly in the management control or capital of an enterprise of another State, or

(*b*)   the same persons participate in the management control or capital of an enterprise of the other State, and

(*c*)   non-arm's-length conditions are made between the enterprises.

No re-writing of the accounts of associated enterprises is authorised if the transactions between them have taken place on an arm's length basis.

Interest and royalties: special relationship clauses — Articles 11 and 12

14.15   Article 11 allows interest to be taxable in the country in which the recipient resides and also in the country where the interest arises: in the latter case at a maximum rate of 10%. Article 12 allows royalties to be taxed only in the country in which the 'beneficial' recipient resides.

14.16   In relation to interest the tax authorities may adjust the amount of interest paid if a special relationship exists and arm's length prices are absent. The UK has reserved its right to use in its tax treaties its preferred wording in substitution for the OECD wording. The UK wording (encompassed in *ICTA 1988, s 808A*) is intended to make the special relationship clause contemplate all factors; excessive interest rates and also unrealistic terms and an excessive amount of loan are all to be taken into account, even to the extent that should they be non-arm's length, the loan may be regarded as not viable in the real world and accordingly dismissed. For all UK tax treaties, *section 808A(3)* puts a burden on the taxpayer to show that there is no special relationship or show the amount of interest which would have been paid in the absence of the special relationship.

14.17   As to royalties the tax authorities may adjust the amount of royalties paid where a special relationship exists and arm's length prices are absent. The special relationship clause is almost identical to that in the interest Article, but there is no *section 808A* equivalent.

Mutual agreement procedure — Article 25

14.18   A taxpayer may initiate the mutual agreement procedure within three years of the first notification of the action resulting in the disputed taxation, i.e. the taxation that is not in accordance with the provisions of the Convention. This may particularly include a mis-match of tax arising from the implementation of Article 9. The mutual agreement procedure requires the competent authorities to negotiate but there is no requirement to reach agreement or work within a timescale.

Exchange of information — Article 26

14.19   The competent authorities of the contracting States are required to exchange such information as is necessary to carry out the Convention or the domestic laws of the contracting States concerning taxes covered by the Convention. Information can be exchanged.

(*a*)   on request, in relation to a specific case;

(*b*)   systematically to the other State;

(*c*)   spontaneously, where information is thought to be of interest to the other State.

Indirect tax rules

Introduction

14.20   Value added tax and customs duties may apply on importation, manufacture or processing and frequently, a company's transfer pricing policy will conflict with *direct* taxation considerations or with *indirect* taxes, and sometimes the transfer pricing and valuation rules of these respective taxes will conflict with each other.

Customs valuation

14.21   Customs authorities now apply valuation methods which are analogous to direct tax transfer pricing methods and co-operation between direct tax and customs authorities is growing. Customs duties valuations (which also apply for VAT purposes) are regulated by the General Agreement on Tariffs and Trade (GATT) valuation Code which is based on the commercial value of imported goods. This is largely in accordance with OECD transfer pricing rules, but it should not be taken for granted that a customs valuation will accord with an Inland Revenue value.

The GATT customs valuation basis will not automatically take the price paid as being the dutiable amount if that price is determined by related parties — the definition of related for these purposes is very much wider than for direct tax purposes. Typically an importer will declare (and duly evidence) for custom's purposes the manufacturer's price for goods where he has acquired the goods from an intermediary who has not processed or handled the goods except as middle-man. This will not automatically follow where the parties are related.

Customs valuation will be based on prices paid for identical or similar goods in transactions between unconnected parties, or actual customs valuations of such goods. Customs require the price to conform with industry pricing norms, and to be arm's length and commercial or to accord with one of the acceptable methods of valuation.

14.22   Certain additional costs or ascertainable value may be required to be included in the dutiable amount of the goods, such as:

(*a*)   freight and handling charges,

(*b*)   insurance, brokerage fees and commission,

(*c*)   packaging and containers,

(*d*)   intangibles,

    (i)   royalties and licence fees for trademarks, patents etc. related to the goods (if part of the conditions of sale);

    (ii)   technical services (including engineering and development costs) provided before importation;

    (iii)   interest (but not commercial purchasing financing);

    (iv)   software (includes the carrying medium and the program);

    (v)   distribution rights;

    (vi)   other payments to the seller such as from the resale of the goods by the buyer.

Other costs may be included in a price for the goods. These may not actually be required to be included for customs valuation purposes but being included would fall to be assessed for duty. 'Unbundling' is the exercise of removing from the price all elements that are not required for customs valuation purposes and is an important element in any pricing exercise to minimise duties whether or not for transfer pricing purposes.

Valuation for VAT

14.23   For VAT on imports from a place outside the EU, the value is that determined in accordance with customs rules plus all taxes, duties and other charges levied outside the UK; all UK import taxes and charges (other than VAT); and all costs of commission, packing, transport and insurance to the port or place of importation. The value may be reduced by prompt payment discount (*Value Added Tax Act 1994, s 21*).

The value of goods from another EU Member State is the value of the transaction under which the goods were acquired.

A transaction for a consideration in money is valued at the amount of the consideration. If that is less than the open market value, and the supplier and the acquirer are connected, and the person who acquires the goods is not entitled to credit for all the VAT on the acquisition, an open market value may be imposed (*Value Added Tax Act 1994, 6 Sch 1; 7A Sch 1(4)*). A transaction for a consideration including something other than money is valued at such amount in money as is equivalent to the consideration. The value of a transaction for no consideration is:

(*a*) the consideration in money that would be payable by the supplier if, at the time of the acquisition, he were to purchase goods identical in every respect, including age and condition, to the goods concerned;

(*b*) the consideration in money that would be payable by the supplier if, at the time of acquisition, he were to purchase goods similar to the goods concerned and of the same age and condition (if the value cannot be ascertained in accordance with (*a*)); or

(*c*) the cost of producing the goods concerned at the time of acquisition (if the value cannot be ascertained in accordance with (*a*) or (*b*)) (*Value Added Tax Act 1994, s 20; 6 Sch 6; 7 Sch 3*).

Excise duty charged on the goods and any EC customs duty or agricultural levy to which the goods are subject, may also have to be included in the value (*Value Added Tax Act 1994, 7 Sch 2*).

The OECD Guidelines for Multinational Enterprises

Introduction

14.24 The Committee on Fiscal Affairs of the Organisation for Economic Cooperation and Development (OECD) has produced a number of important Transfer Pricing Reports including the '1979 Report on Transfer Pricing and Multinational Enterprises', and three 1984 Reports: 'Transfer Pricing, Corresponding Adjustments and the Mutual Agreement Procedure'; 'The Taxation of Multinational Banking Enterprises'; and 'The Allocation of Central Management and Service Costs'. The latest Report commenced to be issued in draft form in 1994 and throughout this chapter it is referred to as the 1994 Report, although parts of the Report are being issued over time. Its published title is 'OECD Transfer Pricing Guidelines for Multinational Enterprises and Tax Administrations', and it updates the 1979 and 1984 Reports. This Report comprises Part I (Principles and Methods), Part II (Applications) which includes Intangible Property, Services, Mutual Agreement Procedures, Simultaneous Examination, Safe Harbours, Advance Transfer Pricing Agreements and Arbitration; and Part III dealing with Permanent Establishments, Thin Capitalisation and Cost Sharing. The basic point of reference throughout transfer pricing is the *arm's length price*.

Transfer pricing methods

14.25 The OECD identifies a number of generally acceptable methods for determining an arm's length price. The principal methodologies are based on a comparison between the controlled transaction and comparable transactions between independent enterprises. The 1994 Report identifies the methodologies as transaction-based methods and profit methods.

Transaction-based methods

14.26 The three transaction-based methods for determining arm's length prices are: the comparable uncontrolled prices method (CUP), the resale price method, and the cost plus method. For each of these methods a third party transaction is comparable to a controlled transaction if either:

(*a*) there are no differences between the transactions being compared or between the enterprises undertaking those transactions that could materially affect the price in the open market; or

(*b*) there are differences but adjustments can be made to eliminate their effect: the 1994 Report emphasises that a flexible approach should be taken to enable the CUP method to be used and to be supplemented by other methods according to their particular accuracy.

The comparable uncontrolled prices method

14.27 This is the method favoured by the OECD. In the right circumstances this can be the easiest and the most decisive method to use as it is a direct reference to third party prices in comparable transactions. Unfortunately, this information often cannot be easily obtained by ordinary businesses. Tax authorities may be able to identify such prices from the commercial information they receive but it may be difficult for proof of comparability of these prices to be provided to the taxpayer because of requirements of confidentiality. The transactions must be comparable and important comparability factors are:

- time and place of supply;
- physical features;
- quality and reliability;
- availability of product;
- shelf-life;
- volume of sales;
- transport costs;
- delivery terms and speed;
- packaging and insurance;
- brand name and advertising;
- market characteristics;
- terms of payment or other financial arrangements;
- auxiliary services (guarantees, transfer of technology, technical support, support hardware, etc.);
- condition (whether subject to processing, labelling, assembly, checking etc.).

An adjustment to eliminate differences between prices that are being compared can only be made in respect of *measurable* differences in the comparability factors.

The CUP may be identified by reference to third party sales made by or to the taxpayer company in question or of an associated enterprise.

Resale price method

14.28 The resale price method identifies the arm's length price for a sale between related parties as the price for which the reseller sells on to a third party buyer, less the resellers mark-up (the gross margin on net sales). This mark-up will be derived from the following factors appropriate to the resellers functions:

(*a*)   any added-value;

(*b*)   ancillary services or guarantees;

(*c*)   risk;

(*d*)   costs such as marketing, advertising, testing, financing, distribution;

(*e*)   the original cost of the goods (and of any ancillary goods or services) to the reseller;

(*f*)   exclusivity or distribution etc. rights.

The reseller's functions and responsibilities from acquisition to disposal require analysing to underpin the profit element.

So far as possible, the mark-up should be derived from comparable transactions between third parties or between the reseller and third parties, and be adjusted to take account of measurable differences between the actual transaction and the comparable transaction(s).

Cost plus method

14.29 If no open market for the goods or services exists and they are not supplied to third parties, as is often the case in transfers of technology or semi-finished products, the arm's length price should be determined by adding a mark-up to the cost of production.

Profit methods

14.30 Where the transaction-based transfer pricing methods are unworkable because data is inadequate, an alternative method or methods, must be considered. Profit methods look at the transfer pricing issue at the bottom end of the comparable transaction — namely the profits that arise from the transaction — and work upwards from there to determine the acceptability of the controlled price.

The profit-split method

14.31 The profit-split method looks at the allocation of the profit for the whole transaction from start to finish on an arm's length basis between the associated enterprises involved: however, a sensible allocation may only be achievable in simple short-length transactions or in industries where all facets of operations are standard and well known. The method first requires the profit to be identified, and then for it to be split between the enterprises upon some economically valid approximation of profit division according to the contribution of each enterprise arising from the function of each. Values related to functional analysis should be determined according to available external data, such as, profit-split percentages between independent enterprises carrying on similar functions.

The 1994 Report says that tax administration must acknowledge that in the arrangements for controlled transactions associated enterprises could not be said to know what the profit result would be, because independent enterprises in similar circumstances could only have relied upon projections.

14.32 Two approaches for estimating the division of profits are contribution analysis, and residual analysis.

14.33 Under *contribution analysis* the total operating profits from the controlled transactions are divided between the associated enterprises according to the relative value of the functions performed by each. External market data is needed to identify how independent enterprises would divide profits in similar circumstances. A valuation of the contribution by each enterprise might be made by comparing the nature and degree of the contribution and assigning a relative percentage to each contribution, supported by any available external market data.

14.34 The *residual analysis* approach divides the combined profit in stages. In the first stage, each related enterprise is allocated a profit as a basic return for the transactions in which it is engaged. This is determined by reference to the returns achieved for comparable third party transactions. The second stage looks at the residual profit (or loss), which is allocated to the parties as though they were independent enterprises. Matters such as intangible property and relative bargaining positions would have a bearing. The return earned by each of the participants should be the lowest price that an independent seller would accept and the highest price that the buyer would be willing to pay. The OECD Report suggests that as part of a residual profit split a discounted cash flow approach (see Chapter 8) might be appropriate looking at the anticipated life of the business.

Transactional net margin method; comparable profits method

14.35 The transactional net margin method (TNMM) identifies the net profit margin, adopting an appropriate financial ratio such as net profits on sales, that is realised from the controlled transaction, and this margin is compared with the net profits that might be expected to arise from a comparable uncontrolled transaction. The comparable profits method (CPM) also considers the level of profits resulting from a controlled transaction by reference to financial ratios, but there may be other approaches that are less analytical and these would not be endorsed by the OECD. One of the problems in looking at operating profits, as such, is that they can be influenced by factors that have no affect on prices or gross margins. A functional analysis will be necessary to apply these methods.

'Global' methods

14.36   There is a category of transfer pricing valuation methods known as 'global' methods which are not endorsed by the OECD and are classified as arbitrary, and contrary to the OECD Model Double Taxation Convention. These methods may allocate profits by reference to the respective costs or turnover or labour force, etc. of related enterprises, or may fix transfer prices by reference to pre-determined formulae for allocating profits between related enterprises. Concern is expressed by the OECD about methods that create an 'intolerable administrative burden' on a multinational enterprise and particularly complex analysis of the different functions of the various associated enterprises.

The arm's length price

The arm's length price range

14.37   The 1994 Report recognises that an appropriate transfer price method can produce a range of equally reliable figures and that therefore the determination of the arm's length price requires the exercise of good judgement. The use of a range of prices may be appropriate where the *comparable profits* method is applied. A range of prices may also result where more than one method is being applied to evaluate a controlled transaction.

Underlying realities

14.38   Although tax authorities should determine arm's length prices on actual transactions there may be instances where the form of the transaction has to be ignored. For example, interest on a loan may in reality be a disguised dividend. The 1994 Report emphasises two circumstances where a tax administration may disregard the form or structure of a controlled transaction. One, where the economic substance of a transaction differs from the form of the transaction. Two, where viewed in their totality the arrangements made in relation to the transaction differ from what would have been adopted by independent enterprises and the structure impedes the determination of an appropriate transfer price.

Associated enterprises make a greater variety of contracts and arrangements than unrelated enterprises do because of the absence of conflict of interest. Cost-contribution arrangements for research and development expenditure are a case in point. Contracts between associated enterprises can be altered or terminated according to the overall strategy of the multinational enterprise, and in such cases the tax authorities have to determine what the underlying reality is in order to establish an arm's length price. This may require an evaluation of linked transactions rather than looking on a strict transaction by transaction basis.

Functional analysis

14.39 Functions, risks and responsibilities of associated entities are key elements. It is becoming increasingly necessary to analyse and attribute these elements because tax authorities need to see and understand the structure and organisation of the group and which entities assume risks and responsibilities in order to determine where concomitant profits arise. The 1994 Report suggests that in making price comparisons between controlled and uncontrolled transactions or entities a comparison of the functions taken on by the uncontrolled parties is also necessary.

14.40   Functions will include, for example:

- treasury;
- management;
- manufacturing;
- assembling;
- processing;
- testing;
- research and development;
- packaging, labelling;
- after-sales servicing;
- warehousing, preserving, storing;
- distribution;
- branding, marketing;
- retailing or wholesaling;
- transportation;
- advertising;
- intellectual property ownership;
- other asset ownership, management and use;

- sales administration.

Responsibilities and risks include:

- commercial risk exposure;
- guarantees and comforts;
- third party liability;
- environmental and political risk;
- financing, leasing, treasury etc. services;
- employee related liability;
- management expertise;
- asset management skills.

Evidence

14.41   If controlled transactions are not supported by adequate evidence it will be difficult to convince tax authorities that they actually took place as claimed or that the transactions compare with arm's length transactions. A history of loss-making is often interpreted by tax authorities as the result of shifting profits to a controlled party.

Composite benefits

14.42   Controlled party 'package' deals may be rational (e.g. a package may constitute a transfer of technology including equipment rental, related specialist products etc., though would not usually include independent goods for sale) but they have to be unwound in an analysis to see if different elements are to be treated differently, for example, a withholding tax may be applicable to one of the elements and not to another.

Set-off

14.43   A similar situation to composite benefits applies in the case of 'set-off', e.g. where one service is provided in exchange for another. This type of arrangement may definitely be found between unrelated parties but in a controlled situation some of the consequences may be different and especially the motives could be different.

Market share strategy

14.44   Controlled parties often have special arrangements to deal with start-up situations or in implementing a market share strategy. The 1994 Report suggests that where a company explains away its transfer pricing

14.45 *UK Transfer Pricing Rules*

approach by a business/market share strategy the tax administration may wish to pay particular attention to the transaction at an early stage because by virtue of the timescales involved it may become too late to redress the tax position later. It is possible to find special arrangements between independent parties and the Report identifies five conditions that must be met for the market share strategy to be allowed:

(*a*)   similar pricing would occur between uncontrolled parties in similar circumstances;

(*b*)   the strategy must result in future profits for the controlled seller;

(*c*)   the strategy must be adopted by the controlled distributor;

(*d*)   the strategy must be documented before implementation;

(*e*)   the strategy time scale must be reasonable, perhaps three to five years.

Goods

Outline

14.45   Prices paid for goods supplied by one associated enterprise to another should be those which would have been paid between unrelated parties for the same or similar goods under the same or similar circumstances. In summary, the OECD methods for ascertaining an arm's length price for goods sold by one party (let us call it the original vendor) to a related party or purchaser are:

(*a*)   adopting the uncontrolled market price for the same or similar goods, or the price of the same or similar goods sold by the original vendor (or sold by other parties related to the original party) to independent third parties — *the CUP method*;

(*b*)   taking the price at which the goods are sold by the related purchaser (the reseller) to independent customers and subtracting a mark-up to arrive at the arm's length price for the sale by the original vendor — *the resale price method*;

(*c*)   taking the original vendor's cost and adding an appropriate mark-up to arrive at the arm's length price for the sale by the original vendor and thus for the purchase by the reseller — *the cost plus method*;

(*d*)   any other method which is found to be acceptable — *profit methods*.

The method to be adopted is that which provides the best evidence in any particular case. However, an arm's length price may not be precisely ascertainable, in which case it will be necessary to seek a reasonable approximation to it.

The elements of each supply of goods which is being compared must be the same, otherwise compensating adjustments should be made provided that the differences are measurable.

196

14.46   In relation to the comparability of prices for goods in an uncontrolled sale:

(*a*)   an uncontrolled sale is one where at least one party to the transaction is not a member of the controlled group;

(*b*)   sales not representative of the market are not uncontrolled sales;

(*c*)   for prices of goods to be comparable they must be sold on markets that are economically comparable;

(*d*)   prices must be compared at the same point in the chain from producer to consumer;

(*e*)   if the goods being compared are different it may nevertheless be possible to make appropriate adjustments;

(*f*)   quality differences are an important determinant of price;

(*g*)   product differentiation may affect the relative prices of otherwise apparently similar goods, and is usually achieved through the medium of:

    (i)   a brand name,

    (ii)   a trade mark,

    (iii)   packaging,

    (iv)   singularity in quality, design, colour or style,

    (v)   in any case, supported by targeted marketing,

(*h*)   pirate sales (basically counterfeit production) may force down prices in some markets;

(*i*)   the uncontrolled sales must have been realised at or around the time of the controlled transaction.

Resale price method factors

14.47   The elements of the resale price method are explained at 14.28.

Cost-plus method factors

14.48   Prices fixed on a cost-plus basis are often found in arm's length transactions, e.g. where the product is tailor-made or where the costs are unpredictable. The first element to consider is the cost, and the second is the mark-up, the 'plus'. As to the costs, which in most cases should be easily identifiable, at least on an historical basis, tax authorities will review costing methods to see how actual costs are related to the product. Mark-up is a more open-ended matter unless it can be determined by reference to the seller's mark-up on uncontrolled sales. If not, gross profits must be estimated by reference to uncontrolled parties performing similar activities.

As a matter of practice this is one area where for many years some tax authorities have often taken a pragmatic approach and have readily agreed a mark-up that is considered reasonable rather than scientific, especially in smaller cases. However, this can well be to the advantage of the tax authority if the taxpayer entity does not actually know precisely what mark-up is made by its direct competitors, or by others carrying on the same sort of business whether or not they are in open competitive combat. Neither of these scenarios is unusual.

Although one tax authority may be prepared to discuss and agree a pragmatic solution to a profit mark-up for the supply of goods (and the same may be said in respect of services), another tax authority which is considering, or may in due course consider, the same transaction(s) may well not agree. The taxpayer entity needs to remind itself, especially in the area of cost-plus agreements with tax authorities, that a one-sided pragmatic resolution of transfer pricing issues is, by definition, likely to be only half the answer, and more dangerously might actually contribute to the creation of additional tax liabilities.

A future phenomenon, well beyond the cost-plus question, will be a growing area of dispute between tax authorities over the pricing, accounting and other profit determinants of a related party taxpayer with the taxpayer sitting uncomfortably in the middle effectively being ping-pong ammunition between warring economies. This will be especially the case for businesses involved with intellectual property.

Other methods

14.49   In some cases, tax authorities will compare enterprises' overall performance, and in some industries and businesses profit levels will conform to a rigid pattern or market response. Innovative goods or goods produced by innovative means may enjoy higher profits than standard products. The success of some goods depends more upon marketing skills than intrinsic value or cost of production and in these cases profit may be greater in companies associated with marketing or distribution.

Intangible property (intellectual property)

Outline

14.50   Industrial intangible property (in the sense of production and marketing activity) refers to patents, trade marks, trade names, designs or models, literary and artistic property rights, know-how and trade secrets and promotional names, symbols or pictures. Production intangibles are patents, know-how, designs, and models etc., and marketing intangibles are trade marks and trade names. However, an item of intellectual property can fall under either heading.

The standard methodologies for determining arm's length prices apply for intangible property as they apply generally to goods and services. These are the transactional bases (at 14.26) and profit bases (at 14.30).

Where the owner of intangible property licenses it to related parties and to independent parties, the CUP method may be workable; it is also possible that some industry-wide practices and prices apply to the not too sophisticated end of intellectual property products, so that the CUT method may be applicable. In the field of breakthrough technology it may be impossible to use any method satisfactorily and a profit based method may be all that is available.

The transfer pricing issues concern the transfer of particular intangibles, the facilitating of group research and development, and trade marks.

(*a*)   Transfer of particular intangibles comprise (see 14.51):

   (i)   sales (or gifts) and licensing of intangibles, and

   (ii)   sale of goods benefiting or derived from R&D activity. If intangible property is sold with goods and they are separable a valuation of the intangibles may be necessary and there may be customs duties or VAT implications. Where the value of intangible property is included in the transfer price for goods or services but the purchaser has no access to the use of the intangible property as such, the transfer is of goods.

(*b*)   Facilitating of group research and development comprise (see 14.53):

   (i)   cost-contribution arrangements, and

   (ii)   contracts for specific research and development activity. The norms of comparative arm's length pricing apply but the issues relating to services may be relevant.

(*c*)   Trade marks (see 14.54).

It is important to distinguish between the making available of rights, know-how and technical assistance which constitutes personal services. The tax treatment can be markedly different around the world.

Sales and licensing

14.51   There are many and varied arrangements for the utilisation of intellectual property within a group. A parent company may simply license property to its operating subsidiaries for a stated term, but some multinationals have research operations in foreign subsidiaries which licence the parent company or directly licence subsidiaries. Sub-licence arrangements, or cross-licensing arrangements may also be used. Certain intellectual property, such as know-how, can have a short life if it can be easily learnt or easily loses its stamp of derivation. In these cases the property may be sold outright for a capital sum.

To earn a tax deduction for licence payments a real benefit must be conferred by the license. A license agreement should be evidenced in writing. The benefit must be demonstrable and the prices and contract terms should be those which would apply between independent enterprises acting at arm's length.

If a royalty is payable by reference to output or sales, stepped royalties of some nature are acceptable to the tax authorities if they would be usual between independent parties.

Evidence of arm's length prices includes licence contracts concluded by the licensor with unrelated parties concerning similar intellectual property licensed under similar market conditions. Also, offers to unrelated parties, bids for competing licences and the terms of sub-licensing arrangements may be considered.

14.52   Other factors to be taken into account in comparing values for intellectual property include:

- the territory of exploitation;

- export and political restrictions;

- exclusivity of the rights;

- ancillary services (such as training);

- development or completion costs required;

- on-going or product launch support expenditure required;

- the duration of the rights;

- renewal and special terms;

- legal protections;

- pirating problems;

- trade mark or trade name quality;

- the degree of quality control and R&D support;

- distribution network and availability of product;

- marketing success and follow-up;

- the value of the market share and prospects for further gain.

The 1994 Report suggests that *expected* profits from intangible property might be determined through a *net present value calculation*, with 'added value' applicable to 'breakthrough' patents. The fair market value of a production intangible might be determined using a discounted cash flow technique (see Chapter 8). The actual cost of research and development rarely bears a direct relationship to the present value of developed intellectual property — see Chapter 13.

In relation to marketing activities undertaken by enterprises that do not own the brand name or trade mark of the goods (or services) they distribute or provide, in assessing the arm's length return attributable to the marketing activities weight must be given to the actual conduct of the parties over a period of years, and in relation to promotional expenditure of the distributor, a functional analysis should be carried out, including a cost-benefit analysis to the distributor bearing the costs.

If there are no concrete comparable prices, it will be necessary to consider more than one method to find a satisfactory approximation to an arm's length price. The 1994 Report suggests that in cases involving high value intellectual property account should be taken of profit methods as a last resort.

Where the ownership and exploitation of intellectual or other intangible property carries through several group entities, and if they pass the real benefit test, it will be necessary to identify what added value may be contributed by each company or operation.

Cost contribution arrangements

14.53 There are two categories of cost contribution arrangements: cost-sharing and cost-funding. *Cost-sharing* is where group members share the actual costs and risks of research and development and in return each member is entitled to its fair share of research and development results. *Cost-funding* is where group members contribute to a research and development programme but not directly in relation to the actual costs. The ownership of the research and development results remain with the R&D company and the benefits are made available in different ways to the contributing members.

In cost-sharing only net costs of research and development are allocated to participants. Specifically contracted research or development work undertaken would not be included in a cost-sharing charge and receipts from such work would be deducted from costs to be apportioned to participants. Surpluses and deficits are shared among the participating members, perhaps by reference to the use of the property under development by the members, or by reference to turnover or sales of each member. Some indirect costs of research and development can also be shared, such as supervisory, administrative and other overhead activity. Capital expenditure may be allocated by reference to depreciation allowances.

If a profit mark-up is to be made by the R&D company this should take into account any financial risk the company is taking. Tax authorities will be concerned to ensure that costs of research and development under a cost-sharing arrangement are not also passed on in the price of goods or other services or facilities offered to the members of the group.

Trade marks

14.54 Creating a trade mark (or brand) may or may not be expensive but often it is costly to give it value and to maintain or increase the value, such as through advertising and marketing campaigns and maintaining quality controls or other marketing standards.

A trade mark licence is exploited in two main ways. Either the licensee uses the trade mark in selling products that are manufactured by the licensor; or the trade mark owner licences the trade mark to an enterprise which applies it to its own produced goods or to goods that it buys in from other sources. The licence may include other matters such as quality control and technical assistance.

If the licensor also licences trade marks to unrelated enterprises it may be possible to utilise the CUP method instead of the CUT method: the volume of sales, the prices and the profits realised for trade marked goods can be compared with those of similar goods that do not carry that trade mark but may carry another trade mark or be unbranded.

Services

Scope

14.55   Services includes central management and services cost allocation as well as specific administrative, technical and commercial group services. The two main issues identified in respect of intra-group services in the 1994 Report are the transfer price on an arm's length basis, and whether the services have actually been provided.

Whether the services have actually been provided is determined according to whether a comparable enterprise would regard the service as having provided economic or commercial value and would thereby be prepared to pay for it, or perform the service 'in house'. If not, the 1994 Report says that the services should not be considered as an intra-group service under the arm's length principle.

Administrative, technical and commercial services

14.56   Intra-group services fall into two categories: where services are provided exclusively for the benefit of the parent company, and where the services are provided for the benefit of one or more of the members of the group. Costs properly belonging to the parent company will not be accepted as chargeable to subsidiaries: for example, costs relating to shareholder matters, consolidating group accounts, administering and financing group equity positions (see 14.60).

Technical services will often be linked to transfers of technology, sales, new production plans, rationalisation, quality control, administration matters such as finance, leasing arrangements, legal matters, management and finance supervision, employment services, investment expertise, production assistance, marketing, auditing, computer services, property services and so on.

14.57   The cost of central guardianship and control of a group (as opposed to actual specific intra-group services) is the responsibility of the parent company and notwithstanding that the services also benefit members of the group not all may gain equally. It is necessary to look at the actual benefit to individual members.

If the intra-group services are on-call (that is, available as and when needed) an annual flat rate fee or a contribution on a cost-plus basis would not be unusual. In fact, the charging practices for intra-group services and allocating central expenditures differs amongst multinational enterprises and there does not appear to be any fixed pattern.

To determine the benefit it may be necessary to analyse the responsibilities and functions of the members of the group as well as to look at their performances and profits (perhaps over several years): expenditure on marketing operations might seem too heavy to be borne by one member unless the long-term effect is considered.

The prices paid for services between associated enterprises is that which would be paid between unrelated enterprises. Transactions between independent enterprises are usually specific services, not the assortment of services often provided in multinational enterprises.

Even so, it may be possible to find comparable arrangements: lawyers and accountants may provide various types of advice for an annual retainer; but where there is a range of services being provided it would be necessary to satisfy a tax authority that there is no doubling up of charges to group members through other conduits. In the absence of information about third party transactions it may be necessary to look at the charges that the services provider is making for similar services to unrelated enterprises.

14.58   In the absence of any satisfactory third party comparisons a cost based method may work. In applying a cost-based method, the full cost and a mark-up would have to be charged and not just the incremental or marginal cost. Direct costs are identified by reference to employees, materials and supplies consumed in providing the services. Indirect costs will include office expenditure, rent and related overheads and possibly a share of costs of other departments and companies that support the provision of the service. As to profit mark-up, in an arm's length situation an independent enterprise would take a profit and therefore this must be expected in a controlled situation.

14.59   To prove the reality behind an intra-group service evidence will have to be produced to the tax authorities and in relation to costs adequate books and records have to be maintained. An actual service agreement or cost allocation agreement might be expected and other evidence might include invoices, time records, etc.

Central management and service costs

14.60   Central management and service costs include, *inter alia*:

- planning, co-ordination, budgetary control, financial advice, computer services;

- production, buying, distribution and marketing advice;

- recruitment and training and staff management;

- research and development or administration and protection of intellectual property.

As to charging for these services, the first question is 'who benefits from the activities?'. The next question is whether a profit margin should be included. Shareholder costs to be borne by the parent company and which thereby should not be charged to other related parties arise from:

- the legal structure of the parent company, such as meetings of shareholders of the parent, issuing of shares in the parent company and costs of the supervisory board;

- reporting requirements of the parent company and the consolidation of accounts;

- raising funds for the acquisition of participations;

- management control, monitoring and protection of the investment in participations.

The costs of management and co-ordination performed to improve the operation of a subsidiary benefits the subsidiary in question but problems of evidence and attribution may be expected if the services are performed by the same persons who provide services in relation to the parent and its investments as such. In these cases it may be appropriate to split the total costs on a time basis.

A subsidiary should not pay for indirect benefits derived simply because it is a member of a group: for example, where a higher credit standing is obtained merely as a consequence of the group itself having a higher credit standing than other concerns. Benefit must be related to specific activities of the provider of the service or benefit. A higher credit standing derived from a guarantee by another group member constitute an intra-group service.

The function of central services is sometimes to reduce the costs of the group as a whole and in these cases it may be acceptable for the company not to seek to recover more than its costs from other group members.

Allocation and apportionment of services costs

14.61 Most OECD member countries' tax authorities recognise that for many services the allocation of the cost is on an approximate or estimate basis (*indirect charge method*) and that to insist upon a direct charge for services on an individual basis (*direct charge method*) would in many situations impose a disproportionate administrative burden on a multinational enterprise. Nevertheless, comparison with open market transactions is still the primary requirement, but if this is not possible a cost based method may be acceptable.

14.62 In terms of indirect methods of allocating costs or charges (e.g. by reference to staff numbers, turnover, etc.) they will be more acceptable to tax authorities if they adhere to the following:

(*a*) the method should be laid down in clearly formulated and binding contracts made in advance;

(*b*) the contract should be observed consistently over several years;

(*c*) the contract should apply to those associated enterprises which will benefit from the activity;

(*d*) the costs should be determined on the basis of generally acceptable accounting principles;

(*e*) the group members which share the costs should have full access to the services concerned;

(*f*) where the services are also provided to third parties but the prices charged thereto cannot satisfactorily be used as the basis for the use of the direct charge method, the costs recoverable from affiliates should be reduced by the income from the third parties;

(*g*) the contracting group members must not pay for the services in any other way;

(*h*) alterations in the responsibilities and activities of group members which would influence their benefit position should be taken account of as soon as possible in the contracts;

(*i*) the 1994 Report, considers 'buy-in' and 'buy-out' rules and requires that the contract addresses the consequences of a participant entering or withdrawing from the arrangement. These rules must adhere to the arm's length principle having regard to the remaining members of the arrangement.

In the case of an indirect charge method, there is still the question whether a profit mark-up should be included. This may depend upon whether the cost to the related entities of the service without the mark-up would be less than if they were to acquire the services from an independent party, but other factors may also be relevant including whether in the circumstances of the above factors a profit mark-up is appropriate.

14.63 Where a direct charge method is possible but a comparable open market price cannot be found, a cost based method may be appropriate. A profit mark-up will be appropriate:

(*a*) if providing the services is a main activity of the enterprise;

(*b*) if providing the services is not a main activity but the enterprise is capable of supplying them and the value of the services to the recipient is considerably greater than the cost of supplying them;

(*c*) if the cost of the services represents a substantial proportion of the expenses of the recipient's business.

When a direct method is being used and the service company is working at under-capacity the business may run at a loss even though a profit element is charged. This may mirror an arm's length situation but the approach may not be accepted by all tax authorities. Nevertheless, the 1994 Report states that 'it need not always be the case that an arm's length price will result in a profit for an associated enterprise that is performing an intra-group service'.

Loans and interest

14.64 For loans, there are three questions to address. Should a particular transaction be regarded as a loan? Should interest be paid on it if it is? If it is at what rate? It is necessary to distinguish between loan capital and equity. If equity, it follows that interest will not be payable. Generally speaking loan interest is tax deductible whereas a dividend will not be, and withholding tax considerations are different between these two payments. The main factors to take into consideration in determining the character of stock or a debt instrument are as follows:

(a) Is there an unconditional promise to pay a fixed amount of principle at a maturity date?

(b) Are the rights of other creditors superior to the loan?

(c) What is the debt/equity ratio of the company?

(d) Is the debt convertible into equity?

(e) Do the shareholders hold the debt pro rata to their shareholding?

(f) Can the holders of the debt instrument sue the company for the principal in default of payment of interest?

The same financial transaction may be treated for tax purposes as loan in one country and equity in another country.

The transfer pricing principle is that a loan should bear interest if interest would have been charged in similar circumstances in a transaction between unrelated parties. The matter may also be dealt with under the appropriate double tax treaty to which reference must be made.

Financial facility offered may include trade credit following normal trade practices such as regards delays in making settlement. If in similar circumstances unrelated parties would not have charged interest on outstanding balances it should not be necessary to charge interest between group members.

Some multinational groups make loans to subsidiaries in financial difficulties or in start-up years, but most tax authorities do not accept that an intra-group loan should be interest free. Interest always has to be charged unless an unrelated lender would waive the payment of the interest in the same circumstances. As to the UK Inland Revenue view on intra-group interest charges, see 14.16.

With regard to the rate of interest chargeable, it is necessary to look at the time the indebtedness arose and transactions with or between unrelated parties under similar circumstances. Current market rates when the interest is payable may have some bearing but it is likely that an interest rate was specified when the loan was advanced. Tax authorities will insist on a rate adjustment only if it significantly deviates from the market rate, or if the amounts concerned are substantial. It is also necessary to look at the conditions in the financial markets for similar loans, to take into account the amounts and maturity date, the nature or purpose of the loan, the currencies involved and the exchange risks, the security and the credit standing of the borrower. The starting point may be the central bank rate or prime rate but such rates must be weighted by the above considerations. It may also be necessary to consider the difference in the financial markets between the countries of the lender and the borrower.

Appendix 1

Model Valuation Report

International Shipping Company Limited

Share Valuation at 1 April 1993

Valuation of 2,000 ordinary shares of £1 each in International Shipping Company Limited, which were transferred on 5 April 1993 by Mr. John Smith (the transferor) to the trustees of the John Smith Discretionary Settlement dated 10 June 1991 (the transferees).

Purposes of the valuation

The shares were transferred for no consideration and are to be valued both for the purposes of inheritance tax (IHT) and capital gains tax (CGT). The shares were acquired by way of arm's length purchase on 20 October 1984.

As the transfer is to the trustees of a settlement in which there is no interest in possession, it is immediately chargeable to inheritance tax at lifetime rates (*Inheritance Tax Act 1984, ss 3* and *3A*). Capital gains tax is not to be held over under *TCGA 1992, s 165*. No business relief is available for inheritance tax purposes since the shares were acquired by the transferee by way of gift less than two years previously.

Capital structure

Before the transfer the fully paid issued share capital of 30,000 £1 shares was owned as to 29,000 by the transferor and 1,000 by Mrs M Smith (the transferor's wife).

Basis of valuation

The company is to be valued as a going concern. The company does not pay dividends and there is no intention to do so in the future. For IHT purposes it is the reduction in the value of the transferor's estate that has to be ascertained. The 'earnings basis' of valuation is to be applied because the holdings by the transferor before and after the transfer are substantial majority holdings, in both cases exceeding 75%.

For CGT purposes, the value of the 2,000 shares is to be arrived at by reference to a shareholding of that size in isolation. The value is to be calculated on a dividend basis without regard being had to earnings because of the insignificance of the percentage of shares transferred (6.66%), but with some regard being given to any surplus assets in the company, discounted heavily to reflect the shallow likelihood of receiving any actual benefit therefrom.

Tax bases of valuation

The shares, which are not quoted on a recognised stock exchange, are to be valued for Inheritance Tax in accordance with *Inheritance Tax Act 1984, Part VI. Section 160* provides:

'Except as otherwise provided by this Act, the value at any time of any property shall for the purposes of this Act be the price which the property might reasonably be expected to fetch if sold in the open market at that time; but that price shall not be assumed to be reduced on the ground that the whole property is to be placed on the market at one and the same time'.

and *section 168* provides:

'In determining the price which unquoted shares or unquoted securities might reasonably be expected to fetch if sold in the open market it shall be assumed that in that market there is available to any prospective purchaser of the shares or securities all the information which a prudent prospective purchaser might reasonably require if he were proposing to purchase them from a willing vendor by private treaty and at arm's length'.

Under *Inheritance Tax Act 1984, s 3(1)* the chargeable transfer for inheritance tax is the amount by which the transferor's estate is reduced by the transfer.

The transferor's wife holds 1,000 shares which are to be included for valuation purposes as related property under *Inheritance Tax Act 1984, s 161*.

The shares to be valued for IHT purposes are therefore:

Before transfer	—	transferor	29,000
		wife	1,000
			30,000
After transfer	—	transferor	27,000
		wife	1,000
			28,000

For *Capital Gains Tax* purposes the valuation provisions are contained in *TCGA 1992, s 272(1)(2)* which provides:

'In this Act "market value" in relation to any assets means the price which those assets might reasonably be expected to fetch on a sale in the open market.

In estimating the market value of any assets no reduction shall be made in the estimate on account of the estimate being made on the assumption that the whole of the assets is to be placed on the market at one and the same time'.

And *TCGA 1992, s 273(3)* which provides:

'For the purposes of a determination falling within subsection (1) above [a determination of the price which the unquoted shares or securities might reasonably be expected to fetch on a sale in the open market], it shall be assumed that, in the open market which is postulated for the purposes of that determination, there is available to any prospective purchaser of the asset in question all the information which a prudent prospective purchaser of the asset might reasonably require if he were proposing to purchase it from a willing vendor by private treaty and at arm's length'.

For both IHT and CGT, various principles emerge from case law which assist in the interpretation of the statutory provisions:

(1)   The test is what the purchaser would pay not what the then vendor would receive after costs: *Duke of Buccleuch v IRC*.

(2)   The market must be an open market without specially excluding anyone or specially including anyone: *Re Lynall, Lynall v IRC*.

(3)   Where the Articles of Association restrict the rights of transfer, nevertheless it is assumed that the hypothetical purchaser will be entered on the register of members, but thereafter will hold the shares subject to the restrictions in the articles: *A-G v Jameson*.

(4)   The sales to be assumed are hypothetical sales and the fact that the transfer is by or to a director has to be disregarded: *Re Aschrott; Winter, Sutherlands Trustees v IRC; Duke of Buccleuch v IRC*.

(5)   Directors owe no duty to a shareholder-vendor to disclose either orally or by way of documents the secrets of the boardroom: *Percival v Wright*.

(6)   The directors would be under a positive duty not to disclose confidential information. What the directors would be prepared to disclose in a sale by private treaty is a question of fact: *Re Lynall, Lynall v IRC*.

(7)   The hypothetical sale is deemed to take place at the time of the transfer: *Duke of Buccleuch v IRC*.

(8)   Any subsequent placing of the ordinary shares, unless it were known to be in contemplation at the time of this transfer has no relevance since it would be a totally different sale in totally different conditions: *Earl of Ellesmere v IRC; IRC v Marr's Trustees*.

(9)   Subsequent accounts can only be used to see what sort of forecast would have been given if the purchaser had asked for one, not to find out what actually happened: *Trustees of Johan Thomas Salvesen v IRC*.

Articles of Association

The articles carry severe restrictions on the right to transfer shares, the directors have power to decline to register transfers and there is a pre-emption clause under which an independent 'fair selling value' may be determined.

Previous transfers

There has been no previous commercial transfer of shares (see note at end of valuation calculations).

Valuation assessment of shareholding

The shareholding to be valued represents a proportion of a controlling interest in a private unquoted company in the shipbroking, chartering and forwarding agents sector. The company is trading satisfactorily and there are no plans to liquidate the company in the foreseeable future. It is expected by the current owners and management that the company will continue to prosper.

General economic conditions

Data: (reported in FT of 6 April 1993).

At 5 April 1993 the FT Actuaries Share Index for Transport stood at 2,890.36; twelve months previously this was 2,277.91.

The FT All Share Index was 1,392.18; twelve months previously this was 1,148.96.

Clearing banks base rate was 6%.

The flat yield on irredeemable gilts was 8.41%; twelve months previously this was 9.84%.

The rate of exchange against the dollar in London was £1:$1.514.

Outlook for the sector: For some years the shipping and international transport industry had been improving from its previous depressed state. The recession which has prevailed over British industry has had an adverse effect on the company's levels of turnover and profit. It is considered within the shipping industry, however, that the abolition of the dock labour scheme and the privatisation of the former trust ports and certain council-owned ports should benefit the industry generally. Although the company itself is buoyant by virtue of excellent management, it is clearly dependent upon factors largely outside its control in terms of demand, and therefore high returns would be required to justify investment in this sector of the economy.

Appendix 1

Company financial history

The company was incorporated on 1 September 1972 with an authorised and issued share capital of £30,000 fully paid. The company has traded satisfactorily since incorporation.

Valuation approach

The trading activities and performance of the company prior to 1986 were unexceptional with commission never exceeding £130,000 and trading losses being made in each year. It is believed that a realistic view of the company's future cannot be taken by reference to those years.

Recent years' trading activities (see Table 1) have been turbulent and considerable caution would be exercised by a prospective purchaser in taking the latest year's results as typical and an indicator of future years' profits.

Because of the peculiarity of a large windfall profit in 1992 and a loss in 1991, an average of averages has been used to identify what can be regarded as reasonable future maintainable profits.

Table 1

Earnings Year ended 31 December	1987	1988	1989	1990	1991	1992
Commission received	400,000	400,000	610,000	540,000	760,000	700,000
Other income:						
Rent	1,000	1,600	1,600	3,000	3,000	3,000
Foreign exchange	1,000	(3,000)	(15,000)	–	–	1,000
Sale of investments	–	–	–	30,000	–	–
Investment income	2,000	2,000	16,000	14,000	25,000	30,000
Total per Profit & Loss Account	404,000	400,600	612,600	587,000	788,000	734,000
Net Profit/(Loss)	40,000	60,000	90,000	(86,000)	60,000	190,000
Adjustments						
Pension fund increase in 1990 over 1989						
(200,000–30,000) at 75% (say)	–	–	–	127,000	–	–
Sale of investments	–	–	–	(30,000)	–	–
Net trading profits	40,000	60,000	90,000	11,000	60,000	190,000
RPI at December	101.9	106.9	115.2	126.1	133.5	138.4
RPI (139.3) to nearest thousand	55,000	78,000	109,000	11,000	63,000	191,000

Notes:

1. The pension fund extraordinary contribution in 1990 represented pre-tax appropriations of profits and for valuation purposes are not normal annual expenses. However, only 75% has been added back to the profits because ordinary annual contributions are a normal annual expense and these could reasonably vary considerably on a year by year basis.

2. Exchange profits and losses are the result of accounting requirements only. The trading activities are conducted in $US and it is not considered that there are risk factors attendant on the international trading. The results of the translation have not been removed from trading results for valuation purposes because it is considered that the likely purchaser of the shares in the company would be a UK resident and therefore conversion to sterling would possibly be a relevant factor in determining the benefit from dividends and earnings in the hands of the shareholders.

Balance sheet and investments

An analysis (see *Table 2* below) of the company's investments that could be regarded as standing to one side of the business assets shows a decline in those assets as a percentage of the annual net asset value of the company. Nevertheless it is considered that the value at 31 December 1992 of the investments at 4.8% of the total net asset value of the company is material enough to be brought into the share valuation for consideration of additional value. Cost of sales and liquidation is estimated at £500, and because a minority shareholding is being valued the discount for uncertainty of realising the benefit in this case must be 75%. The value to be brought into account would therefore be:

Value of investments (ex leasehold property) — see *Table 2* below, col (9): £12,000

$$(£12,000 - £500) \times 25\% = £2,875.$$

In view of the high earnings value of the company, this amount is *de minimis* for an earnings basis of valuation, and in any event the income arising from these investments is included in the capitalised earnings.

The leasehold is regarded as a business asset that is not to be separated from the valuation of the company on a going concern basis because of the importance to the business of having premises of the same character and in the same locality.

Interest arising and cash

Interest accruing to the company up to 1992 should be regarded as a concomitant of the business activities. The interest arises from cash on deposit and this cash is necessary to meet urgent demands for funds by ships and agents around the world. For 1992 the net current assets are considerably in excess of cash and bank balance.

Profit trend — future maintainable earnings

(a)	1992	191,000	× 5	955,000		
	1991	63,000	× 4	252,000		
	1990	11,000	× 3	33,000		
	1989	109,000	× 2	218,000		
	1988	78,000	× 1	78,000		
			15	£1,536,000	=	£102,400

213

Appendix 1

(b)	1991	63,000	× 5	315,000		
	1990	11,000	× 4	44,000		
	1989	109,000	× 3	327,000		
	1988	78,000	× 2	156,000		
	1987	55,000	× 1	55,000		
			15	£897,000	=	£60,000

The weighted average (a) includes the exceptional 1992 profit.

The weighted average (b) excludes that exceptional profit.

The average which includes the 1992 results, over-emphasised the large exceptional profits for that year. The average of the averages is:

$$102,400 + 60,000 = 162,400/2 = \qquad\qquad 81,200$$

Taking the last two years together, the average earnings would be:

$$191,000 + 63,000 = 254,000/2 = \qquad\qquad 127,000$$

Maintainable future profits might then be estimated somewhere between these figures at, say, one-quarter of the difference up on the lower figure, i.e.:

$$127,000 - 81,200 = 45,800/4 = \qquad 11,450$$
$$\text{add } 81,200 = \qquad 92,000$$

Management projections for 1993 suggest profits of £100,000. It would be reasonable to increase the estimate of future maintainable profits by one-half of the difference up on £92,650, i.e.:

$$100,000 - 92,650 = 7,350/2 = \qquad 3,675$$
$$\text{add } 92,650 = \qquad 96,325$$
$$= \text{Say } £97,000$$

Comparison with quoted companies

The Price to Earnings ratios on 5 April 1993 for quoted companies in the transport sector are too at variance with one another to draw a conclusion for the purpose of this valuation.

Inheritance Tax valuation — earnings basis

The view has already been expressed that a high return would be expected, especially when there is no substantial asset-backing equivalent to that of the quoted shipping companies.

A Price to Earnings ratio of 7 would appear to be realistic in terms of the wider economic risk.

Corporation tax rates for the future may be taken to be 33%.

	£
Pre-tax future maintainable profits	97,000
Less: corporation tax @ 33%	32,010
Anticipated maintainable profits post tax	£64,990
PER @ 7 = say	455,000
Less: discount for non-marketability @ 25%	114,000
	£341,000
Value per share on earnings basis (30,000 shares)	£11.37p
For Inheritance Tax — chargeable transfer shares transferred 2,000 @ £11.37	£22,740

Capital Gains Tax valuation — Dividend basis

	£
Anticipated maintainable profits post-tax	64,990
Reasonable distribution, say 1/3rd	21,663
Grossed for ACT @ 100/77.5	27,952
Required yield — not less than 12% Capitalised value	233,000
Discount for non-payment of dividends — 50%	116,500
Capitalised dividends	116,500
Additional asset-backing £2,875 (already discounted)	2,875
	119,375
Discount for non-marketability @ 40%	47,750
	71,625
Value of 2,000 of 30,000 shares	£ 4,775

Note

It will be recalled that the whole shareholding had been acquired by Mr. Smith within twelve months previously by way of gift. It is likely therefore that a value was struck for tax purposes at the time of that transfer. Although that transfer was (presumably) not an open market value, nevertheless the value could be brought into the final determination of the current value — but, of course, only with regard being had to all the features that distinguish the economic and company profile at that time with those existing at the current valuation date.

Appendix 1

Table 2: Investments

(1)	(2)	(3)	(4)	(5)	(6)	(7)	(8)	(9)	(10)
	Leasehold property*				Investment†		Balance Sheet	Value of Investments	Value of Investments
Balance sheet Net asset value	Book value	Estimated Realisable Market Value	Revaluation Surplus	Balance Sheet Book Value	Estimated Realisable Market Value	Revaluation Surplus	Net asset value after revaluation surpluses (Cols 1, 4 & 7)‡	(ex leasehold property) (Col 6)	(Col 9) as %age of revalued balance sheet (Col 8)
1992	225,000	40,000	60,000	20,000	8,000	12,000	4,000	249,000	12,000	4.8%
1991	200,000	40,000	70,000	30,000	8,000	15,000	7,000	237,000	15,000	6.3%
1990	80,000	40,000	70,000	30,000	4,000	10,000	6,000	116,000	10,000	8.6%
1989	100,000	40,000	60,000	20,000	4,000	9,000	5,000	125,000	9,000	7.2%
1988	80,000	40,000	50,000	10,000	12,000	20,000	8,000	98,000	20,000	20.4%
1987	80,000	40,000	40,000	–	8,000	8,000	–	80,000	8,000	10.0%

*The leasehold property (Cols 2–4) has been valued by Jones & Co (Auctioneers, Valuers and Estate Agents) at April 1993 at £60,000. Its annual market value each year back to 1987 (when purchased) has been estimated from that valuation.

† The estimated realisable market values of the investments (Col. 6) have been provided by a director and are recorded in the notes to the annual accounts.

‡ The revalued balance sheet (Col. 8) does not include any revaluation of plant, machinery, fixtures and fittings which are estimated to have the same value as their book value for a going-concern, it therefore represents the full net asset value of the business as a going concern excluding goodwill.

Alternative Investment Market

1.   The Alternative Investment Market has been introduced to replace the Unlisted Securities Market to offer a lower cost and accessible entry to the public market than the alternative of a full listing under the requirements of the London Stock Exchange's 'Official List'.

2.   Admission to AIM is open to public limited companies, irrespective of the country of incorporation, and to any class of share or security. The market will be regulated and managed by the London Stock Exchange.

3.   The principal benefits which admission to AIM might offer are:

— access to finance

— the opportunity to create a market for shares in a company which does not have a long trading record

— wider trading in the shares of smaller companies

— the facility for shareholders to realise a value for their shares

— a way of raising the profile of the business

— a lower cost entry to a public market which might lead to a full listing

4.   In particular, the market will be appropriate for the following:

— growing companies with high growth potential

— young companies with a short track record where capital is required for expansion or product development

— companies formed under the Business Expansion Scheme or the Enterprise Investment Scheme ('EIS') where shareholders require a market for their shares

— established owner managed companies which do not want to incur the cost of a Full Listing. Once shares have been traded on AIM for two years it can apply to join the Official List of the Stock Exchange without producing full listing particulars

— family or owner managed companies which otherwise may have sought a trading facility under Rule 4.2 of the Exchange

— companies currently trading on the USM which do not wish to join the Official List

— companies incorporated overseas where local capital markets cannot meet their funding requirements

— companies previously subject to a management buy-out or buy-in

— companies financed by institutional venture capital where the investors are seeking a controlled exit

5. It is important to note that companies can join AIM without seeking to raise finance on entry.

Joining AIM

6. Companies seeking to join AIM will need to satisfy the admission requirements and the ongoing obligations. In both cases the processes are considerably more straight forward and less onerous for the company than for companies on the Official List.

7. To gain admission to AIM, companies are required to appoint a nominated adviser and a nominated broker.

8. The nominated adviser assists with the application process by explaining the rules of AIM to the entrant, ensuring that all admission documentation is complete and correct. Prior to admission the adviser will confirm to the Exchange that the company has complied with the market's regulations. Thereafter the nominated adviser should provide guidance to the company on any specific issues concerning the requirements of the market.

9. The nominated broker will be a member of the Exchange and will form the point of contact with investors, thereby advising the directors on pricing issues, market conditions and maintaining interest in the company's shares. Brokers will also place shares with institutions and act as market-maker.

10. The rules of AIM also require that companies meet the following conditions at all times:

— be a public limited company or equivalent

— have published accounts which comply with Generally Accepted Accounting Principles or International Accounting Standards

— ensure that the securities traded on AIM are freely transferable

— adopt a model for share trading for directors and employees in possession of unpublished price sensitive information

11. Where a company has been earning revenue from its main activity for less than two years, the directors and all employees must agree not to sell any shares in the company for at least 12 months from the date of admission.

12. Applications for admission to the market are submitted directly to the Exchange, either in London or in a regional office, and must be supported by:

— a prospectus (see below)

— an application form signed by each of the directors

— a declaration by the nominated adviser that the rules of the Exchange have been followed

— a letter from the nominated broker confirming his appointment

13. The application must be submitted at least 72 hours before the shares are to be admitted to the market.

The prospectus

14. A company's prospectus must comply with the specific requirements of the Public Offers of Securities Requirements 1995. In particular it must contain all information which potential investors would reasonably require and expect to find, for the purpose of making an informed assessment of the company, its prospects and the rights attaching to the shares which are being traded. The information required includes:

— a description of the securities to be traded on the market

— a description of the company, its principal activities and its capital

— historic and current financial information about the company, its trading history and performance

— details of the management, administration and supervision of the company

— recent developments and prospects

— details of directors, including all directorships in the previous five years, any unspent convictions, bankruptcies, receiverships or liquidations of companies where they were directors, either at the time or within the 12 months preceding these events and any public criticisms by regulatory or statutory authorities

— details of the company's promoters

— names of substantial shareholders i.e. anyone entitled to exercise or control the exercise of 10 per cent or more of the votes able to be cast at general meetings

— confirmation that the directors are satisfied there is sufficient working capital in place to meet the present requirements of the company

— a notice drawing investors' attention to the fact that AIM is a different market from the Official List, being a market for smaller, emerging companies

15. Directors are responsible for ensuring that the Prospectus is accurate and that there are no material omissions.

Ongoing obligations

16. Companies have to meet the ongoing obligations of the market but these are considerably less onerous than the requirements of the Rules of the Official List. The obligations are designed to ensure that effective communication is maintained with the market, thereby allowing investors to make informed investment decisions. The principal obligations involve the need to:

— notify the Exchange of any price sensitive information, including changes in shareholdings of directors and connected individuals or significant shareholders, the appointment or resignation of directors, further issues of shares and details of dividends

— publish audited accounts within six months and interim unaudited accounts within four months of the period ends

— advise the Exchange of changes in nominated adviser or broker

— notify the market of transactions (acquisitions or disposals) equivalent to 10% of the company's assets, profits or value of the company

— notify the Exchange and shareholders of transactions involving a director, associate or substantial shareholder where the transaction accounts for 5% of assets, profits or value of the company

— obtain shareholder approval where an acquisition would result in a reverse take over, in which case the company would need to seek re-admission to AIM

— disclose related party transactions in annual audited accounts

17.   It is important that the rules of the Exchange are complied with to maintain investor confidence and to protect shareholders interests. Failure to comply with the obligations can lead to cancellation of trading in the company's shares.

Relations with investors

18.   Companies joining the market may choose to exceed the ongoing reporting obligations referred to above to increase investor confidence and awareness. Implementing and developing effective shareholder relationships is particularly important if the company expects to raise finance in the future to fund acquisitions. Although companies on AIM are not required to comply with the Code of Best Practice on the Financial Aspects of Corporate Governance ('the Cadbury Code') consideration should be given to adopting certain of the guidelines, in particular those in relation to non-executive directors and the use of audit and remuneration committees where appropriate. Institutional finance is likely to be directed towards those companies which are perceived to adopt sound management and control procedures.

Taxation implications

19.   Securities dealt in on AIM are treated as 'unquoted' securities for tax purposes. This means that family and owner managed qualifying trading companies traded on AIM where certain conditions are met will enjoy a

considerable tax advantage over fully quoted companies. In summary these include the following:

   (i)   *Inheritance tax business property relief* — shares in AIM qualifying companies which represent more than 25% of the voting rights potentially qualify for 100% business property relief, whilst smaller holdings qualify for 50% relief.

  (ii)   *Capital gains tax reinvestment relief* — gains on disposal of any assets can be deferred by reinvesting the proceeds in an AIM qualifying company.

 (iii)   *Capital gains tax hold-over relief* — gifts of shares in AIM qualifying companies should be capable of being held over.

 (iv)   *Income tax for shareholders* — relief for interest on loans to acquire shares should be available to an investor who owns more than 5% of the capital of an AIM qualifying company which is also a close company. On a more cautious note, shareholders may be able to claim an income tax deduction for an allowable capital gains tax loss should one arise where there was a subscription in an AIM qualifying company.

  (v)   *Enterprise Investment Scheme* — shares issued by AIM qualifying trading companies are potentially eligible for EIS reliefs.

20.   The treatment of AIM traded securities as 'unquoted' for tax purposes means that the shares could be attractive to Venture Capital Trusts that will be looking to invest funds in qualifying investments. AIM securities do not qualify for inclusion in Personal Equity Plans.

Summary of the British Venture Capital Association's 'Guidelines for the Valuation and Disclosure of Venture Capital Portfolios'

Information about the British Venture Capital Association may be obtained from BVCA, 3 Catherine Place, London, SW1E 6DX.

The current UK national guidelines, issued in November 1993, are an update of original guidelines issued in March 1991. The guidelines evolved over a period of time and had their origins in the work of a committee of the European Venture Capital Association which was set up in mid-1989 to develop a set of common European principles for the valuation of venture capital Portfolios.

What follows is a brief summary of the 'Valuation Guidelines' which cannot be attributed to the BVCA. Potential users of this information should contact the BVCA for better particulars. These guidelines are not designed for general application outside the specific audience to which they are addressed, namely members of the British Venture Capital Association, and for the specific purposes that they have been written. The reason for including the summary in these Appendices is to provide comparative information for those enquiring into share valuation techniques. The disclosure guidelines are not summarised here.

Background

1.   The guidelines constitute the BVCA recommendations for carrying out venture capital valuations and for making disclosure of valuation information. Venture capitalists need to make valuations for their investment appraisal decisions and for periodic reporting and assessment purposes in relation to the success of the venture capital vehicle (as well as for the performance of their individual venture capitalists). The point is made that the valuation of individual unquoted investments is very judgmental. Valuations must be prepared with integrity and common sense and subject to a review procedure and the valuer should have an appropriate level of experience and ability.

2.   There are different disclosure requirements because, on the one hand, portfolio valuations may be contained in accounts of quoted investment trusts and, on the other hand, may be confidential to a limited number of investors. The point is made that full disclosure of valuations to the public could be damaging to the investment; also, it is suggested that where there is a close relationship between the investor and the venture capitalist (for example, limited partnerships or captive funds) a greater level of disclosure may be required by the providers of the investment funds. The disclosure guidelines are not summarised here.

Valuation guidelines

1.   The overriding principle is to show the investor a fair valuation of the investment, avoiding unwarranted optimism but also excessive caution.

2.   *Early stage investment* — immature companies, seed investments and start-ups etc—should be valued at cost less any provisions thought necessary. A different approach may be taken only where a significant third party transaction takes place which values the investment at a materially different price (see below).

3.   A provision may be made if the performance of the investment is significantly below the investment expectations — indicators include missing significant milestones and failing to service equity or debt, and breaches of covenant. Provision would be made, as the valuer sees fit, as a percentage of cost (in bands of 25%) against the appropriate instrument (e.g, whether equity or loan).

4.   *Development stage investments* — those unquoted companies including management buy-outs and buy-ins not being early-stage investments — should be valued on the basis of —

(*a*)   *Cost (after provisions).* This basis should be used for one year at least, unless it is no longer a reliable indicator of value.

(*b*)   *Third party valuation.* An independent third-party material valuation should be the precedent basis unless a change in circumstances dictates otherwise. A change from another value or another basis of valuation may be justified if there is a cash transaction, or a price is struck for a new issue of capital, involving a significant investment by a new investor.

(*c*)   *Earnings multiple.* Probably the most common basis, the suggested method is to apply a discounted price/earnings ratio to post-tax profits, usually taking the full corporation tax rate, but leaving open to the valuer whether to take profits pre- or post- interest (with a warning note that a valuation of highly geared companies is sensitive to interest rate changes). The earnings should be taken from the most recently completed audited accounts, or the current earnings should be used if they are likely to be lower than those of the previous period or they are predictably higher. Comparable quoted price/earnings ratios (by reference to comparable business activities and magnitude of sales and profits) should be used, or alternatively the appropriate sector FT-SE

Actuaries Share indices can be used. The discount to be applied to the quoted price/earnings ratio is to recognise the lack of liquidity, the risk attaching to unquoted investments and the approximate nature of valuations based on earnings. The minimum discount is set at 25% unless an early realisation of the value is a strong possibility and justifies a lower discount.

(*d*) *Net assets*. Rarely applicable, the basis may be appropriate where, for example, there is a significant real estate element to the business of the company. Some discounting of the assets will be appropriate to reflect the lack of liquidity of the investment. In valuing quoted investments, the mid-market price can often be taken to be a fair value, subject to any restrictions that may apply to the holding or if the holding is a large proportion of the issued share capital and in these cases the discount range is 5%–25%.

5. *Loan stock and preference shares* held by the venture capitalist in the subject company should not be valued on the basis of their yield but on cost together with any fully accrued premium or interest after appropriate provisions or discount.

6. *Warrants, options and performance ratchets* whose effect is to dilute earnings should be reflected in the valuation. Warrants and options are to be valued at the excess of the share value over the exercise price: conservative valuations tend to put the value of these at nil.

7. *Guarantees and commitments* between subject company and investor which appear likely to crystallise must be recognised in the valuation and, where appropriate, any resulting new investment should be valued.

Index

Index

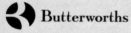